Autism's Politics and Political Factions: A Commentary

By Thomas D. Taylor

The author gratefully acknowledges the editorial and technical assistance, and words of encouragement provided by Elyse Bruce in regard to the publication of this book.

This book is dedicated to Mom, Dad, Sis, Elyse Bruce, Lewis, and Lola, with a special thanks to Elyse Bruce, for providing excellent commentary, suggestions, and constructive criticism while this work was in progress.

Table of Contents

Introduction

This book does not attempt to be scholarly in any regard, but offers some general opinions about the topic of autism's politics, and political factions. The discussion of this topic here represents a logical extension of some of the discussion included in my previous book <u>Autistic Authors, and Autistics, and Autism in Literature: A Commentary</u>. In that book, where I have asserted that the motives of many autistic and non-autistic authors might not be entirely altruistic, it became necessary to list out factions in the autism world so that readers of literature could better understand how and why an author might influence something that they have written.

The list in that book, while extensive, was not all-inclusive or all-encompassing, nor did it go into much detail about the mindsets of the people who belong to one or more factions. My feeling is that it is very important for people to know what the factions are, what they believe, and how they act on their beliefs. Earnest information seekers, or people looking to interact with others whom they share commonalities with, may find themselves unknowingly joining factions which may harbor ill-intent, and they may become subject to the manipulations of those factions. In the more extreme cases, speaking against a faction's viewpoints, refusing to follow its mandates, leaving it, or opposing it, can result in online or offline bulling, or outright harassment.

You will find a longer -although *still* not all-inclusive or all-encompassing- list of factions here than the one that was given in <u>Autistic Authors, and Autistics, and Autism in Literature: A Commentary</u>, but this time, wherever possible and/or relevant, I will be talking about the "politics" behind each faction. This in addition to talking about autism politics elsewhere in this publication in more general terms. I will also be discussing the ways in which factions overtly and covertly try to destroy one another, and give examples of some of the unlikely alliances that can and do happen between them.

Readers will notice that some of the material from <u>Autistic Authors, and Autistics, and Autism in Literature: A Commentary</u> has been republished in this book. While this is so, not *all* of the material has been transferred, and that which has been transferred has been revised in many cases. People looking for more information on autistic authors, and autistics, and autism in literature would do well to read the other book.

I have heard it said that many kinds of autism politics are misguided and corrupt. I have heard it said that there is a similarity between some autistics' political factions and street gangs (or religious cults). However, the intent here is not to attack autistics, or autism politics or to attack one faction or another, but merely to produce a book that attempts to list out and discuss real online and offline autistic political viewpoints, and autistic political factions. If a reader should construe some commentary I have made about a particular political viewpoint or faction as negative, he or she should recognize that this is *their feeling*, and not necessarily a correct assessment of what my personal opinion may be.

This commentary should be regarded as an editorial, and should not be taken as anything else. At the same time, readers should understand that my perspective is that, were there no basis or foundation to write the opinions put forward in this book, this book would not need to be written.

It is hoped that people interested in this subject will view this work as a point of departure from which will stem further research and investigations into the topic.

One final note: Although medical issues are discussed in this publication, it should be understood that neither I or the editor are licensed medical professionals. No medical advice is given by myself or the editor, and no medical advice is sought by the readers. People seeking medical advice about autism are urged to seek the advice of a board certified medical professional.

Autism's Politics and Political Factions: A Commentary

The Dawning Of The Age Of Aspergia

Circa the late 1990s, there were a number of message boards and chat rooms in existence online for people on the autism spectrum. Some of these boards were diagnosis-specific, and others were for anyone who was autistic.

These boards were a godsend for spectrumites who, offline, were unable to find, or effectively communicate with others like them. Whereas today, in some locations, the number of people on the spectrum is thought to be 1 in 64, in those days, the rate was one in many hundreds. Back then, in a sparsely populated area, a person with autism wishing to have a real life interaction with someone like themselves might have had to do something extreme to find someone -such as attend an autism convention.

I cannot offer any insight as to why some online social media sites have become more popular than others. I personally do not like Facebook, Twitter, and many of the other online places people these days go to interact with one another. But I can offer some insight as to why autistics began to flock to one site in particular many years ago.

The site I am speaking of is Aspergia, or www.aspergia.com. It's now closed, but in its heyday, the site at one time hosted the biggest online forum for people with autism on the net.

In the beginning, Edan Dagan created a message board, a mythos, and a website. People surfing the net on search engines that are no longer in existence were fairly likely to come across it by typing "Asperger syndrome" into the search window. When they clicked through to the site, the page they were most likely to hit was one that asked "Do you have Asperger syndrome?"

You could read a little about Asperger's, click through to the "Aspergian Mythos" (where you could read a sort of fictional mythological theory about how Asperger syndrome came to be) and, whether you were diagnosed with Asperger syndrome specifically, or were diagnosed with some other form of autism, or thought you were diagnosed, you were given the option of joining Aspergia, which was a message board populated by people on the spectrum, and by people who thought they were on the spectrum.

Initially built in the EZ Board format, the message board was easy to use. Topics were plainly visible, and if you clicked on a topic, you could see the thread beneath it. People there in those early days felt free to speak on anything that came to mind, and for the most part, everyone on the board got along well.

They compared notes with one another about Asperger Syndrome, Autistic Disorder, Pervasive Developmental Disorder, Not Otherwise Specified (PDD-NOS), Rett Syndrome, Childhood Disintegrative Disorder, and then they shared a little about themselves and about their interests and experiences. It was soon discovered that no matter where they lived in the world, no matter what ages they were, or what their socio-economic circumstances, no matter what religions they belonged to, or what type of relationship status they had, there were certain commonalities between them. For many of these people, it was the first time in their lives when they ceased to feel different and apart from the rest of society and began to know the feeling of belonging, and true and meaningful (albeit virtual) friendship.

What was interesting was that Edan Dagan himself seldom participated on the board, didn't moderate the board very much, and allowed people to associate and socialize as they pleased. So as not to offend their host, the board members policed themselves as best they could, and they did a good job. For a few months there, sniping, trolling, and all the other "bad" things one commonly saw on *other* message boards were absent from Aspergia.

There were no written rules as to how to behave on the board, but it was customary for people to identify themselves, either as diagnosed or undiagnosed, and *if* diagnosed, with what specifically. No one thought less of anyone else when one declared their status, and people accepted one another easily. The term neurodiversity -which can be defined as the universal acceptance of everyone, no matter what their psychiatric diagnosis might be, (with that definition also accepting people who do not have a diagnosis of any kind, be it psychiatric or physical) - will be discussed at some length later on. The term was not so widely known when the Aspergia board was in its infancy, but in a sense, the Aspergia board was a typical example of the neurodiversity concept in ideal operation. Aspergia was nearly an utopia, and looked to stay that way as long as the board remained small.

But then, as the board became more populated and popular, change came to the forum in the form of trolls, and other people who were less likely to obey the unspoken "rules" of the board. Open disrespect of the older members was plain, despite those older members' attempts to lead by example, or else to mentor new members.

To digress for a moment, it is worth noting that given that a rigid adherence to rules is accepted by many as a symptom of autism, and given that people on the autism spectrum are socially awkward, and given that autistics are supposed to possess a singular lack of empathy, it is interesting to note that though there were no actual rules on Aspergia at first, there were no problems with how the board members socialized initially. That some older members later stepped up to lead by example, or to act as mentors to newer forum members after the problems began, is equally remarkable, and subverts the misperception among some people that autistics are incapable of doing such. To be able to mentor requires that the mentor empathize with the person they are mentoring, and then deftly steer them in the right direction through words of encouragement and praise. To the extent that rules were absent, socialization among the membership seemed easy, and empathy by Aspergia's users was widely demonstrated, it could be argued that in its early form, the board was very healthy for people with autism because it helped them "come out of their shell" and helped them to think and behave more like people who circulated offline in the rest of society.

It must be acknowledged, however, that none of the early posters on Aspergia offered proof of their diagnoses. Therefore, it cannot be stated with any degree of certainty that those who claimed to be diagnosed were telling the truth.

But if they *were* telling the truth about their diagnoses, some of those who came later to Aspergia were almost certainly lying.

It was not uncommon during that time in the board's history for someone to come to the board, claim they had symptoms that were similar to Asperger syndrome, and within weeks were claiming to be "Aspie" and that they had received a diagnosis years earlier. All anybody had to do to catch them in a lie was to go back and reread old threads, but by the time it got to the point where people were lying about their diagnoses, and where others were looking back to prior threads to find out what the truth was about these people, there were so many threads that one was hard pressed to go back and find the exact one needed to expose the lies.

Some people -primarily ones whose perseverative interests were categorizing information- *did* go back and investigate, however, and actually began to make lists of who was diagnosed and who wasn't. Thus it was soon shared among a core group of Aspergia's original posters who was telling the truth and who was lying.

Unfortunately, by this time it didn't matter. Self-diagnosed autistics and fakers were asking diagnosed autistics whether or not they had a diagnosis, and if the diagnosed ones answered "Yes," the self-diagnosed autistics and fakers would say "Prove it!" And since no one wanted to post their personal information online, nothing was ever proved.

But the self-diagnosed autistics and fakers were thereafter hailed as heroes for exposing the autistic "liars" for "what they were."

To this very day, some of Aspergia's latter members continue to lie about their diagnoses, saying that they were diagnosed in childhood when in fact they stated in Aspergia's threads under their own user names that they were in their earlier twenties and seeking a diagnosis. Some of these people are in leadership positions in autism advocacy organizations today, or they have "grown up" to be "autism advocates." This is quite disturbing to when one reflects that many of these people also stated on the Aspergia board that -though they were not (yet) on the autism spectrum- they had diagnoses like bipolar disorder, ADHD, OCD, ODD, antisocial personality disorder, sociopathy, psychopathy, or no diagnosis at all.

Today, even some of the *diagnosed* people might not fit the description in the DSM IV TR (Diagnostic and Statistical Manual of Mental Disorders, Fourth edition, Text Revised) for Autistic Disorder 299.00, Asperger's Disorder 299.80, Rett's Disorder 299.80, Childhood Disintegrative Disorder 299.10, Pervasive Developmental Disorder Not Otherwise Specified (Including Atypical Autism) 299.80, nor would they fit the description in the DSM V (Diagnostic and Statistical Manual of Mental Disorders, Fifth edition) for Autism Spectrum Disorder [299.00 9F84.0)], nor would they fit the description in the ICD 10 (International Statistical Classification of Diseases and Related Health Problems, 10th edition) for any of the (F84) Pervasive developmental disorders [F84.0 Childhood Autism, F84.1 Atypical Autism, F84.2 Rett syndrome, F84.3 Other childhood disintegrative disorder, F84.4 Overactive disorder associated with mental retardation and stereotyped movements, F84.5 Asperger syndrome, F84.8 Other pervasive developmental disorders, F84.9 Pervasive developmental disorder, unspecified, and might instead be classified under the DSM V's Social (Pragmatic) Communication Disorder [315.39 (F80.89)].

Be that as it may, some of those that would no longer be diagnosed "autistic" today *were* diagnosed on the autism spectrum and accepted as autistic then, and while no one can say with certainty if members of this select population of people were among the troublemakers on the board, one must acknowledge that it is a possibility, as many of the traits and characteristics of the troublemakers seemed to be ones the DSM V would categorize into the Social (Pragmatic) Communication Disorder [315.39 (F80.89)] delineation. Indeed, many of the troublemakers on boards today who call themselves "autistic" have traits that fit the definition of Social (Pragmatic) Communication Disorder to a tee.

And Then There Were Trolls

Trolls interfered with the interactions on Aspergia by inserting themselves into any discussions they could, and then pitting both sides against one another. In the discussions about who was diagnosed with what, they would defend the diagnosed people against the "posers" and then the "posers" against the diagnosed people.

They would incite fights between users in all the ways which have since become familiar to any person on any board (autism-specific or not) but interestingly, they would particularly go after diagnosed individuals, which would suggest to me that either these trolls were prejudiced against diagnosed autistics, or were jealous of diagnosed autistics for having a diagnosis.

We must acknowledge however that some of the people causing this kind of interference might not have been trolls. They may have been affected by disorders of their own which caused them to shift opinions and alliances as arguments and counterarguments made sense to them.

Alternatively, they may have been friends or allies of those who felt wounded in the diagnosed/poser fracas who entered the forum to support their friends, or to derail discussions to keep their friends from getting hurt.

Nevertheless we can see an example of fracturing in Aspergia, and by proxy, the autism community. Whereas before, everyone was getting along successfully whether they were diagnosed or not, people were now in one of three "camps." They were either diagnosed, self-diagnosed, or undiagnosed.

Around this time, Dagan switched Aspergia over to a new message board format now commonly used by most of the familiar autism hangouts. This new format allowed for people to have "emoticons" and private message boxes. There were other features that made the posting experience enjoyable for most users, though I was not then and am not now a fan of those features.

The new format was very popular, and drew a larger membership much faster from that time onward.

However, the trolls and troublemakers quickly found a way to unify against those they opposed: They used the PM boxes to message each other in real time to better coordinate their attacks. Now, multiple users, who each had three or four different accounts, could gang up on people instantaneously and drive them into the ground if they chose. The targeted people fought back valiantly, sometimes having defenders come to their aid, but no firm bonds ever seemed to get established between targeted people and defenders. Occasionally during these fights, someone would try to muster an opposing force to go after the bullies, but these coalitions -when established- were weak at best, with most potential allies saying they were afraid of being targeted themselves, and so did not want to participated too much in any online fights...unless maybe there was a clear sign of victory. Then they would come in at the last moment to "deal the final blow" to the bullies.

These tenuous anti-bully coalitions would usually dissolve after the arguments had come to an end, with only a very small powerless core of members occasionally coming together to participate inconsistently in other arguments, and with varying degrees of determination, until around the time the Aspergia message board was about to close down.

Dagan continued to keep a low profile through all of this, administering the board without moderators, though from time to time, there was someone who oversaw the board while he was away.

A chat room was added somewhere along the line too, much to the pleasure of the membership.

But with the real time chat came real time trolling, and close to the time of Aspergia's closure, the chat room became a very unpleasant place. Two people, or three, or four or more could be having a peaceful conversation, and in would come another person, whose intent appeared to be to disrupt, derail, and destroy the talk. For some, it was enough that threads were being disrupted and derailed on the *forum*, and now it was happening in chat!

Soon, swarms of trolls populated the chat, and it became

impossible to have an intelligent conversation there.

A few longstanding members began to quit.

Edan patiently tried to settle everyone down, but to no avail. It could be argued that he wasn't firm enough with the members, yet many believe one of the reasons Aspergia had been successful in Aspergia's early stages was that there were no rules back then. Edan didn't really impose any rules near the end of the board either. In fact, to my recollection, there was only one person who had ever been banned from Aspergia, and that person was later readmitted, just before Edan finally closed the door to the Aspergia board for good.

Dagan shut down the board and chat in 2004, citing personal reasons as an explanation for the closure.

After the board's shutdown, Dagan seemed to disappear from the net, although he promised to post as himself when he appeared in an autism forum somewhere.

My feeling is that initially, the Aspergian Mythos was as enticing as the prospect of meeting other people on the spectrum. The idea that people with Asperger syndrome could have a *culture*, let alone a gathering place, was appealing to many. Though I will not reproduce it here, the Mythos spoke of a gathering together of an ancient people after separation by eons of time.

However, the Mythos may arguably have been just as responsible for the demise of Aspergia as it was Aspergia's success. Asperger syndrome is not -medically speaking- a culture. It is a psychiatric disorder defined previously in the DSM IV-TR (Diagnostic and Statistical Manual of Mental Disorders, Fourth edition, Text Revised). It is possible that for some people with Aspergers, it was too much to ask for them to create or interact within a culture that was specifically their own, whatever that culture looked like, especially when one considers that some people with Asperger syndrome *are* known to have difficulty with social interactions.

At any rate, with Aspergia's closure, all of the *good* that was birthed from the Mythos seemed to have ended.

Aspergians were not without hope, however. New Aspergia successor boards were opened up with Dagan's permission and technical assistance. All one had to do to use the

Aspergia name, its Mythos, and the "Min" symbol was ask Dagan and cite him as having given permission.

Former Aspergia Members - Secret Society (now Fellowship of the Aspergian Miracle – Secret Society) was the first of the new boards to spring up that carried the Aspergia name. Administrated by Zoologist, a former Aspergia member, the Yahoo group was sanctioned by Dagan to be the "life raft" for some of the former members until newer, more complex boards could be set up. Other publications suggest that Zoologist was partially responsible for the breakup of the original Aspergia, but proof to the contrary can be seen in Edan's posts in FAM, where he thanks Zoologist for supplying the life raft.

Many members from the original EZ board populated this little Yahoo group, while others moved on to the bigger boards, which had the "look" of Aspergia, and carried the Aspergia name.

FAM expanded into a series of Yahoo groups (some public, and others hidden and invitation only) which still exist today. At the time of this writing, they are the *only* message boards in existence which carry the Aspergia name with Dagan's approval, the other successor boards having been closed down.

Rivalry soon developed between all of the successor boards for a number of different reasons, most of them ideological, and it is in this rivalry where we can begin to see some autistic political factions in their most naked forms.

Edan Dagan Is *Not* Responsible For Factionalization

Before beginning to delineate these factions and explain their viewpoints, it must be stated that neither Edan Dagan, nor Aspergia can be seen as the cause of the factionalization, and my using Aspergia as an example should not be seen as giving the website, its message board, or its creator a black mark. I think highly of Edan and his earnest attempt to bring people with Asperger syndrome together.

My use of Aspergia here is, as I have said, to illustrate how factionalization happens. I could just as easily have picked any other board to serve the same purpose, although no other board that I recall was as populated and as popular at the time than Aspergia was.

Why Aspergia Matters

It would have been necessary, however, to include Aspergia in this book somewhere regardless, because the site and board seem to have become legend. I could hardly write this book without touching upon it.

Why should Aspergia matter in the first place? And why should the dissolution of the board matter?

It's creation and dissolution both matter and don't matter, depending on who you talk to.

However, one thing the original EZ Board Aspergia was good for was earnestness and honesty among its membership. If you came to the board with a problem, there were people there who genuinely wanted to help you, and those people seemed to be in the majority -at first.

Early on, members and prospective members seemed inclined to reveal their diagnoses out of *etiquette*, not due to probing. This was especially true when a prospective member did not have Asperger syndrome specifically. The board, after all, seemed mainly to be created for people with Asperger syndrome. If, for example, one was on the spectrum, but diagnosed with something else besides AS, one felt the need to declare themselves so that their presence didn't give offense to those who had Asperger syndrome.

But no one on the autism spectrum was ever in my memory cast out because they were not AS. Using the DSM IV-TR, (Diagnostic and Statistical Manual of Mental Disorders, Fourth edition, Text Revised) as a reference, the five categories of autism were:

- Autism
- Asperger Syndrome
- Childhood Disintegrative Disorder
- Rett Syndrome
- Pervasive Developmental Disorder Not Otherwise Specified

An Aspergia member on the spectrum could be any one of the above.

The ICD-10's definitions were accepted as well.

A Quick Note About Diagnosis

There were and are some autistics who believe themselves to be diagnosed with more than one form of autism, but many psychiatrists have stated clearly that a person may only be diagnosed with one form. If a person has -in their lifetime- been labeled with two different kinds of diagnosis, it is because their specific diagnosis is undetermined, and/or the current diagnosis vacates the previous. Additionally, it is not uncommon for a diagnosis to be changed throughout an autistic person's life depending on which doctor they are seeing, or how functional they may appear to the diagnosing physician during evaluative periods.

The DSM V (Diagnostic and Statistical Manual of Mental Disorders, Fifth edition) effectively eliminates the need to ask the question "What is your autism diagnosis?" because the five categories are eliminated in favor of one single category: Autism Spectrum Disorder.

More About Diagnosis

Returning to Aspergia, when people without an autism diagnosis began to join that board, another thing people felt necessary to reveal about themselves was whether or not they were diagnosed, and if they were not yet diagnosed, what the status of their diagnosis was.

A person could be:

☐ Diagnosed
☐ Self-diagnosed
☐ In the process of getting a diagnosis
☐ Seeking a diagnosis
☐ Wannabee

While the labels seem self-evident, in order to illustrate where factional differences exist, each label will be discussed in detail.

1. Diagnosed

This meant that a person had received a diagnosis from a reputable physician, most preferably one who was a specialist in autism spectrum disorders. However, as time went there came into being a dispute over just what a "reputable" physician was.

A "reputable" physician was thought to be:

- A doctor who was a specialist in pervasive developmental disorders (PDDs)
- An autism researcher
- A psychologist
- A psychiatrist
- A doctor

It was preferential that any of the above be licensed and/or board certified, or otherwise properly credentialed, and that they provide the battery of testing necessary to *rule out* disorders outside the PDD category while *ruling upon* a particular one within it.

Testing for and diagnosing an autism spectrum disorder can be an exhaustive task. It usually isn't a matter of having a patient fill out a short questionnaire. Patients are in many cases given tests for other disorders, given self-assessment tests, given intelligent quotient tests, emotional quotient tests, achievement tests, aptitude tests, tests for comorbidities, mental age assessments, and the patient's behaviors may be observed by the diagnostician over a period of time. Parents and caregivers may also be interviewed to give the diagnostician a more comprehensive view of how the patient is seen by others, and school transcripts may be taken into consideration as well as work and medical histories.

A less reputable physician could be:

- A school psychologist
- An autism researcher
- A doctor without much background in autism

spectrum disorders

☐ A doctor practicing "quack" medicine

About School Psychologists...

One would think that a school psychologist wouldn't be any less practiced, or any less ethical, than another psychologist, but some schools and school districts can be guilty of engaging in deceptive practices, and some school psychologists can be complicit in those deceptive practices.

One of the biggest scams going in government today is one presented and perpetuated by our school systems on the populace. I can say this because, having done my teacher training in various school districts, and having advocated for autistic students since my teacher training days, I have witnessed this scam being pulled on unsuspecting kids -and their parents and caregivers- many times.

What is the scam?

If you have a child who has a behavioral problem, or if your child is a slow learner, or if your child has a mental disorder that's not easily identifiable, quantifiable, or diagnosable, your child may need assistance in the classroom, and rightfully so.

This assistance doesn't materialize out of thin air. It needs to be paid for, and the primary source for funding comes from one or more forms of government. It comes from states and/or counties if you live in the US, and it comes from counties and/or provinces, if you live in Canada and other countries. In many cases, federal funding may be available too.

Have you ever noticed that autistic adults who apply on their own for disability benefits from the government –no matter where they live- are almost always turned down on the first try? Yet it seems that for kids, when funding is applied for by schools on their behalf, the dollars fly into school coffers.

Have you ever stopped to wonder why that is?

How does that happen?

Children get funded because schools fill out the necessary application forms in a way that demonstrates a child is grossly developmentally challenged, and has special needs that are so expensive as to be unaffordable by the school district. An

ADHD diagnosis used to get schools much of the funding they needed for a child.

Now it's an autism diagnosis.

But the fact is, most of the kids diagnosed with autism these days don't have autism. It's the biggest secret kept in many school systems. The psychologists many districts have on staff are on their payroll, and it has been made known to some of them that if they expect to stay on the payroll, they had better do everything in their power to secure the necessary funding the school requires to put accommodations in place for problem students.

These psychologists know *exactly* what to write on forms to get funding from county, state/provincial, and federal sources.

Sometimes, more than a "diagnosis" is needed, and so parents are coached about what to say to their child's pediatrician to get a secondary "diagnosis." Some parents are told something along the lines of "Have your pediatrician put XXXXXX on the form and give it back to us. We'll submit the paperwork for you."

Then the child in question gets an Educational Assistant, a laptop with assistive technology, a weekly pass to the Snozelen room, and a bunch of other nonsense. I say it's "nonsense" for the child to get these things because, if a child actually *doesn't* have autism, but is diagnosed as being on the spectrum anyway, it means the school is actually wasting money and resources, and probably not properly educating that child. They are in fact shuttling the child through the educational system using costly, time consuming "aids" that do nothing to actually educate.

Put another way -and using a hypothetical example- why would a school provide a visually impaired student with a touch screen computer when what they may really need is a Braille writer, voice readers on their computers, and a seeing eye dog?

These schools wind up socially promoting autistics on a tiered system of lowered expectations rather than providing proper supports for them. Given that many children who are "diagnosed" with autism are actually kids with behavioral problems, schools would be better off, in these questionable days of political correctness, forcing these misdiagnosed children to buckle down and study harder.

Parents of behaviorally challenged or special needs children are similarly victimized. Many are ignorant of what the schools are doing, and, because they have not done the research into autism or any other diagnoses that their children might have, they do not know what their children actually need. Because no parent wants to admit that they are ignorant, or poor disciplinarians, or that they don't know how to handle a kid with special needs, schools seize on that fact, prey upon it, and use these kids to gain funding which they can use to their advantage.

Why would schools do this?

Partly, it is to help schools on a more comprehensive level. School populations in total have special needs kids, and providing for the *general* needs of *all* of them means that schools can serve a wider segment of the student population than just a select few, but the way they acquire the necessary resources to provide for those kids is to inflate the number and severity of a few students and say on grant application forms that they require extreme and expensive accommodations.

Still, many times, those students who really need accommodations are not getting them to the extent that they need them.

You will find that a common complaint many parents have about educational assistants, for example, is that there are not enough of them to go around. Funding may have been obtained for an EA to sit with a single student for the entire school day, yet, for some inexplicable reason, this EA is made to divide his or her time between two or more students. This is because, while the other students may in fact need educational assistants, they by no stretch of the imagination meet the qualifications for the school to secure funding for assistants. Thus a behaviorally challenged individual may be deliberately misdiagnosed so that the acquired aid may serve the other students who *really* need the assistant.

But wait a minute? Didn't I say there was a scam here somewhere? If *some* students at least are getting the help they need, or if *all* students are at least getting *some* help, how is applying for funds a scam?

Well...

Sometimes, funding *is* secured for many EAs, or maybe

for certain alterations to a classroom, but only one or two EAs are hired in the former example, or, still in the former example, the proper number of EAs are hired, but worked for fewer hours than necessary. In the latter example schools use the money for other purposes, like doing structural repairs. Or maybe the schools never get around to hiring an EA or making the alterations and simply pocket the money.

Have you ever noticed that sometimes a full time EA is hard to come by, but a school may have a Snozelen room? This indoor playground is expensive to build, and requires huge allocations of space in an age when many of our schools are overcrowded and underfunded. Yet these rooms seem to be making their ways into schools a lot these days.

How many times do we see a school push its students to sell candy bars to raise money for itself while students' needs go unaddressed even as a Snozelen room sits empty?

How does a thing like that happen, and why?

It happens for two reasons: One, the district has received a grant to build the room, and if they build it on the cheap, they can pocket the difference, and two, for schools and districts that are guilty of this financial shell game, it's all just a show. "We're doing something for our autistic students," is the message these schools are trying to get across.

But the saddest part is, most of the kids they are saying are autistic may not really be autistic at all, and may be improperly diagnosed by their own psychologists.

Aside from improperly diagnosed students not being properly accommodated, and not getting a proper education, the one *other* major problem associated with these misdiagnoses is that students will carry this label with them out of the school system and into real life.

And so today, there is a whole generation of people in society, believing themselves to be autistic who really are not. Some of these people may go to talk to therapists about unrelated issues, and they may begin by saying, "Well, I have Asperger syndrome..." and the therapist will respond by saying "No you don't. You don't have any of the symptoms."

Won't these people be surprised and angry that they have been rooked by the educational system! That they have been living a lie through most of their youth and part of their adulthood! That their real diagnosis continues to be a mystery, and that they are in for a lengthy and expensive round of diagnostic testing to find out what diagnosis they may really have!

And what if these people have been demanding accommodations from their employers based upon the fact that they are "autistic?" We hear so many times that people on the autism spectrum have applied for disability (and other) benefits on the basis of their diagnoses and have been turned down. Could it be because government agencies know that their diagnoses may be incorrect? Could it be because government agencies know that the "autism epidemic" is largely fueled by erroneous diagnoses given, not only by schools, but by others as well, like researchers, unqualified doctors, and "quacks"?

Some states now have "autism registries" so that people on the spectrum can get autism-targeted health services. How would these misdiagnosed people feel if they were on a registry when in fact they did not have autism? How would they feel if they had to get themselves de-listed from the registry before they could receive proper treatment for their *new* diagnoses? How would they feel if they were prejudiced against if it was found out by -for example- employers that they were on the registry?

When some schools scam the system, the consequences for the victims can be long-lasting, worrisome, burdensome, and far-reaching. Some adults who have been victims of their school districts are now harboring animosity at their parents for not catching on to the scams in the school systems so long ago, and for not pushing the school psychologists to properly diagnose them way back when.

About Researchers...

I had mentioned that some autism researchers may be unqualified to make a diagnosis.

How can *this* be? Aren't they on autism's front lines? If anyone is qualified to make an autism diagnosis, wouldn't it be *them*?

This depends on whether or not the researcher is doing

legitimate research that will be peer-reviewed. *Anyone* who conducts a study can bill themselves as researchers. And if a dishonest researcher, or a researcher with dishonest motives, wants to skew a study, or skew the interpretation of the study results in a biased way, it can be done.

While it is generally understood that there are certain methods by which a study may be conducted, and a certain way the resulting data ought to be correlated, some researchers may not adhere to those methods, and given that there are so many studies that are produced at any given time, it is unlikely that all research will wind up being peer-reviewed.

Sloppy science, faulty interpretation of the results, and biased conclusions can make for poor studies. And if such a study should begin by requiring a sample of people on the autism spectrum, and if those autistics are in short supply, it could well be that they will be produced...through off the cuff rapid-fire diagnoses.

So while it is true that some autism researchers are honest, their work "iron clad", their study results unassailable, and the study samples properly diagnosed by other doctors (and properly re-diagnosed by the researchers), other researchers may not be so ethical.

About Doctors...

It may seem obvious that some doctors who are not trained in the area autism spectrum disorders may not be qualified to issue a diagnosis. Some doctors will, however, fortify their backgrounds as they conduct their lengthy diagnostic examinations and attempt to properly diagnose their patients. Yet their training may still be lacking, substandard, or insufficient for *accurately* diagnosing someone with an autism spectrum disorder.

About "Quacks"...

Doctors who practice what some call "quackery" that is to say, medically unproven treatments and cures, may not have qualifications to diagnose autism spectrum disorders either even though they may have began their careers with regular medical training.

Not all doctors who practice "bad medicine" are "quacks" by definition. It may be that they have alternate but unproven theories about the origins of autism spectrum disorders, and may not only employ unproven treatment methods, but may be "treating" people who may be "diagnosed" autistic based upon theoretical diagnostic criteria.

Yet for all of that, they may just as well be listed as "quacks" by virtue of the fact that the medicine they are practicing in relation to ASDs is not commonly recognized by health-related government bodies and/or by medical organizations.

About Other "Diagnosticians"...

Least reputable of all in some people's minds would be a diagnosis from anyone not of the medical or research profession, such as a

- ☐ Public speaker, or
- ☐ Someone on the spectrum

Public speakers who have read the existing research, and who speak about autism spectrum disorders are unqualified to give a diagnosis because

- ☐ They may not have the medical background to properly understand the research or properly interpret the results,

- ☐ Nor is it probable that they have the medical knowledge to rule out other diagnoses which may account for autism-like symptoms.

- ☐ And if they *do* possess such medical knowledge (i.e., they *are* doctors) they would need to examine someone very carefully and extensively before issuing a diagnosis -something that cannot happen at a public speaking event.

The same can be said for someone on the spectrum.

Thus (getting back to online discussion boards) people claimed to be diagnosed, and believed themselves to be diagnosed, when in fact, there was really the possibility that they were either misdiagnosed, or "diagnosed" by a person or people not properly qualified to make a diagnosis.

Blurring the lines between whether a diagnosis was a "true" one or not was the idea that a person could be "officially" or "unofficially diagnosed.

"Officially" meant that:

1.A person was subjected to what was commonly considered to be the proper battery of tests which would result in a solid, almost irrefutable diagnosis.

2.The tester was presumed to be properly qualified to conduct those tests.

"Unofficially" meant that:

1.A person was not as rigorously tested, and/or

2.The tester was not properly qualified to conduct the tests.

3.Testing by a qualified tester was still in progress.

4.The results were inconclusive, but leaning toward the test subject being on the spectrum.

Thus a person could be diagnosed:

- "Officially" by a psychologist
- "Officially" by a school psychologist
- "Officially" by a psychiatrist
- "Officially" by an autism specialist

- "Officially" by a doctor
- "Officially" by a researcher
- "Officially" by a public speaker
- "Officially" by another autistic
- "Unofficially" by a psychologist
- "Unofficially" by a school psychologist
- "Unofficially" by a psychiatrist
- "Unofficially" by an autism specialist
- "Unofficially" by a doctor
- "Unofficially" by a researcher
- "Unofficially" by a public speaker
- "Unofficially" by an autistic

You can now begin to see how a message board could begin to fracture, and how political factions could begin to emerge.

Common questions which one would observe flitting back and forth on a message board or in chat would be:

- Are you diagnosed? Self diagnosed? In the process of getting a diagnosis? Seeking a diagnosis? A wannabee?

- If you are diagnosed, who diagnosed you?

- Was the diagnostician reputable, or not?

- Was it an official or unofficial diagnosis?

2. Self-Diagnosed

There are those who "self-diagnose" and they may do it in a number of different ways:

- They may have a friend on the spectrum, and identify with some of his or her symptoms, and diagnose themselves.

- They may read a newspaper article or magazine article and see themselves as being similar to the people mentioned in the newspaper article or magazine article, and diagnose themselves.

- They may identify with a fictitious autistic character in a book, magazine, television show, movie, etc, and they diagnose themselves.

- They may read the DSM IV-TR (Diagnostic and Statistical Manual of Mental Disorders, Fourth edition, Text Revised), DSM V (Diagnostic and Statistical Manual of Mental Disorders, Fifth edition), or ICD 10 (International Statistical Classification of Diseases and Related Health Problems, 10th edition) and identify with the "symptoms" listed therein, and diagnose themselves.

- They may read a study and see themselves as being similar to the test subjects, and diagnose themselves.

- They may take a comment from a diagnosed person or doctor as being a diagnosis (e.g. "You share a trait or two with people on the autism spectrum.").

- They may transfer a diagnosis from a family member, or relative to themselves. (e.g., "My brother has a diagnosis, and I share many of his 'Aspie Traits' so I must have Asperger syndrome too, only much milder.").

- They may take an informal online test or quiz, (e.g. The Aspie Quiz) which may suggest that they *might* have Asperger syndrome, and diagnose themselves. However, they may ignore any disclaimer on those quizzes that state that only a professional clinician can make an informed diagnosis.

- They may take a respected online assessment test or quiz (e.g. The Australian Scale for Asperger syndrome by M.S. Garnett and Tony Attwood) and diagnose themselves. However, they ignore any disclaimer on those tests which state that only a professional clinician can make an informed diagnosis. (**Note:** Oftentimes people who use this online diagnostic test will stretch the truth and say things like "A professionally developed and recognized test diagnosed me with Asperger syndrome," or "Tony Attwood diagnosed me," or "I was professionally diagnosed.")

- They may be made an "honorary autistic" by other people who are or who believe themselves to be on the spectrum, and consider this to be an informal or formal diagnosis.

The Dangers Of Self-Diagnosing

Sometimes, when people think they know better than professionals, they really don't, and what they *think* they know can actually hurt them in the long run.

- Self-diagnosed people may actually have other disorders that are not being diagnosed, addressed, and treated, and believing actual medical attention to be unnecessary, they do not seek medical attention for their *true* disorders.

- When a self-diagnosed person does not seek a true diagnosis, *real* undiagnosed disorders may not only go unaddressed and untreated but may worsen, or become life-threatening.

- If the undiagnosed disorders are ones which may cause an individual to be, or to become a danger to themselves or a danger to the public, they are not only their own worst enemy, but the public's enemy as well.

- Self-diagnosed people who have received approval by their diagnosed peers may soon come to see themselves as being able to speak for autistics, when in fact, their self-diagnosis may not be a *true* autism diagnosis at all.

- Self-diagnosed individuals may at one time or another see themselves as authorities in the area of autism spectrum disorders, and write books, magazine articles, give lectures, etc., when in fact, their personal experiences and world view might really be influenced by some other disorder or disorders altogether.

- Other unsuspecting people may come to see the self-diagnosed individual as an authority or a reference, not realizing that the self-diagnosed individual may not have autism at all.

Can we really believe that an autism diagnosis can be *faked*? After all, for self-diagnosed "autistics" to "look the part" on demand, they have to appear autistic to anyone who may question their diagnosis.

Can it be done?

Yes.

As proof, I offer Dustin Hoffman and Claire Danes, who played Rainman in <u>Rainman</u>, and Temple Grandin in <u>Temple Grandin</u> respectively on the big screen. While any moviegoer knows that people who portray other people on the screen are actors, both Hoffman and Danes convinced millions of people around the world that they were watching an accurate portrayal of autism. And, in the case of <u>Rainman</u>, Kim Peek, the autistic man upon whom Rainman was based, shares only a few qualities with Hoffman's character. Thus while Hoffman's Rainman isn't exactly a lie or a fraud, it's not exactly true either.

Hoffman and Danes didn't instantly fall into their roles. Rather, they were coached, and told how to behave. In fact, Hoffman was actually coached by Temple Grandin. It is not so much of a stretch, then, to posit that, like Hoffman and Danes, *anyone* could learn how to imitate someone with autism and carry out this act for an extended period of time, and perhaps a lifetime, if the people carrying out the act were particularly manipulative.

Realistically speaking, however, living a lie for one's whole life is not easy, and is not something someone would likely do. Yet, when you factor in that many self-diagnosed people naturally have some traits similar to those displayed by real autistics, faking might not be so hard.

Some Additional Words On Self-Diagnosis

There are many more ways people can self-diagnose, but my point ought to be clear: Self-diagnosis is specious and unreliable. Aside from that, a self-diagnosis is not recognized as an official diagnosis by medical professionals. My opinions about self-diagnosis are shared by many others in the autism community at large.

My further opinion is that, for their own good, people who self-diagnose who are told repeatedly by medical professionals that they don't have autism would be wise to listen to the diagnosticians rather than themselves. And if these self-diagnosed people, after being told by many doctors that they are not autistic, "diagnosis shop", and find one lone doctor who tells them they *are* autistic, they would be wise to question whether or not what that one doctor is telling them is true.

On a related note, we cannot put much faith in a self-diagnosed individual if they disbelieve the majority of qualified medical practitioners who tell them they don't have autism, and who instead choose to believe their self-diagnosis to be accurate.

Similarly, I don't believe anyone can take a self-diagnosed person's "personal experiences with autism" seriously until they are *truly* diagnosed.

I have been circulating in the autism community online since just about the time the internet became widely used.

Sixteen years ago I was seeing kids joining autism forums who were saying things like "I've been diagnosed with Oppositional Defiant Disorder, but I think I'm really autistic because people don't understand me. I'm going in for testing to get checked for autism." Invariably, people like these reported that autism was ruled out, but, interestingly enough, more diagnoses were tacked on that were behaviorally related.

One woman specifically, who now claims to be an "autism warrior" was diagnosed as being psychopathic, and this diagnosis, to my knowledge, remains unchanged to the present day. "Autism" as far as I know, was never her diagnosis, yet she claims to be autistic.

These "posers," many of whom have been repeatedly - and in no uncertain terms- told by licensed board certified medical professionals that they are not by any stretch of the imagination autistic (regardless of whether or not they were previously "diagnosed" by school psychologists) are now giving lectures, making tapes and videos, writing books, and billing themselves as "autistic life coaches" and "autistic advocates." Some of them are now running -or serving in leadership roles in- autistic advocacy organizations.

There is an avid critic of the Midnight In Chicago blog, (www.midnightinchicago.wordpress.com), who claims to be autistic. He (or she – I'm not going to spill the beans on who this person is) has *not* to my knowledge been diagnosed autistic, but *has* stated elsewhere that he or she has been diagnosed with bipolar disorder. This person has a video-blog and a series of other blogs designed to tell anyone who will listen about how autism has impacted his or her life, and what people can do to make life easier for autistics. This person has written one "book" (never published, except for free distribution in the form of an electronic file) and has been trying to write other books for many years now.

Supposedly, according to this person, s/he has one "novel" that is being "considered by agents" whatever that means. Whether or not the "novel" and the "book" are one and the same, I do not know. But I must say that I find the assertion about agents misleading. Having once been in the market for agents, I've spoken with a few of them about their services and what they could potentially do for me. I know that before they would solicit my writing, they would "consider" whether or not what I had to submit was worth soliciting. To say that an agent is "considering" something is like saying Readers Digest is "considering" a joke for publication. *Sure* your piece of writing is being "considered." Yours and many others.

But when it comes to publishing something as significant as a "novel," I don't think it is acceptable to imply that it is on the road to being published when it hasn't even passed an initial informal review and critique.

There is another "autistic" person who was living in (his or her) parents' basement until recently, who lectures, makes videos, and writes books. The books he or she publishes tell autistics about how to make successes out of their lives. Autistics and parents of autistics alike buy into his or her spiel, probably never realizing how unsuccessful the person is they are buying the books from.

To "identify" with someone on the spectrum is understandable, but to take that one step further and "diagnose" oneself may not be healthy or medically sound. To self-diagnose for the express purpose of making money off of one's diagnosis is potentially fraud and, when it victimizes those with *real* diagnoses, exploitation.

We can see, then, why it is that a fracture might develop between diagnosed and self-diagnosed individuals, and why some of the former and some of the latter have developed their own factions.

3. In The Process Of Getting A Diagnosis

People in this category can be of a number of different types.

- They may be undergoing an assessment by qualified diagnosticians.

- They may be in the beginning stages of the assessment process by qualified diagnosticians.

- They may have just begun the process of getting assessed by qualified diagnosticians.

- They may be undergoing an assessment by *unqualified* diagnosticians.

- They may be in the beginning stages of the

assessment process by *unqualified* diagnosticians.

☐ They may have just begun the process of getting assessed by *unqualified* diagnosticians.

☐ They may be seeking a qualified physician who is capable of diagnosing them.

☐ They may be thinking about getting a diagnosis.

While we can say that thinking of getting a diagnosis, or seeking a physician to get diagnosed is part of the process of getting a diagnosis, some people think of getting a diagnosis for years and decades, and their search for a physician who can give them a diagnosis may be half-hearted, lackadaisical, or entirely fictitious.

It's true that ultimately, these people *may* wind up on the spectrum, but until they do, they are *not* diagnosed as being on the spectrum, thus they may not be not looked upon favorably by diagnosed individuals, especially when these diagnosis-in-process individuals assert viewpoints about their experiences as though they do in fact have autism.

We can see arguing and fighting in chat rooms, on forums, on message boards, and in real life between people who are diagnosed, self-diagnosed, and in the process of getting a diagnosis. Depending on where they rank themselves in the hierarchy, any one of these types of individuals may see themselves as "higher" than people who are seeking a diagnosis, and even more will rank themselves higher than "wannabees."

4. Seeking A Diagnosis

Some will use this term to mean that they are in the process of getting a diagnosis, and vice versa. Generally speaking, those seeking a diagnosis may:

☐ Be undergoing an assessment by qualified diagnosticians.

☐ Be in the beginning stages of the assessment process

by qualified diagnosticians.

- ☐ Have just begun the process of getting assessed by qualified diagnosticians.

- ☐ Be undergoing an assessment by *unqualified* diagnosticians.

- ☐ Be in the beginning stages of the assessment process by *unqualified* diagnosticians.

- ☐ Have just begun the process of getting assessed by *unqualified* diagnosticians.

- ☐ Be seeking a qualified physician who is capable of diagnosing them.

- ☐ Be thinking about getting a diagnosis.

But the last two bullets best represent the term. For these people, they are not yet in the process of getting a diagnosis, but are seeking to get one.

Some of those who are diagnosed, self-diagnosed, or in the process of getting diagnosed, may think of these people who are seeking a diagnosis, that they should: "Just do it! Stop thinking about it. Stop looking around for someone to diagnose you. Settle on someone and do it!"

It is easy for these people to make such remarks, particularly if they are self-diagnosed or if the people who are/have diagnosed them came cheap, or were paid for by someone else. A diagnosis by a board certified doctor who is qualified to diagnose autism spectrum disorders may take many months if not years, and lots of money. In addition to other considerations, the cost alone is reason enough to choose carefully when seeking someone to give a diagnosis.

However, many who say they are seeking a diagnosis may not be seeking a diagnosis at all but may be just saying so in order to fit in with those who actually *have* a diagnosis. Deep down, they may know or suspect that if were they to be properly assessed, they would not fit the criteria for any autism diagnosis.

Yet for them to admit this publicly risks anything that they stand to gain (be it merely social acceptance of real autistics -as I have just stated-, or public sympathy, or government or scholastic benefits) from being thought "autistic."

5. Wannabee

A wannabee can be said to be someone who identifies with people on the spectrum -usually with their more preferable traits, like the high IQs many with Asperger syndrome seem to possess- but who is not diagnosed. They would, however, *like* to be diagnosed.

Some people on the spectrum find the wannabee perspective offensive. Why would someone *want* the label and all the negatives that come with it? Wannabees fail to take into consideration that people on the spectrum may have sensitivity issues, processing difficulties, learning impairments, and social interaction problems. They may have trouble with life skills, may be unable to live alone, may live in impoverished conditions, and may be reliant on government programs and assistance, such as food stamps, disability, and welfare. They may have problems in school, or finding and keeping jobs, and they may face bullying, prejudice, and discrimination in school or in the workplace.

Even autistics who are self-assured, self-actualized, and happy with who they are, recognize that not all of their traits are spectacular, or advantageous to have, and that some of their traits cause them trouble. They may see wannabees as having an unrealistic and uninformed view about what autism really looks like.

Wannabees might look at people who are rumored to be autistic, such as Bill Gates and wish that they could be diagnosed, but seldom are wannabees keen on autism being equated with autism like we see portrayed in Rainman, nor are wannabees interested in being identified with someone like Kim Peek, on whom Rainman was based. Similarly, they don't want to be subjected to the more extreme forms of autism therapy that autistics with less desirable traits are forced to endure, nor do they talk pleasurably about the prospect of being looked down upon by a society that is generally prejudiced against people with diagnosed mental disorders.

Sometimes, when diagnosed individuals try to make wannabees understand the negative aspects of having a diagnosis, the wannabees rebut them rudely, challenging whether or not the diagnosed person is really diagnosed

> "Do you even know what autism is? *You* might have difficulties, and *you* might have problems, but *you* are surely the exception to the rule. In fact, you're probably just *lazy*. You're probably *lying* about even *having* a diagnosis. You're probably just *self-diagnosed!*"

They may even go further than that, and gather a party of individuals to challenge the diagnosed person.

From a psychological standpoint, it could seem like wannabees are in a state of denial. In other words, if wannabees see autism the way it actually is, it might mean that they would be forced to accept that they are not autistic, but instead are suffering under some other (less acceptable to them) kind of diagnosis. Or it might even mean that they don't have another kind of diagnosis at all, but might just be suffering from some bad character flaws. Thus they may re-frame all of autism into their own warped definitions, and may accuse some diagnosed autistics of being fakes just to maintain the fiction that they *might* have autism.

Alternatively, and speculatively, the wannabee could be seen as a narcissist, or someone with an insecure ego who needs to be perceived a certain way in order to feel good about themselves. If this last is the case, we can see how wannabees could be so volatile on social media sites. Trying to explain the reality of autism to them, and how negatively autism is perceived by many, may be a direct threat to fragile egos.

There is yet one more label heretofore unmentioned under the category of diagnostic status, and that would be

6. Misdiagnosed

This is an individual who may have received a diagnosis, but that diagnosis may have been given either by an unqualified individual, or for an untoward purpose. I have already illustrated how some school systems will misdiagnose an individual to get funding. Doctors outside the school system who are *not* autism specialists may be complicit in similar schemes (usually so that the "diagnosed" individual can get special services or funding that might be useful for their *true* diagnosis but which would not be normally provided or funded by organizations for that diagnosis), or so that insurance companies will reimburse doctors for services rendered at a higher rate than they otherwise would.

Because there is no way for anyone except for a qualified physician to reverse a diagnosis, these people can claim to be diagnosed with near immunity to attack even though they may not be on the spectrum at all.

The exception to the rule is when someone is diagnosed by a school psychologist.

Person #1: "Oh, you've gotten one of *those* diagnoses."

Person #2: "What's *that* supposed to mean?"

Person #1: "It means you're not really autistic. Congratulations! You've been used! You're just a moneymaker for the school system!"

Person #2: "No I'm not! I'm autistic! The school wouldn't do that to me. And mom and dad wouldn't allow it."

Person #1: "Your mom and dad don't know their butts from holes in the ground. They don't know jack-shit about autism. *And*, they're suckers. That's why you've been diagnosed with something you don't have. Idiot!"

Person #2: "Oh yeah, well *fuck you!*"

Levels Of Functionality

The next area of contention is concerned with how functional a diagnosed autistic, self-diagnosed person, person in the process of getting a diagnosis, person seeking a diagnosis, a wannabee, or a misdiagnosed individual may be.

In *reality, if* they are autistic, they may either identified as:

- High-functioning, or
- Low-functioning

by their physicians.

But diagnosed autistics, self-diagnosed people, people in the process of getting a diagnosis, people seeking a diagnosis, wannabees, and misdiagnosed individuals *may consider themselves to be* either:

- High-functioning, or
- Low-functioning

regardless of how their physician has identified them.

Many times diagnosed autistics, self-diagnosed people, people in the process of getting a diagnosis, people seeking a diagnosis, wannabees, and misdiagnosed individuals will call themselves high-functioning when they aren't.

They may not do well in school or college, may not be able to hold jobs, may function poorly in relationships, may not be able to handle finances, may not be able to live alone, but at the same time, because they are proficient in their perseverative interest (whatever that interest may be) they may say that they are superior to non-autistics, and that they are high-functioning.

They may deny that they are low functioning for *honest* reasons: Perhaps they cannot see that they *are* low functioning. Perhaps circumstances legitimately prevent them from functioning well *at the moment*.

Then of course there are some who know they are low functioning but refuse to admit it to themselves or others. Perhaps they are simply embarrassed that they are not more capable.

However, there is a third type of person who claims that they are high-functioning when they are not: They are the type who do this in order to avoid working on counteracting their own deficits.

> "My brain is lopsided. I have superior intelligence in one area, and am lacking in others. So I use the superior portion of my mind to my advantage and just accept that I will never be capable in other areas."

It is not unheard of that when faced with the prospect of discipline or punishment in life-skills classes, some people who previous "couldn't" do something will respond favorably, promptly, and exactly as required. This shows that some on the spectrum are simply lying when they say they cannot do something. Yet their determination to prove incompetence in a certain area up till that point, even while claiming to be high-functioning over all, caused them to be labeled as low functioning.

They may also claim to be high-functioning so that their peers and lesser peers will hold them in good and admired esteem. Even in the autism community, there is considerable prejudice against lower functioning autistics. Some even go so far as to describe lower function autistics as "retards."

Alternatively, diagnosed autistics, self-diagnosed people, people in the process of getting a diagnosis, people seeking a diagnosis, wannabees, or misdiagnosed individuals will sometimes call themselves low-functioning when they aren't. What they may be instead is lazy, and they may use their diagnosis or their alleged diagnosis to obtain special privileges throughout life, such as:

- An IEP (Individualized Educational Program) in school
- Subsidized housing
- Work accommodations they would otherwise not be entitled to have
- Disability benefits

- Tax breaks
- Reduced admission costs at public and private functions and venues

When it is discovered by people in the online and offline autism community that some people are not as functional as they say they are, or are *more* functional than they say they are, arguing and fighting can break out, and this results in factions forming. The more a faction's members have in common with one another, the stronger the bond between the faction's members.

In addition to being either high-functioning or low functioning, diagnosed autistics, self-diagnosed people, people in the process of getting a diagnosis, people seeking a diagnosis, wannabees, or misdiagnosed individuals can be:

- Capable of functioning adequately in society
- Incapable of functioning adequately in society
- Educably mentally handicapped

Using Functionality To One's Advantage

Online and offline, but online especially, it is easy for someone to pretend to be that which they are not. Thus it is not uncommon for unscrupulous people to bill themselves as high-functioning autistics who are capable of functioning in society one year (when all is going well), and then bill themselves as low-functioning autistics incapable of functioning in society another year (when they need money or find themselves falling on hard times).

In addition to the special privileges described in the previous section above, money and sympathy seem to be the things manipulative "autistics" try to obtain the most.

It is not uncommon for someone to ask for money for some seemingly plausible purpose.

- They anticipate being short on the electric bill this month and need a few extra dollars to make sure their power isn't cut off.

- They need to get away and want to go on an overnight vacation but cannot afford a hotel room.

- They need special lenses to shield their eyes from light because their eyes are photosensitive, but it will take them months to save up to get them.

They may even set up a PayPal account to make it easy for people to send them funds.

People offer to send them money and do, not bothering to actually watch what these people are posting elsewhere on social media sites: Things like:

"Whoo hoo! Just bought a new set of headphones for my stereo system!"

or

"Yes! Three new games in three days for my PS 3!"

or

"Going to the Katy Perry concert next week. Tickets for me and my girl cost cost $64.00 a pop!"

Sympathy may not seem like much to ask for, but it's a lot to give when you look into why people are asking for it.

"I'm being bullied and have been for 35 years! Help me stop these bullies and vile trolls!"

But then you see that the person making this plea is the instigator in most of these incidents, doing the equivalent of punching someone else first and then running to someone for help after the person they hit strikes back at them.

Or maybe you see something like:

"I *hate* having Asperger syndrome! I am *so* misunderstood!"

But scrolling further back in that person's page, you discover that this adult believed himself or herself to be "diagnosed" by an 11 year old kid with Asperger syndrome who said he or she "might be an Aspie."

Comorbidities And Their Usefulness

Diagnosed autistics, self-diagnosed people, people in the process of getting a diagnosis, people seeking a diagnosis, wannabees, or misdiagnosed individuals may have:

- Comorbid diagnoses (or, if it proves they aren't actually on the spectrum, other diagnoses)

Or they may "compete" with one another to find out who has the most comorbid diagnoses. Thus while they may or may not have a comorbid diagnoses to begin with, they may add on some that they don't have to beat their opponent.
They may also have:

- Allergies
- Sensitivities (including...)
     -Hyper
     -Hypo
- Synesthesia
- Perseverative Interests

Observe enough people over time, and informal conclusions can be drawn about between people with similar comorbid diagnoses, and one can also postulate that some comorbidities are driving autistic-like behaviors. However, because there is no way to verify whether or not these people actually have the comorbid diagnoses they claim to have, such conclusions and postulations are purely speculative.

A Digression - Sensitivities

Many autistics experience heightened, dulled, or impaired sensitivities that affect their sense(s) of taste, and/or touch, and/or smell, and/or hearing, and/or sight. Should these autistics be given special allowances for having these sensitivities?

Some would say no. After all, *everyone* on the planet has their own way of filtering the world through their senses. But people who make that statement may not understand the concept of hyper-sensitivies and hypo-sensitivities.

Hypersensitivities occur when sensitivities are strongly heightened, many times uncomfortably so. Hypo-sensitivities occur when there is a lesser reaction to a sensation than one would expect, or else a delay in the reaction between the stimulus and the response.

Given that many people cannot imagine what an autistic's sensory processing capabilities look like, it might be wise to give autistics the benefit of the doubt when they say they have sensitivities.

Unfortunately, some self-diagnosed individuals, misdiagnosed individuals, and wannabees will simply claim they have sensitivities when in fact they are making those claims for selfish purposes. If they don't want to eat something they are served, they will say they have a sensitivity to the meat, fish, or vegetable so they do not have to eat it. If there is a dirty job they don't want to do -say, planting a bush- they will say they have a tactile sensitivity to avoid doing the job.

And so, because of certain people abusing the "privilege" of having sensitivities, all autistics are negatively viewed by some.

Some autistics will try to claim they have sensitivities that are worse than others have, and these autistics may be *right*. But they may be argued against by self-diagnosed autistics, misdiagnosed autistics, and wannabees, who will tell their own stories so convincingly, that the true autistics are disbelieved.

A Further Digression - Synesthesia

I will take a brief break here to mention why having or

not having synesthesia is important to some autistics.

Synesthesia can be described as a blending of senses. A person may be able to see colors when listening to music, for example. This interesting trait or comorbidity, call it what you will, is thought by some "autistics" to be a "super power" or alternatively, a sign that autistics and autistics alone are entering the next stage of evolution. Others see it as a supernatural, or occult like power similar to ESP, déjà vu, or the ability to predict the future. Few see it as the neural cross-wiring or sequence of synaptic misfires which some doctors believe it to be.

People who experience synesthesia are called synesthetes.

If you are an autistic synesthete, you may be held in higher esteem by some than if you do not have it. It may also be regarded as "proof" that a person is on the spectrum, even though synesthesia is not listed as a symptom of pervasive developmental disorders in the DSM IV-TR or V or ICD-10.

An additional problem occurs when people may infer they have synesthesia when they really do not, or they may pretend to have it when they don't. These people can actually harm diagnosed autistics and diagnosed autistic synesthetes, because they blur, cloud, and distort the common understanding of what real autism and what real synesthesia is.

One Last Digression – Perseverative Interest

A perseverative interest is an interest so powerful that it consumes most of an autistic's thoughts. Some interests can seem quite bizarre to people who are not autistic (e.g. safety pins, doorknobs, a specific kind of bug). Some autistics have interests that distract them to such a degree that they may not be able to focus on other things that require their attention.

These interests are stronger than pastimes and stronger than hobbies. A person might enjoy model trains and fill up his or her basement with an extravagant layout, but this is merely a hobby in comparison to an autistic who might have an interest in, say, electric can openers. An autistic with such an interest might not only try to accumulate a collection of electric can openers, but will try to get the specifications for each and every electronic can opener that was ever made, as well as the information on the original inventor and the people who have since made modifications to the design of the original product. They may memorize the serial numbers and model numbers for these can openers. They may memorize the exterior dimensions of them. They might memorize the electrical wattage consumed in their operation.

They may even feel compelled to root through garbage, or even steal, to get electric can openers.

In this and other respects, a perseverative interest can be viewed as a comorbidity.

Most autistics will reveal their perseverative interests when they are interested in finding someone else to talk to about them. Sometimes, however, self-diagnosed autistics, misdiagnosed autistics, and wannabees will come into the conversation and try to "best" autistics with their own supposed perseverative interests. After a little bit of time goes by, it usually becomes apparent that the "perseverative interests" of these self-diagnosed autistics, misdiagnosed autistics, and wannabees are actually just "interests."

However, sometimes self-diagnosed autistics, misdiagnosed autistics, and wannabees spin things in their favor by making it seem that diagnosed autistics aren't diagnosed at all, but are simply people with obsessive compulsive disorder who are hyper-focused on minutia. When this happens, "war" can break out between autistics and those that are speaking against them. Unfortunately, the more fervently autistics argue, the worse they oftentimes look to external observers. But the worst thing that happens is that, because external observers cannot tell the diagnosed autistics from the self-diagnosed autistics, misdiagnosed autistics, and wannabees, they simply assume that everyone who is arguing is autistic, and conclude that all autistics are "crazy."

Specific Factionalization

Now that the *general* characteristics of people who may or may not be on the spectrum are defined, it's time to get into specifics. In the next section, we begin to see the first of the *major* factions emerge where there is constant, unrelenting contention going on even to this day.

We're speaking, of course, about those who do or do not what to be treated or cured.

Those on the autism spectrum who are capable of making their feelings and needs known:

- May want to be treated
- May not want to be treated
- May want to be cured
- May not want to be cured

1. Those Who Want To Be Treated

For some autistics and posers on the spectrum, life seems exceptionally hard for them. These people may feel that they require additional assistance to help them make it day to day. There is nothing wrong with having these feelings and having this perspective. Just as someone who has depression might want a regimen of antidepressants and therapy to alleviate the feelings associated with being in a depressive state, so too, do some autistics want something to help them with their autism. Whether they want medication, services, or a sympathetic ear, this is what they feel they need, and wherever possible, in my opinion, if something is available to them that is medically proven to work, they should be entitled to have it, without facing ridicule, and without feeling guilt.

The problem for autistics and posers who *don't* want to be treated, is that people who *do* want to be treated open up a "dangerous" door.

A demand for treatments creates a demand for people to do research into treatments, and if an effective treatment -or even a cure- is discovered, it means that autistics and posers who do not want to be treated or cured might someday be forced to undergo treatments or cures anyway.

Thus autistics and posers who are looking to be treated are often bullied, and oftentimes they are bullied into complete submission.

2) Those Who Don't Want To Be Treated

These may be autistic and "so-called autistic" people who believe themselves able to cope effectively with the challenges autism presents, or who believe their symptoms are not severe enough to warrant being treated. Still others may resent the idea that they are in need of treatment even though their ability to function adequately in society is severely limited.

To these people, being treated for autism is akin to being treated for having homosexual proclivities. They may see attempts to treat them as assaults on their very beings, and the fact that treatments (proven or "quack") exist may feel threatening to them.

The question at this point is whether some of these people see themselves and their situations realistically. There are those in this latter category who blame the world for their problems, when their autism -or even just their own personal faults- is to blame. Since the world cannot easily be changed, the alternative is to change one's self, and if the person who is affected is unwilling or unable to make the necessary changes, it may be possible -some people will argue- that they do in fact need help.

A valid counterargument to this point is that if autistics were better understood, and if they were given adequate accommodations, be it in the home, in the school, or at work, then they might be able to function adequately without the need for treatment. After all, we have handicapped parking spaces for the disabled, ramps in public buildings for people in wheelchairs, etc. Why can't we have similar accommodations for those on the spectrum?

The answer to that question is probably one of cost/benefit and to what extent homes, schools, and businesses can afford to make accommodations.

One question those having to make the accommodations may ask is: Are the people we are making accommodations for going to meet us halfway? In other words, we see paraplegics using wheelchairs; and homes, schools, businesses, etc., provide ramps for them. In return for this mobility, not only are these paraplegics better able to function on their own, they are able to offer more to the world than they otherwise would be able to, first by not requiring as much assistance from others to get around, and second by being better able to obtain and keep voluntary, educational, and occupational positions in the community, educational system, and workforce respectively, not to mention that increased access to places of business means the possibility of increased levels of consumerism. What will people on the spectrum do to if they are accommodated?

Fighting between people who want autism treatment and those who don't want autism treatment also revolves around the question of who is considered by diagnosed autistics to have "legitimate" needs and who is "whining." There are many real people and posers on the spectrum who strive to be self-sufficient and succeed, but there are others who are just as capable but who do not put in the same effort.

Why do they not put in as much effort as they should?

Are they lazy?

Perhaps.

But it is just as possible that they don't have the stamina to work as hard as others.

At any rate, a problem arises when the competent group tries to argue that treatments of all kinds should be ended: Were the side that wants to eliminate treatments to win, there might be many who would suffer for want of treatments.

They anti-treatment faction will argue -truthfully- that treatments can be painful, or inhumane, and will even suggest that some treatments are a violation of human rights. While there is some basis for this last argument, the United Nations Convention on the Rights of Persons with Disabilities addresses that last point. I am paraphrasing here, but as I understand it, "degrading" medical treatments are not to be given to patients, nor shall patients undergo experimental treatments without consenting, or, if the patients are incapable of consenting, then treatments may not be given without a guardian's consent.

3. Those Who Want To Be Cured

Some real and "posing" autistics want to be cured. There are many reasons why. One of those may be that their suffering is so severe, and the challenges they face so overwhelming, that they wish that their autism was gone entirely.

Others may be very capable of functioning on their own in the world, but use their autism as an excuse to remain dysfunctional or nonfunctional, and clamor for a cure just to prop up their ongoing scam of having other people believe they are autistic and borderline helpless. If other people believe these scammers are dysfunctional or nonfunctional, and are in dire need of a cure, people may be more inclined to do for them so they don't have to do for themselves.

"Curebies" absorb criticism for having their point of view. As they clamor for a cure, those who do not want a cure become threatened.

4. Those Who Don't Want A Cure

To people who do not want a cure -spectrumites and "posers" alike- if a cure were made available, and if they were given the opportunity to have one, they may feel as though they were being *forced* into a cure. For them, it would be akin to being sterilized against their will, or getting forced into a sex change.

Thus we can see how those who do not want a cure will fight bitterly with those who do.

However, as much as anti-cure autistics may see themselves as fighting to preserve their identities -and their whole beings- they may be regarded as callous and unempathetic by autistics who want a cure.

More Commentary On Treatments and Cures

Looking at things from an external perspective, if someone is "normal" -that is to say, for our purposes here, without autism- a "normal" person may see all autistics as being different, as being under the thumb of their disorder, and may see a treatment or a cure as beneficial. Thus in online forums and real world venues, you will often see people without autism - particularly parents and caregivers- becoming proponents of treatments and cures.

Diagnosed autistics and autistic posers and pretenders, on the other hand, may resent these "normal" people, and challenge them on fair grounds: What right does someone who does *not* have autism have to make life changing decisions for people who *do* have it (or who think or pretend they have it)?

A counterargument is that nonfunctional autistics who could benefit from a treatment and a cure but elect not to pursue either of them, are a financial burden on society, and on the healthcare system. Since things such as social services are paid for through taxes exacted on *everyone*, and since insurance premiums for *all* may be based on the spread out costs of treatments that are necessary for a select few, "normal" tax-paying people who may or may not have insurance policies ultimately pay a large percentage of the bill for the care of non-functional autistics even though they receive little or no benefit from this outflow of cash.

At the time of the writing of this publication, there is no cure for autism, so arguing about whether or not someone on the spectrum should be cured against their will may seem premature to most people, but autistics and autistic pretenders alike see the danger in the making. Should homosexuals be cured against their will? If the answer is -according to society- no, then why should autistics be cured?

There *are* treatments for autism -legitimate and "quack" alike- although the effectiveness of the legitimate treatments are debated. Most that are approved by government and medical organizations seem to be limited in their abilities. Those that are considered "quack" have not been validated by peer-reviewed science and/or accepted by government or medical organizations. As in the matter of cures, treatments are usually argued against using patient's rights or civil rights as a defense.

What makes the civil rights defense weak is that, to date, autism is not recognized as a minority population, but as a mental disorder (despite certain factions' attempts to get the UN to recognize autism as a cultural minority).

More Factions

If the five types of autism as described in the DSM IV-

TR can be seen as five branches of a tree, and the fabricated subcategories that I listed out afterward as twigs, now come the leaves.

There are so many factions within the autism community that it will be impossible to list every one of them here, but I will discuss the major ones at some length.

Some of these factions have developed in response to questions. As people answer these questions, they find themselves falling into various "camps." One question would be:

What Causes Autism?

In response to this question are the following viewpoints which I will have to break down into chunks so we can better digest them. I think you will agree that some viewpoints *sound* more outlandish than others, but there have been arguments made that add a modicum of sense to the more insensible sounding ones.

Chunk #1: Autism Is Caused By Vaccines

Specifically:

☐ Autism is caused by vaccines.

☐ Autism is caused by thimerosal.

☐ Autism is caused by mercury poisoning.

☐ Autism is caused by dental amalgams.

☐ Autism is caused by heavy metal poisoning'

☐ Autism is caused by "Big Pharma" "vaccinating" or injecting people with autism (Please note that some people will use the term "vaccinate" and "inject" interchangeably in this context.).

☐ Autism is caused by government "vaccinating" or

injecting people with autism (Please note that some people will use the term "vaccinate" and "inject" interchangeably in this context.).

Though it may seem as though I have written the same statement out a slightly different way seven times over, the differences between each theory and each "camp" is very distinct. Attend please:

A) Autism Is Caused By Vaccines

The idea is that it is the vaccine itself, or else the ingredients in the vaccines, or else the mix of ingredients in vaccines, which causes autism.

The problem with this idea -aside from the fact that no proof has been scientifically established that vaccines cause autism- is that it's based on a faulty premise: Autism, (and Asperger syndrome especially in North America) only began to be diagnosed in great numbers around the time doctors started vaccinating people in earnest.

The thing is, before 1900, there was no word for what we now call "autism" but autism as it is modernly defined has always existed, and has had different names throughout the ages. It has been called everything from insanity to demonic possession!

In the past 100 years there have been a number of different terms for autism and its manners of presentation. It was in 1908 that the word "autism" was first used by Swiss psychiatrist Eugen Bleuler to describe self-absorbed patients with schizophrenia. Dr. Leo Kanner referred to some of his patients as being "autistic" in 1943. Hans Asperger in 1944 was labeling some of his patients as autistic psychopaths. For a while, autistic patients were said to be suffering "Kanner's syndrome" and others who were affected somewhat differently were said to be afflicted with Asperger syndrome.

Bolstering the idea that many names for autism have come and gone is the fact that in 2013 the DSM V eliminated the five categories (Autism, Asperger Syndrome, Childhood Disintegrative Disorder, Rett Syndrome, Pervasive

Developmental Disorder Not Otherwise Specified) in favor of one, called "Autism Spectrum Disorder." "Kanner's syndrome," has also fallen into disuse. Decades from now, people will be unfamiliar with the terms for autism that we commonly use today.

But to restate: The name we commonly use for this pervasive developmental disorder, "autism" came into common usage around the time that vaccines regularly began to be administered to people en masse. Likewise, so did the name "Asperger syndrome." Yet autism existed long before vaccines were invented.

The theory that vaccines cause autism is supposedly reinforced by what is thought by many to be shoddy research. British Doctor Andrew Jeremy Wakefield and his study are most often quoted as "sources," to back up the idea that vaccines cause autism, but many times absent from books, magazines, blogs, and newspaper articles that push this vaccines-cause-autism agenda are counterarguments, such as the fact that Wakefield was sanctioned, his medical license was revoked, and his research was disproved. To date, there is no evidence that vaccines cause autism as it is defined in the DSM IV-TR, DSM V, or ICD-10.

The theory may continue to thrive, however, because autism is many times identified in toddlers after vaccine regimens have begun. However, up until recently, there were very few -if any- well known definitive tests to identify autism in infants, thus a baby could have autism, but the symptoms of autism wouldn't be seen in a person by observers until a time when a child was supposed to meet certain milestones but missed them.

Another reason for the stubborn persistence of this theory is that a small number have people have suffered side effects that mimic autistic symptoms after receiving vaccines. Yet there is quite a difference between these symptoms and autism itself.

In either of these cases (the onset of autism after vaccine regimens begin or some people's negative reactions to vaccines), one can counter argue that a person might ride in a boat for the first time and experience nausea and vomiting. But it does not follow that sea-sickness is the cause of the nausea and vomiting. It could just as well be something that the person ate before getting on the boat. It could be nerves. It could be anything. But just as no cause and effect conclusion can be drawn between riding in a boat and nausea without further study, one cannot conclude definitively that vaccines *cause* autism without further study. The only thing that can be said is that a very limited number of people have experienced autism-like symptoms after being vaccinated.

Yet another reason for this theory's survival is that it fits in nicely with larger conspiracy theories, some of which which will be discussed momentarily. For some people, if they believe an overarching conspiracy theory, they must believe the lesser conspiracies that comprise the larger, and vice versa, never mind that the whole of the theory or its parts may be grossly flawed.

B) Autism Is Caused By Thimerosal

The difference between "autism is caused by vaccines" and "autism is caused by thimerosal" is that thimerosal is an ingredient in vaccines and not the actual vaccine.

This theory holds water with some people because thimerosal is a mercury-based preservative (specifically, it contains ethel-mercury), and since the symptoms of mercury poisoning appear to some to be similar to symptoms commonly associated with autism, thimerosal must cause autism.

The problem with this theory is that

- Thimerosal is not mercury itself, but a mercury compound

- Thimerosal is not the more dangerous methyl mercury compound, but the less dangerous ethyl mercury compound

Why should any of that matter?

Mercury itself can accumulate in someone's system and then stay there indefinitely. The half life of methyl mercury, however, is one and a half months, during which time it is exposed to the blood and may accumulate *in* the body, but the half life of ethyl mercury is one week and is excreted *from* the body.

A secondary problem is that childhood vaccines in modern times do not contain thimerosal (although some flu vaccines do), yet while the number of vaccines which have thimerosal as an ingredient continues to *decrease*, the number of people diagnosed with autism as a percentage of the population continues to *increase*. When confronted with this fact, some who subscribe to the theory that thimerosal causes autism will respond by saying that if it isn't thimerosal that causes autism, then it's something else in the vaccines, such as human fetal cells.

Another counterargument to the thimerosal-causes-autism theory is that if thimerosal causes autism, since it only appears in flu vaccines, we would expect to see the people who are vaccinated for the flu "get" or "catch" autism. Yet arguably largest sector of the population that gets the flu vaccine in any given country - the elderly - do not seem to present with autism after receiving the vaccine.

C) Autism Is Caused By Mercury Poisoning

While it hardly seems necessary to include "mercury poisoning" again after we have just gotten done looking at the thimerosal theory, it does need to be discussed due to its presence in many of the household products we use.

We are often cautioned to be careful cleaning up the "toxic spill" that occurs if we break a mercury thermometer, but I cannot recall anyone being advised to have a hazardous materials team come in to take care of the problem.

Interestingly, while people are so quick to blame the mercury in thimerosal for "causing" autism, we don't hear as many people blaming the mercury in florescent light bulbs for causing autism. Break one of those and you'll have mercury flying all over the house!

If we think about this rationally, what safeguards are in place in manufacturing facilities to ensure that mercury doesn't find its way onto the exterior of a florescent light bulb? Further, what assurance do we have that mercury doesn't leak out of a florescent light bulb as the bulb begins to falter? Finally, when we break a florescent light bulb, or when it breaks if we throw it away, what assurance do we have that we do not inhale the mercury that was previously safely inside the bulb? And how do we know that the thousands of florescent light bulbs which have been buried in our landfills aren't broken, and dripping mercury into the groundwater, or giving off gas that is rising up through the ground to circulate into the atmosphere?

If there is one part of the world that should be suffering from severe autism, it is people who live in the vicinity of Oak Ridge National Laboratory in the state of Tennessee. As much as *18,000 gallons* or *2 million pounds* of mercury has been "lost" by the laboratory. Some reports say this mercury has gotten into the air and seeped into the soil and ground water. Yet neither the laboratory employees or the residents who live nearby are affected by autism in greater numbers than people are affected elsewhere in the world.

We should also expect to see people who believe the mercury-causes-autism theory to refrain from eating fish and shellfish, since it is known that mercury accumulates in these animals. But some of these anti-vaxers have been eating fish and shellfish for years, and, notably, they have not developed autism.

Again, it is true that the symptoms of mercury poisoning can be similar to those exhibited by some autistic people, but as yet, there is no firm evidence to suggest that mercury poisoning is *the* cause, or even *a* cause, of autism.

D) Autism Is Caused By Dental Fillings

Just as some would fear that we would get autism by having mercury injected into our systems via vaccines, some fear that some dental fillings, which use a small amount of mercury, could degrade, with the mercury being absorbed into our system through our teeth and gums.

Just as fearful -and just as insignificant- in my opinion, is the exposure to radiation we receive when we undergo dental x-rays. As any dentist will tell you, the overall risk is minimal. That we wear a lead vest during the x-raying, and that the dentist may stand outside the room to press the x-ray button, is simply to further minimize the risk to ourselves and to him from the x-rays. Yet they are necessary for us to receive proper dental treatment, just as the proper fillings are needed for our cavities.

The dentist doesn't stand outside the room because the risk of the radiation is worse than he is letting on either, by the way. It's just that he takes *lots* of x-rays in any given day, and for that reason, he needs to reduce his own exposure as much as possible.

We must ask ourselves whether or not the risks outweigh the benefits when getting dental treatment in any case. But one question the dental-fillings-cause-autism proponents don't seem to ask very often is: Do x-rays cause autism?

E) Autism Is Caused By Heavy Metal Poisoning

Akin to the idea that mercury causes autism is the idea that so-called heavy metals cause autism. One can easily see why this idea might exist and persist.

In terms of doing damage to the human body, some will argue that the second greatest offender in the heavy metals category next to mercury is lead. Like mercury poisoning, there is such a thing as lead poisoning, and the effects have been documented and are quantifiable. This is why lead-based paint is seldom used in homes, and toys with lead in them are removed from the store shelves when discovered.

As with mercury, adults exposed to high levels of lead can be negatively affected, just like children can. Yet, while both adults and children alike may be diagnosed with mercury poisoning, lead poisoning, and "heavy metal toxicity", it is mostly children who are diagnosed with autism, and to date, there is no scientific linkage between heavily metal poisoning and autism in either children or adults.

Treatment methods abound to reduce heavy metals in the body. Chelation is one of these treatments. When heavy metals are reduced in an affected person's system, outcomes have been shown to be favorable. A few autistics who have undergone chelation have shown favorable outcomes, but the success these few have seen is thought by many physicians to be due to the fact that, as with other people in the general population, some people retain more heavy metals in the body than others, and for these people, it is beneficial to bring the heavy metals in the body down to acceptable levels. To date, the US Centers for Disease Control and Prevention (CDC) does *not* endorse the use of chelation therapy as a treatment for autism, probably because, as I have stated in the previous paragraph, there is no evidence that heavily metal poisoning -including lead poisoning and mercury poisoning- causes autism in the first place. Possibly also because chelation therapy has failed to alleviate the symptoms of autism in the majority of cases where it *has* been employed for that purpose.

F) Autism Is Caused By "Big Pharma" "Vaccinating" Or Injecting People With Autism

With this concept, we have effectively entered the realm of conspiracy theories. Backers of this idea believe that major pharmaceutical companies have an economic interest in making people ill, and then creating expensive, life long "treatments" to profit from those illnesses. What better way to make someone ill then by injecting them with something that causes autism, or by injecting them with autism itself via government mandated vaccines?

It's a specious argument, firstly because:

☐ It suggests that people know how to cause autism

And if autism can be caused, it means that people should not only be able to independently pool their resources and discover how autism is caused, but to afterward expose the conspiracy.

Secondly

☐ The argument presumes that all scientists, researchers, doctors, nurses, nurse practitioners, etc. worldwide, and all the organizations to which they belong, and all the oversight organizations, government and private, are involved in the conspiracy, and will be able to keep "Big Pharma's" secret. It implies that there is not one whistle-blower among the millions that would be in the know, or that all of the potential whistle-blowers have either been paid-off or made to disappear.

Given that not even the White House in the United States of America is able to do something secretive without there being some kind of leak to the press, it is doubtful that a *worldwide* conspiracy can be kept silent.

And third,

☐ It implies that if there is anyone or any entity listed above who is *not* involved in the conspiracy, they either cannot discover the conspiracy on their own, or, if they discover it, they too can be silenced somehow or disappeared.

When one thinks about it, the press would have to be involved in this conspiracy also, because, as much as they are quick to destroy the reputations of *anyone* -or *any entity*- if they can see an opportunity to sell newspapers, or draw people to newscasts and websites, they all seem to be quiet about this particular conspiracy the world over.

Further to this point that this so called conspiracy is bogus, is that we have yet to see any of the people who subscribe to this theory infiltrate "Big Pharma" and/or the alleged conspiracy and come out with solid evidence that such a conspiracy exists. Maybe these conspiracy theorists should employ the activists who expose cruelty to animals. *Those* activists seem to manage to sneak into some of the meat processing plants and some of the science labs and film atrocities whenever they see them committed within. It shouldn't take much more effort to be able to expose "Big Pharma's" supposed nefarious activities.

But people will fervently argue that the conspiracy is for real, and even that all of the world's governments (usually under the auspices of secret United Nations mandates) are "in on it," which brings us to...

G) Autism Is Caused By Government "Vaccinating" Or Injecting People With Autism

One may think that because the conspiracy theories about "Big Pharma" and "The Government" look the same, they must be interchangeable, or identical, but this is not necessarily the case.

While some believe all doctors are mandated by the government to inject a percentage of the population with something that causes autism, others will argue that only certain doctors, (who are really government doctors posing as private physicians) do it.

There is precedence for this idea. It will be remembered by history buffs that in the US, The Tuskegee Airmen were given syphilis as an experiment, and in Japan, some Japanese people were deliberately not treated for radiation sickness by US military doctors after the Hiroshima and Nagasaki bomb fallout began to affect them, just to see what would happen.

However, there are a number of counterarguments which could be used to debunk the idea that the government is "infecting" their citizens with autism.

- Many people who have never gotten vaccinated in their lives have been diagnosed with autism. (Although, admittedly, this argument may not be convincing to some. If a prior generation has been vaccinated -these people would argue- that generation might be a "carrier" who gave it to their children, and -if autism were to skip multiple generations before manifesting itself- to their grandchildren, great grandchildren, and great, great grandchildren, etc.)

- If this deliberate infection is part of an experiment, it is the longest one in history, considering it dates back -according to the conspiracy people- to the times that vaccinations began.

- The health costs the world's government assume by

taking care of autistics via disability benefits -or if and when autistics become wards of the state- are huge.

- ☐ Again, it is unreasonable to expect that there would be no whistle-blowers in this worldwide conspiracy.

- ☐ No one has been able to infiltrate the conspiracy and expose its machinations to the public.

Closing Words On Chunk #I

The number of questions I have asked while discussing these supposed "causes" of autism in Chunk #I ought to give the reader an idea of how one faction could have one view, and another faction will firmly rebut that view.

While some of the above theories may sound ridiculous, if the theories are put forth in such a way that they sound believable, it understandable that these theories may be believed. Regardless of what the theories actually are, however, seldom are they argued against with facts. Instead, counterarguments usually take the form of direct assaults on the characters of those that hold the disputed theories.

But we will discuss *how* the factions argue their points and counterpoints later on.

Chunk# II: Autism is Caused by Genes or Genetics

For most people, genes and genetics are a nebulous concept. We have a basic understanding that humans have something called DNA, and RNA, and that stretches of DNA and RNA are called genes. It is believed that genes hold information central to building and maintaining a body's cell structure, and that some of this information may be passed on from generation to generation.

If a person is knowledgeable enough to have that degree of understanding of genetics, it is doubtful they will have much more. This makes it possible for people to believe *any* theory that is offered as a "genetic" explanation for autism, no matter how much those theories may be seen by professionals in the field as being scientifically implausible.

Just like someone who has no understanding of plumbing may be inclined to believe a plumber who says it's the "flapdoodle" causing the problem, a person may be inclined to believe someone who says that "autism" may be an evolutionary step in a larger evolutionary process.

Yet despite the more wild theories, it must be reiterated that the most compelling and verifiable evidence of a "cause" for autism *can* be found in genetics.

A. Autism Is Caused By Genetics

Dr. Stephen Scherer is a Canadian researcher and was Lead Investigator for the Autism Genome Project, which started January 1, 2006. 170 scientists from 11 countries were involved in this project right from the start.

One point of interest in their finds to date is the identification of a Copy Number Variant (CNV) at chromosome 16p11.2 that is associated with autism."

People interested in learning more about the project can go here: http://www.ontariogenomics.ca/research/project/44

There is other substantive evidence to suggest that autism can be described in the genetic code of individuals. The genetic code of autistic people continues to be mapped, and more and more common genetic elements that all autistics possess continue to be identified.

There is some question, however, about the cause for the onset of the coding. Is it purely genetic in origin, or is the coding influenced/instigated by environmental factors? The answer would seem to be that *both* genetic and environmental factors play a role in causing autism to assert itself in individuals, although the consensus seems to be that the cause is more genetic than environmental. (Some genes, for example, cannot be turned on or switched off or influenced at all by environmental factors, yet many of those particular genes which cause autistic symptoms to manifest themselves have been activated or deactivated, depending on which gene you are looking at. Further, in a percentage of cases, autism appears to be hereditary.) What the exact causes are on a biological level and an environmental level are up in the air.

However, as no environmental trigger has been identified yet, by attenuation, it follows that the vaccines-cause-autism theory is scientifically invalid. Thus we can see how the autism-is-caused-by genetics "camp" can argue so fervently against the anti-vaxers and anti-mercury crowd.

What follows are the other "genetic" theories. We can see as we read through them that they range from the believable to the ridiculous.

B. Autism Is The Result Of Recessive Neanderthal Genes Becoming Active

This theory sounds plausible on the surface, but just as plausible is the idea that autism is the result of recessive genes that we carry from *many* of our pre and proto homo-sapien ancestors becoming active. But the fact is, many CNVs can be used to describe autism, and these genes are ones carried -and not carried- by lots of our primitive predecessors. Thus to peg the genes of *one* human ancestral species as being the culprit of *all* autism is a specious idea.

C. Autistics Manifest Genes That Will Eventually Become Active For *Everyone* When The Next Phase Of Human Evolution Is Complete

This theory arrogates autistics to a level above that of their non-autistic counterparts. It implies that to be autistic is to be superior, if not in terms of the unfinished product, at least in terms of the more supposedly progressive evolutionary status of the autistic person.

The idea that the human race evolves with each generation has plenty of evidence to support it. People in the present day in many Western countries are taller than they were a hundred or more years ago, for example, and if we need to see evidence of physical changes in the bodies of humans over a more extensive period, all we need to do is go to a museum and look at skulls and skeletons of humans from hundreds of thousands and even millions of years ago. The variations are glaringly apparent.

But if the idea animals adapt to their environments holds true, there can be no way that we can predict what men will be like many generations in the future, because we cannot predict what man's environment will be like hundreds of years in the future.

Once in a while we will see articles that will cite studies that project possible evolutionary outcomes for mankind, but these studies admit to having theoretical extrapolations as conclusions. If, for example, mankind continues to be less physically active, and devotes itself more and more towards technology, it will, it is theorized, develop adaptations that will enable it to be better suited for a technological environment. Mankind's fingers will grow longer so as to utilize things like keyboards and mice with better ability. Humans will develop larger eyes and better visual acuity to read computer screens with greater ease. Humans will become more physically frail due to lack of exercise, but cranial capacities will increase to encase mankind's larger, more intellectual brains.

Nice theories, but it's doubtful we will see an evolutionary cycle that parallels what's happening environmentally. Even as this portion of the book is being written, there is talk by major computer and software manufacturers about elimination of the mouse as a method of navigating computer screens and the internet, and it has already been stated years earlier that scrolls may actually take the place of laptops and PCs in the future. No longer would we have the need to keep a stationary PC at home or work, or lug a laptop anywhere. We could, wherever we want to, simply unfurl a fraction of an inch thick scroll and begin typing on it, and this scroll could be any size we wanted so that we could see what was on it better. We'd use our fingers to navigate the display, rather than a mouse, and if you have any confusion as to what this might look like, watch what some of the major news networks are using these days when their commentators navigate digital visual aids. The commentators use hand gestures to expand and contract screens and to move windows around the screens they are using.

In a lab, scientists can raise mice, change their environment drastically, and see the mice adapt physically and mentally in a few generations. For one to expect that humans would respond similarly requires that a human's environment would remain fixed for multiple generations (meaning hundreds and hundreds of years). At the rate that technology currently advances, it is unreasonable to expect that this rate of technological advancement would suddenly halt itself so that humans can complete their adaptation to it.

The fact is, so many CNVs manifesting themselves at once in autistic people suggests more of a "genetic misfire" (my term and idea, not anyone else's) than the onset of an evolutionary phase. What autism looks like genetically speaking is a genetic shotgun blast, not the beginning stages of a metamorphosis.

But that is my opinion, and I have a right to have it, since no scientific evidence exists to prove that autism is part of human evolution.

A Parenthetical Note:

Adding to this concept of autism as an evolutionary process, in my opinion, is/was The Aspergian Mythos. As I understand it, The Aspergian Mythos was never meant to be a theory or hypothesis about the origins and future of autism, but meant to be an entertaining "what if." Having read the mythos, people could then join the Aspergia message board and chat room and become part of "Aspergia" and its "culture." Yet some people familiar with The Aspergian Mythos have adapted it as a theory or hypothesis nearly to the point where they believe in it.

Some would say that Edan Dagan, having been the founder of Aspergia, is a mythical figure and cultural leader. He, his site, and his mythos have been discussed in various online and offline conversations and publications, and in many of these, Edan is revered as though he is a cultural icon, his site is spoken about as though it was a physical (as opposed to virtual) place, and the mythos is discussed in philosophical and even political terms.

Yet the Mythos is pure fiction, there never was an

evolution of people into "Aspergians", and Edan Dagan is not an icon, but a man.

Another Brief Note Before Continuing:

The next seven "camps" squarely blame women for causing autism, if not by genetics, then by behaviors which may or may not have their roots in genetics. This is not to say that the people who hold these views are sexist or misogynistic, but it does seems as though more inferences are made about *women* being at "fault" for their autistic offspring then men.

It should be noted in any case that an association between one "fact" -and we will look at some of these facts momentarily- and another does not indicate a *causal* relationship. Just because a person eats ice cream and gets a headache, it does not mean that the ice cream *caused* the headache, nor does it even mean that what a person has is even what's called an "ice cream headache."

D. Autism Is Caused By Women Having Babies After Age 35

Lending credence to this idea are studies which show that older women give birth to children diagnosed with Down syndrome more frequently than their younger counterparts. Studies trying to correlate autism in children with age of the birth-mother would like to show the same conclusion, and often do, however, some studies suggest that...

E. Autism Is Caused By Women Having Babies Before Age 35

There are studies which suggest that the younger you are, the more likely you are to have a child who will present with autism.

This theory, and the former, are predicated on the idea that poor genetics in the birth mother are the cause for a baby being born that will grow up to present with autism. In the former case, an aged mother would give "degraded" genes to her offspring, and in the latter case, a young mother would give "immature" genes to her offspring.

What people who subscribe to either of these theories fail to remember is that autistics are still in the minority. The majority of babies born to old and young mothers are *not* autistic.

Stated differently, if 1 in 64 babies born today have autism as one of the current figures tells us, 63 out of 64 babies born do *not* have autism, and the majority of these babies are born to mothers above and below the age of 35.

F. Autism Is Caused By Mothers Being Overweight

Again, there is an attempt to make a correlation: Obesity in the pregnant mother causes autism in the offspring.

Amazing how humanity now regards "Rubenesque" figures as something to be loathed, isn't it? Not even "child bearing hips" are considered attractive these days.

But setting aesthetics aside, if one looks at obesity as being a problem purely of genes, then the argument once again is that faulty genetic material begets faulty genetic material.

The problem is, not all obesity is caused by genes. It can be caused by willfully poor eating behaviors, medication, or any one of a number of other things that are not genetic.

The theory *does* make sense if you view the argument in terms of the correlation between alcohol consumption and fetal alcohol syndrome.

If, one might say, a mother drinks, the likelihood that her child will have fetal alcohol syndrome exists, whereas that risk is non-existent if the mother doesn't drink.

The problem is, both obese women and women in their proper weight category give birth to children with autism, just as women in the proper weight range give birth to children with autism.

Additionally, there are many more healthy babies born to obese women than there are unhealthy babies, and there does not, scientifically speaking, seem to be a direct correlation at this time between a mother's weight and whether or not a baby will present with autism.

G. Autism Is Caused By Mothers Who Are Too Thin

If a woman is too thin during her pregnancy, does it mean that the fetus isn't getting the nourishment it needs? And if that is the case, can this affect the fetus's brain? Can an insufficient amount of nourishment in utero cause autism?

No studies have shown this to be the case yet.

This theory may stem from the idea that many women who live in poverty seem to be anemically thin, either due to poor health, malnourishment, drug addiction or something else.

But it does seem that women can be thin during pregnancy and still give birth to very healthy babies.

H. Autism In Children Is Caused By Women With A D Bra Size Or Larger

There are two societal ideas that feed into the myth that a mother's breast size can determine whether or not her child will be autistic.

First, there is a belief that big breasted women are are prone to breast cancer. This belief, if you read what doctors have to say about it, is largely false.

Secondly, there is the idea that "gargantuan" attributes are grotesque, As mentioned earlier, obesity, or largeness, in certain areas of the body, are no longer considered Rubenesque, but something to be frowned upon.

Thus by proxy, it follows that women with "grotesque" attributes give birth to babies with "grotesque" attributes.

The problem is, there is no genetic linkage between big-breasted women producing a higher percentage of children who develop autism.

There was, however, a study that suggested that men who fathered children with autism do *not* prefer big-breasted women, but does this mean the men's genes are flawed, or the genes of the small-breasted women whom they are *presumed* to have copulated with?

Either way, who can tell? The genes of these men and women were not tested.

I. Avoiding Breastfeeding, Causes Autism

Studies show there are many advantages to breastfeeding, one of which may be that certain immunities against allergens and viruses are passed from the child to the mother. Mothers who do not breastfeed do not pass these immunities down to their children, nor do they pass the nutrients to their children that the mammary glands are designed to produce.

A seemingly logical idea is that mother's who do not breastfeed will be more inclined to raise "sick" or "flawed" children. It further seems to follow that some of these children will need vaccinations, which will then "cause" autism.

But there is little evidence to show that any of this is true. Some mothers breastfeed. Other mothers don't. But either type of mother can produce children that develop autism. Similarly, either mother can produce "sickly" children, and when one thinks about it, it makes sense that there should be no direct correlation between breastfeeding and autism, because studies of the autistic genome show that autism manifests itself in the genes, and cannot be turned on or off by environmental triggers.

J. Breast-Feeding Causes Autism

Just as mercury accumulates in fish, which humans in turn consume, it stands to reason that environmental toxins accumulate in the human mother and are passed on to infants via breast milk.

This can be true, although interestingly, it is usually *tainted breast milk* that is blamed for either "poisoning" a child and causing them to develop autism (or for -supposedly- causing autistic genes to be switched on), as opposed to anything that might have been passed to the fetus *via the placenta during gestation*.

Regardless, there is no scientific causal link between anything in the breast milk "causing" autism in children.

K. Autism Is Caused By Refrigerator Mother Parenting

Because "cold" mothers exhibit traits (possibly as the result of genetic makeup) similar to those displayed by autistic children, it was at one time thought that distant mothers produced autistic children, but too many "warm" and "loving" mothers produced autistic children for this theory to remain plausible.

While it could be stated that it is not the genetic traits "cold" mothers may or may not possess that are responsible for autism presenting itself in their children, but instead poor parenting techniques that warp or distort the development of children's mind to the point where they "develop" autism, parenting techniques change from generation to generation, and many different techniques are and have been employed by many different mothers. Yet autism still occurs regardless of the various child-rearing techniques employed.

Other Genetic Theories

L. Autism Is Caused By Men Who Are Over 40 Fathering Children

Just as a woman's ova are thought to be deficient after a certain age, an older man's sperm cells may have a higher percentage of defects in them. The question is, are the children that are sired by older fathers truly exhibiting autism as it is defined genetically, or are these children exhibiting traits that are similar to ones that children with autism have?

The answer to that question is inconclusive, but at least the theory steals some of the blame for autism away from the female parent.

M. Smart Parents Are More Likely To Produce Autistic Children

Studies have suggested that parents who hold professorships and other jobs requiring that type or level of intellect produce a higher percentage of children with autism.

Bolstering these results is that "Silicon Valley" is where there appears to be a disproportionate level of autistic people being born to intelligent people working in the computer field.

That sounds fine, but there are a couple things wrong with this theory.

First is that places like Silicon Valley draw a certain type of people to them. If these people are the type in which autism is hereditary, it stands to reason that they will indeed produce autistic children, yet it does not follow that *other* intelligent people will produce children with autism, nor does it follow that *any* people who are *deemed* intelligent *are* intelligent.

Intelligence to the layperson can mean that someone has an understanding of something that most people don't. Most commonly, people do not understand law, medicine, economics, physics, chemistry, engineering, computer software development, etc. Yet it is *effort*, as much as it is *intelligence*, which gets people jobs in those fields, and it is *achievement* that allows people to ascend to higher levels within those professions. Thus a person can go from paralegal to partner in the course of one's lifetime with effort and study, but these people do not have to necessarily be *intelligent*. In fact, for every class of graduates, someone has to graduate at the bottom. Not all lawyers are *good* lawyers.

And when one thinks about it, a person may rise and ascend in other professions which most people don't understand - and ones that are prejudicially thought to require *less* intellect to perform. One can work their way up from a plumber's apprentice to a plumber, for example.

Which all goes to suggest what?

It goes to suggest that maybe people in the "lesser" professions are of a sort that are not as inclined to get their children evaluated for autism or other socially "unacceptable" diseases, whereas people who circulate in "higher"social circles may seek out diagnoses for their children so as to get an explanation for their "deficiencies."

It requires, for example, a good grasp of math and engineering to be a carpenter, just as it requires a good grasp of math and engineering to be an architect. Why should two people, who may be intellectual equals, produce two different types of children, one type with autism and the other without? Certainly it cannot be the profession or "trade" that is "causing" autism, but it *could* be the prejudice on the part of the researchers who conduct studies. The researchers may be trying to find causal links based on observation, or perception, rather than using scientific methods to lead them to *whatever* the causal link may be.

And so genetically speaking, being born with intelligent brains doesn't necessarily mean that the offspring of two intelligent people will be autistic. This theory, by the way, is almost the antithesis of the refrigerator mom theory -which states that cold and distant mothers produce autistic children- especially if coldness and distant mothering are descriptive and symptomatic of a lack of intellect, or at least some other mental deficiency in the mother.

In other words, whereas with this theory, people believe smart people produce autistic children, earlier, with the other theory, people were believing that people who were in some way deficient produce autistic children.

N. Unintelligent People Produce Autistic Children

Though we've just got done talking a little bit about this concept, more needs to be stated.

The idea that unintelligent parents produce unintelligent babies can be downright offensive. It speaks in favor of the ideas Adolph Hitler put forward in the time of the Nazis, which is that mentally deficient people, if mated, will produce mentally deficient babies which will turn out to be a burden on a country's economic system.

While it is true that people do pass down bad genes from generation to generation, and while it is true that people pass down undesirable behaviors from generation to generation, and while it is true that autism is in some cases hereditary, there is no evidence thus far which firmly and definitively proves that any one segment of the population is more likely that any other to produce autistic offspring.

As an adjunct to the genetic supremacy concept as it pertains to mental illness, it has been suggested that people of oriental extraction are autistic-like -bearing a striking similarity to those with Asperger syndrome in particular- because they avert their gaze when spoken to, and have a higher intelligent than people of European extraction. Could oriental people be a race of Aspies?

But aversive gazes in Orientals are a cultural trait. They believe it is rude to look people in the eyes when talking to them. And as for the intelligence demonstrated by Orientals...could it be they study harder in school, and devote a greater portion of their lives to learning things and meditating upon what they learn?

O. Autistics Are Alien-Human Hybrids

From man's earliest origins, we have now gone to the outer limits of the solar system in an attempt to find an explanation about what may cause autism.

Assuming aliens *do* exist, the only problem with scientifically proving the genetic connection between autism and aliens is that no alien DNA has been found to genetically decode, and so one cannot as yet tell the difference between what part of an autistic person's genetic makeup is human, and what part is extraterrestrial. Thus it cannot be stated with any degree of certainty that autistics are alien-human hybrids.

P. Autistics Are "Rainbow Children," "Crystal Children," Or "Indigo Children"

For those who feel that extraterrestrial explanations for autism are less than satisfactory, there are also Rainbow children, Crystal children, and Indigo children all of which are supposed to have divine origins – or perhaps I am misunderstanding the concept.

At any rate, they are also supposed to have supernatural powers that may either be the budding beginnings of the next stage of evolution, or else these powers may be the empathetic manifestations of half divine, half terrestrial beings.

Or something like that, anyway.

Actress Jenny McCarthy, previously a big believer in the

Indigo children theory as an explanation for autism, has now moved more toward the vaccines-cause-autism camp.

Different sources have different delineations of the three levels of children I've mentioned. If this theory is to be believed, however, all Rainbow children have supernatural powers - perhaps God-given- and that these powers are often perceived by less enlightened people as being negative. The powers that Crystal children have, for example, are the "powers" one sees most commonly associated with autism (synesthesia being one of these) and, ADHD "powers" being most associated with Indigo children.

Because it is scientifically unproven that a divine power exists, it is not currently accepted in medical circles that autistics are divine-terrestrial hybrids.

Lending credence to the concept that autistics -and all people- are divine-terrestrial hybrids is the Bible itself, which states that man was made in the image of God, and that woman was made of man. Thus we arguably have three levels of being according to Christianity. We have the divine (God), We have man, who is made in God's image, and we have woman, which is made from man, who is made in God's image.

If every man, woman, and child on Earth is made in the image of God, it stands to reason then, that all of us possess some shade of God's appearance, intellect, and powers -autism representing one of these shades.

Yet the Bible also talks about diseases, both of the body and mind, and Jesus heals these diseased people. Ergo, while it is true that we can all be made in God's image theologically, it is also true theologically that there are attributes of *our* makeup which are not Holy, and which need to be healed or gotten rid of, physical and mental disorders and affectations comprising some of these, and our sinful nature comprising the rest.

Chunk III: Autism Is Caused By Everything Else

It would take too long to discuss each and every supposed "cause" for autism. Neither would there be a point in attempting to list them all out here, because the list is ever expanding. New (theoretical) "causes" are being added to the list everyday.

However, it would certainly be worthwhile to address some of the more common alleged "causes" that fall under the category of "Everything Else."

A. Autism Is Caused By High Fevers In Children

It makes a kind of sense that people should think high fevers might cause autism. If the body and brain heats up, perhaps brain cells can become "cooked." Certainly the higher a person's fever, the more likely they are to exhibit what could be interpreted as delusions. Maybe if someone's brain was "fried" long enough, that same someone would be permanently afflicted with autism.

However, most science indicates that brain damage does not occur unless the body exceeds a temperature of 107 to 108 degrees Fahrenheit, and very few people who have autism have ever suffered a fever that high.

B. Autism Is Caused By Gluten

There has been evidence to suggest that some autistics show a negative reaction to the ingestion of gluten, although the numbers of autistics with this reaction are not much higher than non-autistic people in the general population. However, to my knowledge, most of the autistics involved in these studies were not tested genetically to see if they possessed the genes commonly associated with autism. Ergo it could be that people who demonstrate behaviors commonly associated with autism might have a higher percentage of their population that is affected negatively by gluten ingestion, but these people may not actually be autistic.

Additionally, there is no scientific evidence to suggest that autism is *caused* by gluten.

C. Autism Is Caused By Celiac Disease

Celiac Disease is a full blown negative reaction to gluten. The idea that the disease itself would attack the body -

and in so doing change the body's chemistry- and produce something like autism makes sense in a convoluted kind of way, but there is no science to back up the theory.

D. Autism Is Caused By Low Levels Of Vitamin B-12 And Vitamin C

Anytime the body experiences a shortfall in vitamins, we can expect that there is a possibility that negative consequences will follow. However, there is no scientific evidence that low levels of these two vitamins cause autism.

E. Fluoride Causes Autism

The theory that fluoride causes autism ties into conspiracy theories which suggest that something in the water is deliberately put there to poison us, or to make us diseased, or to make us more docile, or to control us.

Fluoride occurs naturally in drinking water in some areas, negating the theory that it's "salted" into water everywhere, but fluoride *is* also added when it is missing from drinking water.

The reason?

It's good for teeth and bones, according to dental and medical associations all over the world.

Too much fluoride, however, *can* make teeth fall out.

Even so, if you get "city" water, as opposed to water from a well, chances are you are getting a whole lot more with your water than just fluoride. Aside from the chemical additives that kill bacteria, you are getting trace amounts of all the medications that have been flushed down the drain and been sent through the waste water treatment plant, to say nothing of whatever household chemicals were poured down the drain and into the sewer system and not entirely scrubbed from the water.

Could any of these chemicals and drugs be responsible for autism?

According to believers of this theory, it's just the fluoride.

F. Genetically Modified Organisms Cause Autism

Genetically Modified Organisms (GMOs) are organisms that have been altered scientifically. Crops are oftentimes modified in order to withstand changing climactic conditions, resist blight, etc. Animals may be modified to produce more meat and less fat on the bone.

In looking at some of the animals in particular, one can easily see why there may be cause for concern. Would someone really want to eat something that looks mutated, and what will happen to our bodies if we consume a mutated animal?

This theory ties in with anti-vaccine conspiracies.

There is a new type of vaccine whose viruses will be cultured in caterpillar eggs rather than chicken eggs. The fear for the anti-vaxers is, do we want to risk insect DNA possibly getting swapped with our own?

If that theory were to hold water, they would have a point. The problem with that is that just because our bodies consume contaminants one way or another, it does not mean we are going to become that which we consume.

We eat chicken. We eat eggs. We eat them even if we have cavities, bleeding gums, etc. Yet I have yet to hear of anyone turning into a chicken because they ate an egg, or consumed chicken, nor have we heard of anyone turning into a chicken because the vaccine that was injected into them was cultured in a chicken egg. I doubt anyone is going to turn into a caterpillar (or a butterfly) after being injected with a vaccine that was cultured in caterpillar eggs.

Still, we have no idea what the long term effects of these man-made GMOs might do to people. Nature, via the process of evolution, has a tendency to get rid of its mistakes. People, on the other hand, are not infallible, and keep creating things that nature has either not thought to create, or has (possibly) weeded out of the ecosystem already.

That we are affected by what we eat is undeniable. The energy we get from food keeps us alive, and the vitamins and minerals that come naturally in our food choices nourish us. Even food that has been "fortified" with vitamins and minerals has been good for us.

But we can get sick from what we eat too. If food is in some way contaminated with bacteria, or some foreign substance to which the body is allergic, and we consume it, we will respond with a bad reaction or illness.

Until more is known about the effects of GMOs on the human organism, it would be best to take them with a grain of salt, so to speak.

Even so, there is no scientific evidence to link GMOs with autism.

G. Autism Is Caused By Electronic and Battery Operated Devices Like Cell Phones, Televisions And Other Electronic Gadgets

Look at the warning labels on many products and you will see that we should not get those products on our skin, nor should we get them in our eyes. Is it so unreasonable to assume that the electromagnetic radiation given off by plug-in and battery operated gadgets could in some way affect us too? After all, if we let our laptops sit in our laps too long, they may give our legs a little bit of a burn, right? So what would a cell phone do to our brains if we held them up to our heads long enough?

And lots of autistics like to play video games. How much electromagnetic radiation are they getting, sitting in front of the TV, and holding a game controller than runs on electricity?

We might ask the same question about other electronic gadgets autistics find themselves using: computers, smart phones, tablets, etc.

While those are important questions, no study has as yet cited electromagnetic radiation as being the cause of autism specifically. Furthermore, though it is true that most households have more electronic gadgets and appliances than ever before, it is also true that many of these devices -appliances in particular, use far less electricity than similar appliances in the past used to use. Thus our overall exposure to EM radiation probably hasn't increased much.

H. Autism Is Caused By Electromagnetic Radiation In The Atmosphere

Building on the concept that electromagnetic radiation affects us in negative ways, it pays for some people to ask whether or not the proliferation of cell phones and cell phone towers is filling up our atmosphere with dangerous electromagnetic rays.

Think about it. If a microwave can cook something faster than a conventional oven, what are electromagnetic waves in the atmosphere doing to us?

If one thinks about it, the argument sounds plausible on the surface of it. Once there was a time when there was no way to communicate with anyone long distance other than via mail. Then came the telegraph, telephone, various kinds of radios, television, satellite, cell phones, and all the other hand held gadgets that we have. We have wires carrying electronic current of all types going above and below ground. Within the walls of our habitations, they encircle us like a spider's web.

Yet there has never been any evidence citing electromagnetic radiation of any kind as being a cause of autism.

I. Autism Is Caused By Demonic Possession

That exorcisms have been performed on people with autism does not mean that the people with autism were possessed.

There have been a few deaths among autistics who have undergone the procedure. Those that survived were reportedly unchanged, although some were more obedient to their caretakers, most likely because they were fearful of being subjected to further cruelty.

As the existence of demons is scientifically unproven there is no way to tell whether or not autistics are possessed by demons, but if they are possessed, then it spells trouble for the world. It is currently estimated that 1 in 64 people have autism, and if that number is true, there are a lot of demons running amok amongst us.

And so...What Is Autism? (Still MORE Factions)

We started out this book without defining what autism is. It hardly seemed necessary to do so then, and it hardly seems necessary to do so now. After all, autism is almost a household word, what with so many people being diagnosed with it. And given that all one has to do to learn more about autism is examine the DSM IV-TR, DSM V, and ICD-10, why bother to define it now?

Yet because we can see with the many different beliefs about what causes autism, it seems to go without saying that there may be some disagreement about what autism is. That autism has been defined in the DSM IV-TR, DSM V, and ICD-10 does not matter to some people. Some people have created definitions of autism that are all their own.

Let's remember what the abbreviations of the publications doctors refer to actually stand for:

- The DSM IV-TR is the Diagnostic and Statistical Manual of Mental Disorders, Fourth edition, Text Revised

- The DSM V is the Diagnostic and Statistical Manual of Mental Disorders, Fifth edition

- The ICD-10 is the International Statistical Classification of Diseases and Related Health Problems, 10th edition

Because autism is listed in each of these publications, and the spectrum disorders are delineated in two of them, we can say that both autism and the spectrum disorders are either mental disorders or diseases, or health related problems, depending on which book you read.

And yet, there are still many different opinions about what autism is.

A. Autism Is A Diagnosis

But setting aside all the different kinds of diagnosis that there are as listed in prior pages, and assuming that the autism diagnosis we are talking about *here* is legitimate, having been obtained after an extensive evaluation via a licensed board certified medical professional, there are actually two opinions about what a diagnosis is.

For some, a diagnosis means an actual psychiatric diagnosis. Implied in this definition is that there is something wrong enough or out of the ordinary in the human brain that would cause one to receive a diagnosis.

In the second instance, autism is merely a label, or a descriptor. It does not imply "wrongness" or anything out of the ordinary per se, and there is not necessarily a negative connotation associated with the label.

In the first instance, the meaning is understood by the diagnostician, by the patient and/or by the caregiver.

In the second instance, the meaning is one assigned to by the patient and/or the caregiver, not the diagnostician.

B. Autism Is A Mental Disorder

The DSM IV-TR and DSM V have the words "Mental Disorders" in their names. Ergo if autism, Asperger syndrome, childhood disintegrative disorder, Rett syndrome, and PDD-NOS are in the DSM IV TR, and autism spectrum disorder is in the DSM V, then those diagnoses must by definition be mental disorders.

However, others do not believe autism spectrum disorders are a mental disorder, but something that affects the entire body, like a disease does. Or else they believe that autism is an affectation with unknown origins (such as a disorder, or a diagnosis with undiscovered causation), or else it is a health related problem, or simply a difference.

C. Autism Is A Disorder

I've already pointed out that the DSM IV-TR & V are

manuals describing mental *disorders*, and we know that in the DSM-V that there is a definition of autism spectrum *disorder*. And while it is true that people will call autism a *disorder* as well as a diagnosis, some use the word *disorder* rather than "diagnosis" or "disease." This is because to say that something is disordered implies that something can be put back in order.

Alternatively, disorder suggests *lack of order* rather than something that is very difficult or impossible to be ordered, or something that is very difficult or impossible to treat or cure, such as a diagnosis or a disease. Whereas something that is disordered (brain) may be "organized" to present a better image to external observers, a diagnosis or a disease seem to imply more extreme treatment is needed.

Other reasons abound for describing autism as a disorder. Two more:

☐   Many use the term "disorder" to describe autism simply because they don't *see* it as a diagnosis or a disease.

☐   Others use the term "disorder" because they do not want to accept that what they have is a diagnosis or a disease.

D. Autism Is A Disease

People who refer to the ICD-10 rather than the DSM IV-TR or V would be likely to use the term "disease" to describe autism since the ICD 10 is the International Statistical Classification of *Diseases* and Related Health Problems, 10th edition.

While many see "diagnosis" and "disease" as being interchangeable terms, others see "disease" as the more negative term.

To have a disease can imply that one has something that is debilitating, and because some people see their autism as anything but debilitating, they vehemently oppose the idea that autism is a disease.

But others *do* see autism as a disease, one that impairs

the body's ability to function correctly, and one that prevents the mind from functioning optimally.

Where further conflict erupts is when one throws the idea of a cure into the mix. Whereas a diagnosis may be lived with, the term disease suggests that a treatment or cure is needed. Because many autistics are not interested in being cured, they will defer to the less "pejorative" term.

E. Autism Is A Health Related Problem

Followers of the ICD-10 would be likely to believe in this designation. However, some believe that autism is symptomatic of a larger problem, such as the accumulation of toxins in the system. Viewed from that standpoint, autism is not only a health related problem, but a disorder caused by a slow and cumulative kind of poisoning.

F. Autism Is A Difference

This idea voids any diagnosis and pretends that autism is merely a descriptor for one difference or a set of differences, either innate or chosen, that people have or choose to have. As such, autism under this label may or may not incorporate any of the symptoms delineated in the DSM IV-TR, The DSM V, and the ICD-10.

If a self-diagnosed individual is also a pyromaniac, for example -and enjoys setting things on fire- he or she may say that his or her pyromania is part of his or her [autistic] "difference."

Interestingly, seldom do we see many self-diagnosed "autistics" portray attributes commonly perceived by others to be good, special, or interesting as part of one's "difference." Good, interesting, or special attributes are usually attributed to one's personal traits, talents, or skills. It is only "bad" or undesirable qualities that are part of the "difference" a self-diagnosed "autistic" person may have.

Some self-diagnosed autistics often promote the idea that autism is a difference because it substantiates their own self-diagnoses. In other words, if autism is a "difference," and a person sees themselves as possessing the traits that comprise the "difference," then they are "autistic," even if medically, they do not fit the diagnostic criteria for autism.

Autism *is* a difference in that it is medical condition that some people possess and not others. Having autism makes someone different from people who do not have autism, in other words (and vice versa), but the definition stops there in medical circles, if the term "difference" even exists there at all.

G. Autistics Are A Minority Group

Many on the spectrum and who claim to be on the spectrum will say that autistics are a minority group, but some of these people are unsure of what the term "minority group" actually means.

To the extent that many autistics have similar attributes, share similar traits and so on, it can be argued that they are a minority. However, many take this steps further, arguing that there is a discernible autistic culture in addition to a similarity of autistic traits.

The more fanciful skills and abilities some autistics like to believe they have, such as the ability to read minds, predict the future, etc., and the fact that many may have synesthesia "bolsters" the minority concept because (as many autistics believe) these supernatural abilities seem to occur in a greater percentage of the autistic population than in the population at large.

It has happened that a group of autistics, who were considered radical by many, attempted to petition the United Nations to recognize autistics as a minority group, but to date, the UN has ignored them. Had the UN designated autistics as a minority, it might have given autistics the ability to respond to bullying and teasing with hate crime suits, but it also might have caused them to lose assistance from state and national programs, particularly in the medical arena (in other words, if autism wasn't a medical problem, autistics would no longer be eligible for disability payments and healthcare subsidies).

This movement may also stem from the fact that many supposed autistics who were diagnosed by school psychologists are unable to obtain funding for themselves from government agencies when they are adults. Presenting with no symptoms of autism whatsoever, and unable to get board certified medical professionals to diagnose them, and having been hand-held through school by educational assistants that they probably never needed, they are as adults either incapable of fending for themselves, or in the habit of letting other people help them. And so if they cannot obtain funding they (supposedly) need via state and federally funded programs, they will try to obtain other kinds of "rights" or favors through their minority status.

One of these perks is the ability to sue those who "offend" against them. If it could be successfully argued that someone offended against an autistic person, or autistic people, specifically because they were of a minority, there would be much monetary compensation open to them that they would not otherwise receive. Parents, siblings, relatives, teachers, school administrators, doctors, employers, police, government agencies...*any*one, and *any* entity... could all find themselves facing lawsuits in this kind of scenario.

The problem is, very few people who offend against autistics actually see autistics as being part of a "minority" as the term is defined by the UN. In fact, there is hardly a sizable percentage of the population outside the autistic community who view autistics as a minority group. Therefore, proving that an offender was specifically targeting a "minority" autistic person *because* they were part of a minority group would be difficult.

H. Autistics Are A Separate Race

The concept of race is diminishing in public circles more and more as it seems increasingly that to cite someone with a different skin color as being of a different race is offensive. Ethnologists, anthropologists, archeologists, and other "ologists" might classify homo sapiens into races, but to many free thinkers, race is no longer an appropriate method of categorization for people.

If the autistics from this faction had their way, however, there would be *two* races of men. These would be:

☐   Autistic
☐   Non-Autistic

   While we have all sorts of names (descriptive and pejorative) for mixed races, there would be no such name for autistics. Autistics would be one race, non-Autistics would be the other race, and the four "races" society is currently most familiar with (in layman's terms: yellow, black, white, red) would be subcategories. Thus, if one was autistic, one could be a black autistic, a red autistic, a white autistic, or a yellow autistic, but the skin color, and other qualifiers that some people believe defines a "race", would be incidental to autism itself. In other words, autism would not be considered an attribute of the existing four "races", but a race that exists parallel to the race of non-autistics.
   The concept is not dissimilar to the idea that autism and autistics are an evolutionary weigh station on the human evolutionary journey. However, under *this* definition of autism, it is commonly believed and acknowledged that autistics have existed within the human race since its creation, and have blended in with society up until recently due to the failure of others to properly identify them. Up until the past few decades, in other words, they have been much like the aliens in "Invasion of the Body Snatchers" walking among the general populace unnoticed by many until their numbers began to gain a solid footing.
   Parenthetically speaking, another reason autistics were not so widely noticed in the past, according to some of these people, is because they were afraid to reveal themselves. This is supposedly why, in these modern times, we have an "autism epidemic": Autistics everywhere are "coming out of the closet" and declaring themselves.
   One can see why some self-diagnosed autistics and wannabees subscribe to the idea that autistics are a separate race: It's one of the few explanations for autism that creates a doorway through which self-diagnosed autistics and wannabees may enter into the world of autism... once properly diagnosed, of course.
   And even if they are not properly diagnosed, what of that? Perhaps diagnosticians who elect not to give someone a

diagnosis of autism are "racist" against autistics, those who might be autistic, those who want to be autistic, or those who sympathize and empathize with autistics.

A Note Before Continuing

At any given time, an autistic or fake autistic can and/or will change their views about any of the beliefs about autism heretofore mentioned. Likewise, they may do the same about any autism-related belief (some more of which are to be listed out in the following pages).

Views can change as the result of indecision, the receipt of new knowledge, a shifting of allegiances from one faction to another, or another reason or reasons.

While it is important for a person to be open to new ideas, the frequency with which these shifts in beliefs occur among some autistics or fake autistics can be alarming, if not embarrassing. I've witnessed people shifting views three or more times within the space of a week, every time defending their new views with ferocity.

The implications of such behavior are equally alarming. To know that someone will turn their belief system over on the merest wisp of information tells us that some on the spectrum are highly suggestible, easily led, and possibly easily misled and exploited. Either that, or they are erratic, or indecisive, or mentally unstable in ways not defined by the criteria for autism. Keeping this in mind, we can see why some autistics and autistic posers will turn themselves into virtual suicide bombers for the people they follow, often taking great risks to their online accounts, and to their real persons, for the sake of others. Examples of this behavior will follow much later in the book. For the present, consider, as each additional faction is described, how someone who dwells within the autistic community is likely to feel when confronted with all of these contrary viewpoints, and the constant appeals to subscribe to them.

Factions Ad Nauseam: What Autistics Believe About Autistic Issues

Chunk I: Therapies

In this section, I will be discussing many different kinds of autism therapies one by one, and how autistics feel about them. It may seem that discussions on so many different therapies are unnecessary and that a blanket statement can be made about how autistics view all of them. Such is not the case, however, and you will soon see why. At the same time, I shall not be addressing every single therapy that I can find either, as there are too many to address in just this publication. I will discuss only the ones that seem the most controversial to many.

As before, I am going to state that I have no medical experience whatsoever, and am not qualified to comment medically on whether or not a treatment works. Speak to a doctor about what's right for you.

A Note Before We Begin

With an increased focus on the treatment of autism spectrum disorders in recent years, autistics have been subjected to everything from legitimate proven treatments to outright quackery. As time has passed, and autistic children (and adults) have grown up to be more articulate, one of the combined results of many of these therapies is an aversion by many autistics to the people who subjected them to treatments -and we are not just talking about a hatred of doctors here. There is a great deal of resentment of some autistics towards parents, doctors, counselors, psychiatrists, psychologists, faith healers, and "quacks", and when these autistics see parents online or offline speaking positively about a type of therapy that an autistic found particularly humiliating or useless, they will many times attack that parent. Likewise, they will attack doctors, counselors, psychiatrists, psychologists, faith healers, and quacks when they hawk their therapies, wares and nostrums.

I've heard autistics say that their reason for compliance with some of these therapies was because, even though the therapies were extremely abusive or humiliating, the punishments for not cooperating and undergoing the therapies were even worse than the therapies themselves. Just as when a child is punished -a cost/benefit analysis of the situation caused them to realize that compliance with the parent, doctor, counselor, psychiatrist, psychologist, faith healer, or quack was the lessor of two evils.

But once these autistics reached adulthood, and were out of reach of their former persecutors -or if they were already in adulthood when subjected to the therapies, but were now free-, not only did they revert to their old ways, but they *wallowed* in them, cherishing those ways more for having temporarily lost them than if they had been allowed to continue with them all along. To paraphrase one autistic, "When I got out on my own, I hummed and flapped my hands whenever I wanted. I felt like a pig in shit."

It is also important to remember that "therapy," "treatment" and "cure" are all words with negative connotations to many of those who are subjected to them. The words can imply that there is something inherently wrong with part of an individual, or the entire individual. Thus, as parents and caregivers discuss the autistics they care for, and the therapies, treatments, and "cures" their loved ones are to be given, they sometimes do so in a manner that is not only demeaning to those they care for, but also demeaning to other autistics who may fall witness to those conversations.

Doctors and therapists may discuss autistic people and therapies in a very *clinical* fashion, but autistics may come to see themselves as little more than lab rats as a result. Ergo therapies, treatments, and cures are intrinsically offensive to autistics who are not interested in changing who they are, and the more militant among these autistics will argue angrily against therapies and treatments even if they show some evidence of working.

Interestingly, perhaps the two most vocal factions against therapies of any kind seem to be self-diagnosed autistics, and wannabees. Apparently, these people want the "perks" that come with autism...but not the treatments that come with the diagnosis.

One last word... This hardly needs to be stated, but if a faith healer tries to "heal" an autistic person, the implied message is that the "healer" is doing this with God's power, and - therefore- with God's approval. This in turn implies that God thinks autistics are rejects in His eyes, and *do* need to be treated and cured.

Many autistics have rejected God and rejected religion, because they, or someone they know, have been subjected to the ministrations of faith healers, or, at the very least, they have witnessed or been subjected to, the prayers of pastors and priests who appeal to God for a remission of autism in the "afflicted."

To Resume...

A. Applied Behavior Analysis

The person generally agreed upon by many to be the founder of Applied Behavior Analysis, Dr. O. Ivar Lovaas, described autistics as "Little Monsters" and based the "Lovaas Method" (ABA) on that principal. For this reason alone, many autistics who have never experienced ABA, hate Lovaas and the therapy even though some parents swear by it.

There is also some resentment from people on the spectrum who have been subjected to it, but reports by them about what that therapy looks like are inconsistent.

This is understandable. Allyson Goodwyn-Craine M.S. CCC-SLP, has commented that the area of ABA is loosely structured and poorly regulated, and "anyone can hang a shingle proclaiming expertise in Applied Behavioral Analysis." (See http://www.remedyspot.com/showthread.php/2527683-Ethical-Considerations-When-Asked-to-Collaborate-with-ABA-%93Therapists-%94).

Thus the type of ABA someone receives from one therapist may be different from the type of ABA someone else receives by another therapist.

The result of this, then, are people arguing about ABA as they have experienced it. These people may believe their own individual experiences to be definitive, and see opposing or opposite experiences as fraudulent, or impossible to believe even though those opposing or opposite experiences may be just as valid.

Someone on the spectrum may say that their experience with ABA was pleasant, enjoyable, and productive, while someone else might say it was abusive, oppressive, and humiliating.

Third parties to these exchanges may offer opinions without having any real conception about what ABA is actually supposed to be, and still others may point out (rightly so in some instances) that perhaps it was compliance, obedience, and subservience that caused some people to have a good experience, while it was people's impertinence, defiance, and threatening behavior that caused the other people to have a negative experience.

Compounding the situation are contrary opinions by government officials about ABA. The province of British Columbia in Canada no longer funds ABA in school systems. Yet other government agencies in other provinces and other countries stand by it. So some will say (paraphrased) "The government won't fund it anymore because they disagree with its application and effectiveness," while others say (paraphrased) "The government funds it because they agree with its application and effectiveness." Both are stating facts based upon what they know. In one case, a government entity has *not* funded ABA because it disagrees with its application and effectiveness, and in another case, government funds ABA because it *does* agree with its application and effectiveness. Two opposing viewpoints, both factually correct, yet both diametrically opposed. When we have this kind of "Which came first, the chicken or the egg" kind of discussion, and the answer seems to be "The chicken AND the egg came first" one can understand the conflict that will invariable ensue from that kind of discussion.

We can use these scenarios to understand the conflagrations that arise with other therapies when they are applied inconsistently or when they yield inconsistent results.

B. Antiviral Drugs (Acyclovir)

Now, if you are coming to this book without knowing

anything about acyclovir,and how this drug pertains to the treatment of autism, that's fine. Even many of the people who argue for and against the use of this drug for the treatment of autism don't know what it is alleged to do.

The drug itself combats the herpes virus and is believed by some to reduce the severity of some of the symptoms caused by autism. Why people should think this is not entirely clear. Currently, there is no clear data on whether it really works to combat autism symptoms. Some believe it's would-be success is simply a side effect of the drugs, and to this others will counter-argue that an antiviral drug cannot have an affect on a genetic difference. Eye color is believed by doctors to be determined by dominant and recessive genes. Could aspirin change your eye color?

No. Aspirin cannot do that, but actually, other drugs can: Type these terms into your search engine and see what comes up: "'eye color' warnings indications."

So if it is possible for some drugs to change eye color, could it be possible that an antiviral drug could change how autism manifests itself?

Maybe.

But "maybe" is not a "Yes," and it doesn't pay to speculate. Yet some people are staunch supporters of the "Yes" side of the argument, and others of the "No" side of it.

C. Auditory Integration Training

Autistic conspiracy theorists liken this scientifically unproven "treatment" to Aldous Huxley's conditioning. Are there subliminal messages being sent to the listener while the listener listens to the music provided in this therapy? And if so, what are they?

The American Academy of Pediatrics states this is an experimental procedure.

To the extent that an autistic might not act out while listening to the music – the therapy works. But not too many people believe any lessons learned -if there are any lessons being given, subliminal or otherwise- are carried outside the treatment center.

Given that the treatment is experimental, many autistics will reject the treatment not even knowing what it is for the simple reason that they do not believe autistic people should be used as guinea pigs in any kind of medical experimentation.

D. Chelation Therapy

There are many different kinds of chelation therapy even though there are only supposed to be a few. The reason I can say this is because people will dump all kinds of vitamins, minerals, and chemicals into an autistic's body to get rid of whatever it is they feel is "causing" the autism. For those who do not understand how chelation therapy works, chelation seems to many of these people to be a cure-all, but there is a word that many other people associate with the term cure-all, and that word is "Quack."

Between autistics and parents and caregivers of autistics, autistics are most likely to be the ones who hate chelation, especially if they have been subjected to it.

-DMSA Chelation

This chelation therapy is used to remove heavy metals like lead and mercury from the body. Because it is believed by some that autism is caused by mercury, it stands to reason that they would be fans of this treatment.

Those against the treatment are usually ones that follow the idea that autism is the result of gene variants, and cannot be moderated or reversed with this kind of treatment for that reason. Even if (they might concede) mercury might have caused the gene variations, the damage has been done already. How will leaching out led and mercury from the body improve anything

-EDTA Chelation Therapy

The US Food and Drug Association approves of this chelation therapy as a heavy metal poison treatment. It is sometimes also used for cardiac patients in certain situations as an (unproven) therapy. The EDTA concoction contains disodium ethylene diamine tetra-acetic acid, high doses of vitamin C, B-vitamins, and some other components.

As with DMSA the concept is that harmful elements that "cause" autism are being leached out, but because there are vitamins included in the treatment, it is theorized that autistics are getting supplemented or replenished with vitamins, too.

Regardless, the treatment -most (including doctors) feel- is unproven for reducing the symptoms of autism. Again, if gene variations are responsible for autism, as many believe, there is very little chelation can do to treat autistics, except in this case, to fill them up with vitamins and make them a little bit healthier.

One Other Point About Chelation

People who believe in chelation therapy believe that government agencies are against chelation because for governments to admit that the therapy works would be an admission that "Big Pharma" has indeed caused autism via the mercury poisoning caused by thimerosal in vaccines. And given that the governments mandate vaccine usage, governments bear "responsibility" for the "autism epidemic" just as much as "Big Pharma". However, as has been stated, thimerosal has been eliminated from most vaccines, and in those vaccines where thimerosal remains, the thimerosal itself has a half life of a week and is eventually excreted from the body. Thus mercury poisoning in most people is an improbability.

Ironically, proponents of chelation therapy fail to realize that by prohibiting the use of chelation to "treat" autistics, the government is denying "Big Pharma" all kinds of profits from selling chelation chemicals. Further, were the FDA and the American Medical Association (AMA) to approve of chelation therapy for treatment of autism, hundreds of thousands of doctors could administer this treatment and make lots of profit from it. Yet the AMA seems to disapprove of chelation for treating autism too, as do government agencies and medical associations worldwide.

Very strange how this supposed worldwide "conspiracy" doesn't make very much economic sense when viewed in this light.

E. Coffee Enemas

Yes, some people really do think they can treat autism with coffee enemas...or with other kinds of enemas. To date, there is no evidence that enemas of any kind work to treat or cure autism, but some autistics, and especially self-diagnosed autistics report feeling a sexual pleasure from the experiences, and unnatural sexual attraction towards the administrator of the enemas, including their parents.

The reason autistics would fight against this treatment is obvious, and many autistics are fond of saying to the people who administer it that you should never give a treatment to someone else that you haven't tried on yourself first.

F. Electroshock Therapy

If there is something "out of whack" in the brain, maybe by shocking the organ, the brain can be reset, right?

That's one "maybe" too many for most people on the autism spectrum. Science also doesn't lend any support to the concept, either.

Though this procedure is usually not used as punishment, it certainly seems like punishment, especially when it is done repeatedly with absolutely no favorable results whatsoever.

This does not change the fact that many autistics have, at their parents' or caretaker's request, been subjected to it.

Sometimes, self-diagnosed autistics (in particular, self-diagnosed autistics who, much earlier in their online exploits, declared themselves to be diagnosed with schizophrenia, or depression, or mania) claim electroshock therapy has worked for them. Usually, a skirmish or fight develops between them and diagnosed autistics. Diagnosed autistics can't believe that "their very own" would want to"betray" them by advocating such an "abusive" therapy.

And of course, electroshock therapy *may* have worked for those self-diagnosed autistics, because the self-diagnosed autistics may indeed truly have those previously declared disorders, many of which *can be* positively affected by electroshock therapy.

Some parents and caregivers will stand by the procedure for their autistic charges because *they* see an improvement. This perceived improvement can either be wishful thinking, a figment of their imagination, or alternatively, their charges really *do* improve for a while, the reason being that they are so terrified at the prospect of undergoing electroshock therapy again that they are scared into submission.

But parents and caregivers who support this therapy are usually attacked by autistics, which causes these parents and caregivers to be even more convinced that *all* autistics could benefit from electroshock.

One Other Note About Electroshock Therapy

It has been reported that some institutions have used electroshock therapy inappropriately as punishment. In such cases, anesthesia and muscle relaxants -which are to be used when *approved* therapy is given- are not always administered. Anesthesia and/or muscle relaxants or no, just about whenever electroshock is used as punishment, autistics, self-diagnosed autistics, misdiagnosed autistics, and wannabees are almost unanimously against the procedure. However, some parents and caregivers -and even doctors- who are of the opinion that some of autistics' unwanted behaviors are deliberate, do believe that electroshock is an acceptable punishment.

The battles between autistics and parents and caregivers -or between autistics and doctors- over electroshock therapy that is used as punishment can be bitter and vindictive.

Most autistic advocacy organizations and many -but not all- autism charities have campaigned hard against institutions and organizations that use electroshock for punishment, but some autistic advocacy associations and autism charities support electroshock as a treatment.

G. Exorcism

The Holy Roman Catholic Church is not the only

Church that performs exorcisms in the western world, nor is Christianity the only religion that performs exorcisms in any portion of the world. One sometimes hears about people dying during exorcisms, and these deaths do not only occur in what we call third world countries.

Some people with autism have been subjected to exorcisms. In all fairness, credit goes to the Catholic Church for screening out psychiatric diagnoses and preventing most diagnosed people from having to undergo exorcisms. Other churches may not be so careful. I have no data which says which churches and denominations are or are not doing exorcisms on autistics.

But try to imagine what an atheistic autistic must feel when being subjected to the rite. The absurdity of the situation is readily apparent to almost everyone no matter what their views on religion might be, but for an atheistic autistic, not only is the situation absurd, it is horrific, something akin to the being burned as a witch during the time of the Salem witch trials at the very least.

A second aspect that makes exorcism horrific is that, in cases where a person may be psychiatrically or psychologically disturbed, but has not undergone a psychiatric examination, it suggests that because the administrator of the rite refuses to acknowledge the importance or relevancy a psychiatric diagnosis, the exorcist cannot be reasoned with logically, clinically, or medically -only theologically. And if the autistic is lacking in theological knowledge, or is incapable of expressing himself or herself at all, the autistic has no choice but to endure rite.

Some people with autism are so terrified of the thought of someone (including themselves) being exorcised that they won't even discuss exorcism, and will violently argue against anyone who tries to assert that there is a difference between demonic possession and a psychiatric disorder.

It is known that there are snake oil salesmen and saleswomen of all kinds that try to sell their wares in the autism community, and to parents and caregivers of autistics. Illegitimate "clergy" are no exception to this rule. These people at best represent and paint traditional and established religions in the worst possible light, and at worst may simply enjoy abusing autistics and other people with psychiatric disorders under the guise of "saving the soul" of the alleged possessed person.

It could well be that some "exorcists" are simply sadistic, in other words.

Yet parents and caregivers, believing they know better than the autistics they supposedly love, will attempt to have their autistics exorcised.

I've never read of exorcism curing anyone of autism, and according to what I've read about *real* exorcisms as stated by Roman Catholic Exorcists in books and articles, the worst thing that will happen if a non-possessed person undergoes an exorcism (aside from psychological trauma) is...nothing. Thus if an autistic person comes out of an exorcism un-traumatized, but with no discernible change in presentation of autism, it means either that their exorcist was inept, the exorcism failed, or the victim was never possessed in the first place. This information was inferred and interpreted by myself from the writings of (or articles on) *Catholic* exorcists.

Regarding what I have read generally about exorcisms, and people dying during exorcisms, while I do not know this for sure, I will postulate with a reasonable degree of certainty that it is highly unlikely that a Catholic exorcist in these modern times would exorcise anyone to death. Further, I doubt that if a person is truly possessed that they *could* be exorcised to death, but I may be wrong about that.

I apologize for this, but I cannot help self-promoting here, not because it's an opportune moment, but because part of what I am about to promote is relevant to the point. If you read my book <u>Evil Creeps In: A Tale of Exorcism</u> you will learn quite a bit about exorcism as I have come to understand it (via my extensive research into the topic). Though the book is fiction, the subject of exorcism is discussed at length by two central characters -a Catholic priest, and a Lutheran layman- and the points and counterpoints are based on factual data I gleaned during my research. I will reproduce part of the discussion now. Two words in this passage have been altered to make it more understandable to the readers of *this* publication. Alterations are in brackets. This is the priest speaking:

"The psychologist conducted his examinations outside of our presence so that neither he, nor the old woman would be influenced by our presence, or our reactions. His determination was that while she was showing some mental decline, it was far from the kind we should expect for someone of her age. She had shown small lapses in short-term memory, but nothing unusual. Long-term memory recall was quick and accurate. She seemed in his estimation to be very intelligent, although no formal IQ test was given. Inkblot tests showed no unusual interpretations, though we both know evaluations of these tests are purely subjective.

"She had a slight visual impairment, but was not color blind, showed no signs of seeing hallucinations, was not delusional, exhibited no symptoms of schizophrenia or disassociate identity disorder, did not seem to present with any of the side effects that could come with the medications she was taking. He did see that she was mildly depressed, but not overly so, and he attributed the cause to her being bedridden. He said, in fact, that her depression was healthy, expected, and normal given that she had received a terminal diagnosis of cancer. If she had NOT exhibited signs of depression, or some other behavioral abnormality, he would have found cause for concern because it would have suggested a denial of the diagnosis and a refusal to face the facts. As it was, the woman viewed her oncoming death in a practical manner, stating that at her age, it was doubtful that she would live much longer even without the cancer diagnosis. People in this world rarely [live] beyond a hundred [do] they? And certainly not much beyond that?

The point of that passage is that, in the Catholic Church, psychologists and/or psychiatrists examine possessed people before exorcists are employed, and exorcists are called upon to do their duty only if the afflictions the alleged possessed people are experiencing cannot be explained medically. Thus there is a safeguard put in place by the Catholic Church to prevent what some autistics euphemistically call "The Spanish Inquisition" from happening.

Even so, it is a good bet that historically, the Catholic Church may not have been so careful, and there is nothing in modern times to prevent any pastor or priest from *any* religion from being either ignorant of how psychiatric disorders manifest themselves, or from being overzealous in regards to exorcising demons.

Autistics combat one another over the issue of exorcism for the reasons stated above and for other reasons. Many of these arguments will digress into arguments about religion generally, which inflames things even more.

H. Facilitated Communication

In this form of therapy, a therapist will hold the hand or arm of the person trying to communicate as they use assistive technology. The question is, who is ultimately using the technology? If, for example, it's a keyboard an autistic person is using, who is doing the typing? The therapist or the autistic? Some peer-reviewed studies indicate it is the former. Others the latter.

One objection some autistics have to this therapy is that the therapists, as well as the people who send them to therapy, don't understand that they are not interested in communicating, and so do not make a serious effort to do so. Further, they may not like to be touched, and they may not like their arms and hands to be moved around.

For those autistics, they will respond by attempting to train the therapist by deliberately "typing" gibberish even though they are capable of typing coherently if they desire.

The larger argument, however, is over whether or not the therapy actually works for autistics who otherwise would not be able to communicate effectively. As I have said, some studies say yes. Others no. If you are reading this and happen to be on one side of the issue, you will undoubtedly feel some anger towards people who hold the other view. Either you have "seen" results, or you haven't "seen" any results at all.

Emotion comes into play here. Parents in particular *want*

to see some improvement in their autistic children, and oftentimes they will see improvement where none exists. Conversely, others will *deny* seeing the progress their autistic children are making because it means that prior to this therapy, their children might have been trying to communicate with them without success, and the guilt surrounding that realization can sometimes be overwhelming for some parents.

Thus parents will argue fervently for either side, while those autistics who are articulate enough to argue might either make a joke of the whole thing just to antagonize parents, or will argue for or against the therapy out of their own personal experience. Some of those autistics who fall into the latter category may wind up being negated by the non-autistic adults who are arguing about the therapy.

I. Floortime

Floortime is another therapy that is very often taken advantage of by autistics...according to many on the spectrum.

Theoretically, when someone "gets down to the level of an autistic" -literally on the floor- for twenty minutes or so, one would expect the autistic would respond favorably to this interaction. Rather than the administrator of this therapy talking down to an autistic in an intimidating fashion, the therapist is acting one-on-one -figuratively eye to eye.

If the interaction is enjoyable, the autistic person will many times respond favorably, but transference from anything learned during floortime to the real real world seems to be a choice, rather than a learned behavior, according to those who have experienced this therapy. Thus an autistic may respond well in the therapeutic setting, but behavior outside that setting would remain unchanged.

Doubt revolves around the success of floortime by those who have used it on autistics. Because floortime can be included and integrated with other forms of therapy that have already proven successful, when successful results are seen, can those successful results be attributed to floortime to any degree? Which therapy is eliciting the desired response, floortime, or the other therapy?

The more playful autistics have stated that if people are going to try to get "down" to their level, they will respond as though they are inferior deliberately, just to sabotage the therapist. Given this animosity against therapists by some autistics, it is hard to understand why people who initiate floortime persist with it.

Another thing some autistics have said is that, given that many of them have sensory issues, being in close proximity to a therapist can literally be offensive. Some have described it as being forced to interact with sweaty socks, or even garbage cans. Plus, the very act of being on the floor can be difficult for some autistics, as many have OCD comorbidities. Thus they will do anything to comply to get therapists "out of their face".

But one outside of the therapeutic setting they "let it all hang out".

Finally, some autistics actually reported *enjoying* floortime because it gave them the opportunity to make their therapists act like trained monkeys. Floortime can be implemented in such a way that the therapist follows the autistic's lead, and some autistics have been known to say that there was nothing so enjoyable as getting therapists to do something immature or humiliating.

> "Dian Fossey mimicked apes when she was among them, in order to try to understand them better. When I was in floortime, I had my therapist mimicking *me* to try to get to know *me* better. After I embarrassed her enough, I did what she wanted. But to this day, I see her like one of those machines where you have to keep putting money in and use the claw to get the prize you want. How much effort was she willing to waste -and how much money were my mom and dad willing to spend- to try and win a prize they were never going to actually get? Idiots!"

Argumentation goes back and forth between autistics and parents, and autistics and therapists over floortime for these and other reasons, but many autistics who have undergone floortime agree: The "treatment" is a good study in human psychology. Via floortime, one can learn not only how to manipulate others, one can also learn to what degree another person is willing to let themselves be manipulated.

J. Gluten-Free Diet

This diet can result in protein malnutrition when improperly administered, but this does not stop people from foisting the diet on autistics.

There have been many studies of gluten-free products that were meant to determine whether or not the products lived up to the claim that they were gluten-free.

In most cases, the gluten-free products contained levels of gluten only marginally lower than products containing gluten. While the lower levels of gluten positively affect autistics with celiac disease, seldom does it do anything for autistics without celiac disease.

One would expect this, but many believers in gluten-free diets discount the peer-reviewed studies, often citing "Big Pharma" or purveyors of genetically modified organisms, or the medical community as being conspirators in spreading false propaganda about the effectiveness of the diet, as if *all* doctors worldwide could be "in on it."

Autistics who stand by the diet claim to be either diagnosed or self-diagnosed, but as there is no way of verifying diagnoses, and since the opinion of self-diagnosed autistics may be self-serving, there is no reason to believe their claims that the diets work. It could just as likely be that they have gluten intolerance, or that they are lying, or that they are suffering from the placebo effect, with gluten-free foods being the placebos.

Also, many autistics admit to *liking* the taste of gluten-free foods, and so, in order to ensure the cupboards stay stocked with it, they make sure to become irritable when they get a gluten-filled substitution.

Still others can't tell the difference taste-wise one way or another between gluten-free foods and food with gluten in it, but they pretend to like gluten-free foods so that their parents will buy it for them. Some gluten-free food is more expensive than food *with* gluten, you see, and having their parents buy gluten-free food is a passive aggressive way to get back at their parents attempting to "treat" their autism. In other words, if an autistic with a grudge cannot attack a parent directly, they will do it in a roundabout way, such as hitting their parents in their pocketbooks.

K. Homeopathy

Homeopathy can be so many different things to people who practice it on their children. Coffee enemas, which were mentioned earlier, are one type of homeopathic "treatment/cure."

While there is some evidence that chicken soup may help people who are suffering from a cold, and that duct tape may treat warts, no known homeopathic treatment or cure has been scientifically proven to treat or cure autism.

As with all treatments and cures, a great counterargument to their application is that if they did work, they would be widespread and inexpensive, and they would be passed around the net, and they would be trumpeted from the podium in autism conventions in spite of the media, (which is obviously "owned" or "bought" by "Big Pharma" profiteers). Also, licensed board certified medical professionals would prescribe them.

And yet, while we often see homeopathic treatments and cures being traded like gossip on social media sites, seldom do the people who have been subjected to them report any improvement in symptoms of autism.

So it seems *only* proponents of the homeopathic treatments and cures have "seen" results, although interestingly, these people never seem to be able to produce bonafide treated or cured autistics to back up their assertions, usually explaining that the autistics are still affected with autism too severely to be exhibited -or else the affected autistics have fallen out of remission and are back into their autism again, obviously having developed a "tolerance" to the homeopathic treatments- but sure...the autistics they care for *have* improved -at least for a time. Parents and caregivers alike have *seen* the results after all.

There is reason to believe, however, that people who see results after the use of homeopathic treatments and cures, may not be imagining things. Autism, some scientists, researchers, and clinicians say, is like a wave, with the symptoms and characteristics of autism sometimes getting worse and sometimes waning. So if a person is subjected to a useless treatment or cure *just* as autistic symptoms are on the wane, an observer may attribute the fall-off of symptoms to the homeopathic treatment or cure. [And the same thing often happens when blatantly "quack" treatments and cures are administered.

It is interesting that some people are so quick to believe circumstantial coincidences on the one hand, but may, on the other hand, flatly deny validated peer-reviewed scientific evidence that concludes some homeopathic treatments and cures don't work. But then, some of the people who believe in homeopathic treatments and cures [and "quack treatments and cures] for autism may be mentally unbalanced themselves, or else they are incapable of understanding the research, and would be incapable of understanding the research even if they "saw" the research being conducted with their very own eyes.

L. Hyperbaric Oxygen Therapy (HBOT)

As with electroshock therapy, the brain is at the center of this unproven therapy. This is one is believed in by people who either think autism is caused by an oxygen-starved brain, or that the symptoms of autism are alleviated with an influx of oxygen into the body and brain.

Why shouldn't this therapy make sense? What do we see paramedics do when people pass out. They give people oxygen right? And how often do we hear of people feeling invigorated after a trip to the country where they get "fresh air"?

But as with other types of therapies, this one is unproven.

One other thing to remember is that the most plentiful component in the earth's atmosphere is *not* oxygen, but nitrogen. Could it be that giving someone oxygen who doesn't need it deprives them of the proper intake of nitrogen? I am no doctor, and could not say, but some people will argue this point.

Another argument against HBOT is that some people have died in HBOT chambers, usually from oxygen being ignited. And so why put an autistic person at risk of possible death for a therapy that is unproven? Parents and caregivers will argue that the possible results are worth the risk. However, autistics will argue in response that perhaps parents and caregivers are willing to subject autistics to this therapy because parents and caregivers believe autistics to be of less value to the human race than "normal" people, so if an autistic is killed in one of these chambers, perhaps it really doesn't matter. Or, alternatively, some argue, perhaps some parents and caregivers believe autistics to be expendable altogether, and so even if HBOT therapy has no effect on *some* autistics, why not use autistics as guinea pigs wherever possible to see if HBOT works on *other* autistics?

Even if the therapy itself does not *damage* an autistic person, it can and has traumatized autistics who are claustrophobic. No matter what HBOT chamber construction looks like on the outside, a patient is enclosed in a small, confined area on the inside. But for some parents and caregivers, seeing their autistics traumatized from the experience of claustrophobia is not enough of a consideration for them to abandon this "therapy."

M. Intravenous Immunoglobulin (IVIG)

There are a number of different uses for this procedure, which involves a lengthy injection of immunoglobulin into the system. It may be used to treat disorders of the immune system or to boost immune responses to serious illnesses, but, to date, there is no science that supports its use for treating autism.

There are many possible unpleasant side effects. Worse is the fact that if the hundreds of donors used to make this product are not properly screened, the recipient can end up with any of list of bloodborne diseases. But parents and caregivers who are willing to spend up to tens of thousands of dollars on this treatment may be at the point where "treating" or "curing" autism looks like the lesser of two evils when compared with an HIV or hepatitis infection.

A I have stated, there is no proof at present that it does anything for autism. But this hasn't stopped some people from forcing autistics into receiving IVIG, and *that*, in turn, has caused many people on the spectrum to vehemently and vigorously oppose proponents of the procedure, as well as the procedure itself.

N. Stem Cell Treatments

Given that stem cells can be used to do so many amazing things, one would think they could be used to "rebuild" the autistic mind.

But there is no evidence that this can be done.

Arguments against stem cell treatments are usually made on this basis, but are also made using the argument that fetal stem cells are often used in the treatments. Ergo proponents are arguing with people who will not only rebut them with medical evidence to the contrary, but also from a contrasting ethical, moral, and sometimes religious standpoint.

Closing Words On Therapies and Related Factions

It should be obvious that I have left out a lengthy list of *other* therapies against which people argue on plausible and implausible grounds. My point was to demonstrate that there is significant reason for factionalization, and also to give a representation of how many different factions there are.

Complicating matters further is that some parties may see both sides of a particular issue, and may either be "leaners", "fence-sitters", neutral parties, or peace-makers. People who fall into these categories may irritate those whose opinions are more resolute.

When you also consider that any one of the squabbling parties may be:

- Parents
- Relatives
- Spouses
- Friends
- Teachers
- School Administrators
- School psychologists

- Doctors
- Researchers
- Curiosity seekers
- People with an agenda such as
    -Quacks who are looking to sell something
    -Scam artists who are looking to make money
- Doctors
- Neurotypicals
- Advocates
- Authors

it is easy to see how things can get heated, particularly when these people can have an education about the issues which ranges anywhere from zero to well-versed.

It is not uncommon for a conversation of this type to take place:

Curiosity seeker: "The Autism Genome Project, which included 170 scientists from over 50 research centers around the world, found that-"

Licensed, board certified doctor whose specialty is autism spectrum disorders: "The Autistic Genetic *what???*"

Curiosity seeker: "The *Autism Genome Project!* You're a doctor who specializes in ASDs. You should *KNOW* what I'm talking about!"

Licensed, board certified doctor whose specialty is autism spectrum disorders: "I've never heard of it, And since you are *not* a doctor -as I am- I have no reason to believe anything you say."

And of course, in that conversation, it is the *doctor* who is ignorant. And so the burden of proof is placed upon the curiosity seeker to research offline, or dredge up online, anything about the Autism Genome Project and present it to the doctor, and whether or not the doctor even looks at what is presented, or seriously considers it if he or she *does* look at it, depends upon a great many things. But many times, before the curiosity seeker can even come up with the information the doctor asks for, any spectator(s) to the conversation might side with the doctor simply because it is common practice to assume that a medical professional knows the latest research. Such spectators fail to understand that in every class, there is someone who graduates at the bottom of it.

A Word On Autism "Authorities"

Here is why the following parties cannot always be trusted to provide *informed* opinions on autism:

A. Parents

Assuming parents are honest, and have no ill will toward the autistics they care for, or to anyone they are speaking with, their view of autism is limited to what they have personally observed, and what they have been able to learn. What information they have learned may have been gotten from what they have read, what they have watched on TV, or what they have heard from doctors and other professionals.

Their powers of observation may be prejudiced, however, their interpretations of what they have observed may be based upon ignorance, faulty logic, lack of information, or bad sources or source material, and what they have been told by doctors and other professionals may be misunderstood, misinterpreted, or erroneous.

Let's assume a parent sees a favorable outcome from an uproven "treatment" for autism. While it is certainly possible that the treatment has worked well for his or her child, it is equally possible that other circumstances, interventions, or treatments are responsible for the favorable outcome, or that the observed "favorable outcome" is merely wishful thinking.

One article I read suggests that the more attention a parent pays to their child, the more likely an autistic person will respond favorably to that parent. Thus a parent may dose an autistic with all sorts of quack cure-alls which may have no effect on autism at all, but the autistic person may be responding favorably to increased attention from the parent. Explanations for these favorable outcomes made by professionals to the parent may fall on deaf ears, because for many parents, seeing is believing.

We should not chastise parents for believing in autism treatments that don't work -after all, if they are putting their faith in useless treatments, and believing in favorable outcomes that don't exist, they are probably desperate to the point of believing *anything*-, but neither should we take too seriously what they see and say without first talking with a licensed, board certified medical professional about what the parents are claiming.

One also needs to take into consideration when talking with a parent that they themselves may be mentally unstable, have an ax to grind against autism or autistics, or are not intelligent enough to interpret/compare scientific hard data vs. anecdotal information or biased observations. It is more likely that teachers, doctors, and researchers are not affected by mental instability, as there are many safeguards in place to prevent such people from attaining positions of authority, including peer reviews of their work, and peer observations of their behavior, thus we are better served placing our trust in *them*.

Another thing to remember about "parents" is that people can pretend to be what they want online, and con-artists have swindled people in person. As much as some parents may be good and earnest people, or appear to be good and *honest* people, some "parents" giving advice on autism treatments may really be quack salespeople who are trying to give fake testimony about the treatments they hawk in order to create the perception that the treatments they are selling actually work, and are worth considering.

There are two other reasons to be wary of parents:

1)   They may be less interested in helping than they are promoting themselves and their children for monetary gain, and

2)   They may actually harbor animosity toward autism, and by proxy autistics.

Being a parent to some autistic children is difficult. It can also cost money, depending on what programs or accommodations an autistic person might need. Savvy parents who are unable to hold jobs due to the excessive demands placed upon them by the care they need to give to their autistic children may try to turn lemons into lemonade by promoting their children's artwork, trinkets, or other novel interesting creations for monetary gain.

There is nothing bad about this. Monies earned usually directly or indirectly affect the autistic children for the better. But sometimes parents can become obsessed or consumed with the endeavor. When it gets to that point, they will tell people anything they want to hear about autism in the hopes that people will buy whatever product they are selling, or support them in some other critical and important way.

Parents -again, because of the demands their autistic children can place upon them- can also hold a grudge against their own autistic children, against autism itself, or against autistics. And so opinions and advice they give to others may be given with intent to mislead. It doesn't happen often, but it does happen.

Licensed, board certified medical professionals still ought to be the go-to people for information on autism spectrum disorders, and autism treatments.

B. Relatives

Like parents, relatives of someone who is autistic will show concern for the autistic. While they have the advantage of being removed from the immediate situation, and thus may be able to see the situation more objectively than the autistic person or his or her parents, they also receive much of the information they interpret through the filtered lens of the autistic person or the parents of the autistic.

Thus if a parent says, "I gave my son a B-12 supplement and it's helped his autism immensely. He is now more verbal than he was before," a relative may be inclined to believe what the parent says, especially given that he or she cannot see that some other method was employed by the parent to increase the autistic's ability to become verbal.

Another thing to remember, is that families -including extended families- stick together and defend one another in the face of adversity. If autism is perceived to be the enemy, and the parent of that autistic has come under attack from a third party for employing a treatment which has (apparently) worked favorably, relatives will often defend that treatment without ever knowing or coming to realize that the treatment was in fact useless, or worse, even hurtful to the autistic.

So anytime we hear someone say "My nephew has autism, and his mother and father swear by XXXXXXXX to moderate its symptoms," we should talk to a licensed, board certified medical professional about what we have heard, and not take what the relative has said as absolute fact or truth.

Similarly, we should not trust the advice of a relative of an autistic because, when push comes to shove, they may not have a *vested* interest in positive outcomes for an autistic person. In other words, their responsibility -if any- ends when they put down the phone or leave the scene. Who is to say how much effort they put into collecting information about treatments? Who is to say whether or not they really care about the autistics they are talking about? Who is to say they really care about autism at all?

You will also find that if the parents of an autistic person hate autism, and have spent a good part of their time impressing on their relatives the toll their child's autism takes on their lives, relatives will also take them at their word on *that* count as well, either never stopping to consider, or else refusing to entertain, that the parents could be lying, lazy in their care-giving, or simply poor parents. Thus relatives may cry out in support of a treatment because they wish to see the parents freed from the "misery" that autism brings them.

C. Spouses

Spouses who are not autistic would do well to stay out of arguments going on between autistic people in the autism community. Non-autistic spouses can hardly be neutral in a conversation, because they either love the person they are defending, or they are having problems with their significant other. Thus emotion will creep into their arguments no matter which side they take.

If the spouse loves their autistic husband or wife, the spouse may defend their husband or wife without knowing much about autism or the issues being discussed at all, the result being that they sound foolish. If they are having marital problems, they may side against autistics altogether, rather than be able to see the issues being discussed from a neutral perspective.

If both spouses are on the spectrum, people on the other side of an issue often see both spouses arguing in unison, but it is hard to tell whether or not they are really in agreement, or just supporting one another in order to solidify their matrimonial bond.

At any rate, non-autistic spouses are not reliable sources of information about autism spectrum disorders because they do not actually have an ASD, and thus cannot have a thorough idea of what it is like to have an ASD. Further, their perspective is going to be influenced by the status of the relationship. If, for example, a non-autistic spouse believes that people on the spectrum are closed-minded, that could be the case for his or her autistic spouse, but not the autism community at large. In fact, it could just as much be that the problem is that t non-autistic spouse is too liberal in their thinking.

Additionally, if the non-autistic spouse is actually at fault in the marriage but does not realize it, that spouse risks tainting and otherwise negatively affecting other marriages by spreading bad advice.

Best to leave non-autistic spouses out of the equation when discussing autistic issues, or else to be very careful about taking for granted what they say. It is important to remember also that non-autistic spouses may have other diagnoses that may significantly impair their ability to understand autism, and impair their ability to see autism the way it really is.

D. Friends

Oftentimes, if we see a friend in need, our natural response is to help that friend. If we see a friend being picked on or harassed, we feel the need to defend them. Yet many times, when we come to a friend's defense, we don't understand the entire situation, and the "help" we provide comes at the spur-of-the-moment, in the "heat of the moment", or off the cuff. In other words, sometimes we don't know what we are talking about or what we are doing when we defend friends, and the "help" we provide ultimately does more harm than good.

At any rate, when a friend provides advice or help, it cannot be relied on, even if the emotional component is removed, and if the advice is sound. Unless the friend is autistic, they are partially removed from knowing what autism is like. Unless they have someone in their family who is autistic, they have little conception about what it is like to parent a child with autism. Even if the friend is autistic, a popular saying in the autism community is: If you've seen one autistic, you have seen one autistic. And so inferences cannot be drawn universally for autistics. Further one parent's experience with their autistic child in one family will be different from another parent's experience with an autistic child in another family. One sibling's experience with an autistic in one family will be different with a sibling's experience with an autistic in another family.

Help and advice of any kind needs to come from a licensed, board certified medical professional, and preferably one who is familiar with autism spectrum disorders, if only for the simple reason that they are emotionally removed from the situation. Being emotionally removed from the situation can make them more qualified to view the situation objectively, and without bias.

Another thing to remember is that a friend's support may not be out of a genuine desire to help, but may instead be motivated by a desire to maintain the friendship. In fact, some friends are *most* likely to provide support in a discussion or in an argument when the outcome of that discussion or argument makes no real difference to them, except in terms of showing loyalty to a friend in need.

Finally, people ought to remember that the bonds of friendship are tenuous at best and are seldom lifelong. Loyalties come and go. A friend will defend another to the hilt, only to turn on them at some later time if they see some advantage in it.

It's good to have friends, but when the issue one faces is a medical one, doctors know best.

E. Teachers

Many teachers, as part of their training, will have some background in special education, usually at least one class. They may have some classes in psychology, educational psychology, and multicultural differences. Autism will many times figure into that education, either in passing, as a unit, or it may be a specialization. Additionally, in the course of one's teaching career, additional seminars on special education and/or autism may be required or taken voluntarily by teachers. While this background is commendable, it falls short of what licensed, board certified medical professionals trained in the area of autism spectrum disorders are likely to know, and their knowledge will more likely than not be behind the times.

Who can compare what a teacher may have learned about autism ten years ago with current medical research, for example? Or, if a teacher takes a seminar *this week*, it is possible that the information included in that seminar was obtained and assembled by the lecturer for the seminar many months or years earlier, and who knows whether or not the information that was obtained was obtained from reputable sources? Who knows whether or not the lecturer put their own spin on the material they are disseminating, or infused the material with their own bias?

Coupled with a teacher's knowledge is instruction they will have gotten about how to teach and discipline children, and how to make accommodations for any diagnosis they may have. If any of the children they are teaching have IEPs, teachers act with the full backing of the administration. But disciplining and accommodating children in the classroom is not the same as raising children and teaching and disciplining children in the home.

Further, children act differently in school than at home, so comparing the effectiveness of school discipline and pedagogy to the discipline and instruction a student receives at home may be like comparing apples to oranges.

Yet teachers will stick their noses into conversations with the justifiable belief that they are correct, and with the belief that the parents or autistics they are communicating with are wrong. One thing should be remembered, however: While teachers could be completely in the wrong as far as offering opinions about dealing with autism on the homefront, parents could be completely wrong about offering opinions about dealing with autism at school.

The degree to which a teacher or parent will stand firm on their opinions oftentimes determines how heated a conversation may get. As you can imagine, because both teachers and parents may stand firm in their beliefs, many arguments arise simply because of who is doing the arguing, and not just because of what is being argued.

Casual observers might do well to remember one other, unsavory aspect of battles between teachers and parents: Sometimes, teachers shove autistic kids through school at the behest of administrators to get them out of the school system. If a parent in one of these arguments has experienced this scenario personally, they may see *any* teacher as an agent of the school system who is just trying to make themselves look knowledgeable when (the parents might think) they really don't know anything at all about autism.

It should further be noted that when teachers and parents battle it out in the presence of affected autistics, and autistics are left out of the conversation, or ignored, it may anger autistics to the point where they too, enter the fracas.

F. School Administrators

Some administrators have come to their positions via teaching, but others have had no teaching experience at all.

Many of those who come to administration after teaching possess the most obsolete knowledge because what they've learned, they've learned so long ago. But with promotion comes the false belief in the mind of the person who has been promoted that the promotion would never have taken place had they not demonstrated achievement and success as a teacher. They may view themselves as superior, and the more superior they believe themselves to be, the less likely they are to listen to someone who has not had the education and proven experience they have had.

If the administrator has not had substantial teaching experience, it may be a good idea to question why. Some teachers are shifted over to administrative positions if they have not been successful as a teacher, or if there has been a controversy that has required or resulted in their removal from their teaching position.

For those who have little experience with special needs students, it is possible for them to learn what is necessary to understand the needs of special education students, but unless they see methods and theories working in practice, it is doubtful they will have a true conception of the reliability and success, or lack thereof, of the many methods and theories that are often practiced in school systems.

The types of administrators mentioned above will also fall into conflict with one another, with ego often being the prime factor in preventing mutual and beneficial collaboration for the student, and when any of these people offer advice or opinions outside the school setting, they suffer the same lack of insight that teachers have when offering opinions about people with autism outside the school setting.

Thus their opinions should probably not always be too heavily weighted in discussions about autistic behaviors that occurs inside the school, and especially autistic behaviors that occur outside of school.

A Final Word On Teachers And Administrators

With the negative opinions many autistic people have about teachers and administrators to begin with, contention is often present when teachers and administrators insert themselves into conversations. Autistic people will often refuse to entertain the viewpoints of teachers and administrators simply because they *are* teachers and administrators, even if they have valid opinions.

G. School Psychologists

A popular belief is that *real* psychologists have their own practices, or they work in hospitals. Those who aren't as competent wind up as school psychologists.

I will not impugn the profession by claiming the belief *is* the case. However, the belief did not form out of a void either. Every prejudice has some basis in fact, however slight that basis is, and however wrong that prejudice turns out to be. I have witnessed school psychologists offer their own "diagnosis" of individuals after *one hour-long meeting*, never knowing that extensive year long evaluations of the individuals in question yielded completely different diagnostic results. Similarly, I have seen school psychologists defend their 60 minute diagnoses to the hilt against the extensive evaluations of professional diagnosticians.

Who is to be believed in such situations?

For autistics and their caregivers, it's a judgment call, and every situation is different, but generally, I would suggest that an extensive evaluation is more reliable than a quick one.

Nevertheless, many school psychologists will come to discussions inside and outside of school with the same know-it-all attitude we often see displayed by teachers and administrators, and because the public has been conditioned to respect people in authority -especially doctors- society tends to take the opinions of people like school psychologists as absolute, when in fact their opinions can be the furthest thing from being correct.

Informed autistics and their caregivers know this, and this is why we often see them arguing with school psychologists. Casual observers might think it's the people who are arguing with these psychologists who are the know-it-alls, but the people can actually be in the right and the psychologists in the wrong.

If a school psychologist may be a board certified licensed medical professional, how can we distrust his or her opinion?

Because we must remember that when that doctor works for the school, he or she is working for the school's best interest, and not necessarily the child's. If it benefits the school and the child to get accommodations, and no remarkable harm is being done to the student by issuing an incorrect diagnosis, the school will want the maximum possible funding for the child that they can acquire from external sources, and if getting that funding requires an...exaggeration of a student's need... or a blatant misdiagnosis... unethical school psychologists will make those exaggerations and misdiagnoses.

When they come to a discussion outside the school setting and offer opinions about autism generally, school psychologists' opinions *might* be considered, always keeping in mind what background they may or may not have. However, beyond general opinions, their opinions are valueless. This is true because if they know the patient, it is a violation of the patient's privacy to discuss that person's issues without the patient's or guardian's permission, and, if they do *not* know the patient, then they are hardly in a position to comment at all given that they have not examined the patient.

Another issue that causes confrontation between autistics and psychologists of *any* kind are the negative experiences some autistics have had with psychologists. Some autistics will take out anger for past transgressions on psychologists they have never met before, just to relieve stress. So, in the autism community where autistics are the hosts and psychologists are the visitors, it may be best for psychologists to simply leave the setting when conversations take a bad turn. In cases where psychologists are discussing autism with parents, caregivers, teachers, etc., and autistics are privy to the conversation, but not the hosts of it, it is probably advisable that psychologists, and the other involved parties, be respectful of the feelings autistics have about what is being said.

H. Doctors

Given my familiar refrain about trusting board certified licensed medical professionals, why should we not trust doctors? And why should autistics argue with them so much?

It depends on why and how doctors are making diagnoses and offering opinions, and it depends on the credentials of the doctors themselves.

Is it ethical for doctors to write an incorrect diagnosis on an insurance form? Would you trust a doctor that was that unethical? Even if this doctor offered real and truthful opinions on AS, it would be unwise to trust this doctor as a source because he or she could lie in the future.

There are all kinds of reasons doctors make the unethical decisions they do. I am sure by far, the majority of these unethical decisions are made on compassionate grounds. If writing a false diagnosis on an insurance form saves an impoverished family some money on a co-payment, then why not? Right? The family can use the cost savings to feed themselves, and maybe spend a little more on the one family member who needs it more than others.

But making such a decision forces the insurance company to pay out more than they otherwise would, and causes them to raise premiums on all of their customers.

Everyone pays for unethical behavior, even if that unethical behavior starts off with the best of intentions.

Another reason not to trust what doctors have to say about autism spectrum disorders is that most doctors are not well-informed about them. If they were, they'd know that making a diagnosis after just one visit may not always be the right and correct thing to do. Just like the more a doctor knows about ASDs, the better it is for the patient, the deeper the evaluation of a patient, the more likely a diagnosis is to be accurate. Many of the symptoms displayed by people on the spectrum are shared by people with other disorders. Misdiagnosing someone with an ASD when they might really have something else entirely can mean a lifetime of useless and/or inappropriate treatments, or treatments that can even be physically or psychologically harmful to patients.

It is my personal opinion that, as with psychologists, doctors who are not trained in ASDs should not offer opinions on autism spectrum disorders to or about people they haven't examined without stating clearly in concert with the offered opinion that the only way a person can get valid answers to questions about autism specific to a diagnosed individual, is to ask the autistic's doctor directly. If doctors are not specialists in ASDs, doctors outside of their offices should keep their opinions general, and refer people to doctors whose specialty is autism spectrum disorders, or refer them to peer-reviewed studies directly.

We cannot leave this subject without raising the hackles of some people in relation to "quackery." And you can bet that if what *I* have to say gets some people upset here, some of the things people in the autism community at large say will be even more upsetting to other people there.

The human body is a complex organism, and as advanced as science is today in comparison with The Dark Ages, many years from now, the medicine we practice today will look just as primitive to others as medicine from the past looks to us.

There was once a period in our history when smoking was *prescribed* by some doctors to pregnant women. We know better now, don't we?

Open-minded doctors who believe that alternative treatments may be of some benefit to their patients can be seen either as forward thinkers, or "quacks" or both, and they can *be* one or the other or both. To my knowledge, a doctor should not employ a therapy that is not approved by the FDA, or use a therapy approved for one purpose for another unapproved purpose. Doctors who are willing to take such risks outside of a study, ought to be questioned about their reasoning.

There are some doctors who will stand by their opinions when research points to the contrary. What is a patient to do? What is a caregiver to do? That depends upon how much the patient values himself or herself, and how much the caregiver values the patient. Desperation can also be a factor in making decisions of this type, but it ought not to be. Some of the worst decisions have been made when people have found themselves in crisis mode.

By all means, trust licensed, board certified medical professionals -especially doctors- but as they pertain to autism, trust doctors who recommend a licensed, board certified medical professional specializing in autism even more.

I. Researchers

"Drinking XXXXXX causes cancer."

"Drinking XXXXXX prevents cancer."

"Drinking XXXXXX has no effect on the development or prevention of cancer."

How many times have we seen a study come out that is, months later, contradicted by another study? As the years go by, it seems that so many oppositional study results have been published on the same subjects that people do not know what to believe anymore.

Why is that?

Without getting into the specifics of how a study is set up and executed, I will simply say that there is more than one way to conduct a study, and there are many different ways of interpreting the results.

Valid studies are often ones that have been peer-reviewed. That is to say, the study was examined or redone by people who have no vested interest in the outcome, and the results were either validated (if examined), or duplicated if the study was redone.

Other formal studies, as well as informal studies may never have been peer-reviewed, and thus the results may be completely invalid, despite being written up in a professionally accepted format.

Thus when a researcher budges his or her way into a conversation and starts rendering opinions, it is always important to see if that researcher's reputation is a good one, and even if it is, remember that just because the researcher may be an authority in one area, it does not mean he or she is an authority in related areas.

Recently, I have seen a statement by anti-vaxers advising other anti-vaxers on how to combat pro-vaxer's assertions that Andrew Wakefield's conclusions are invalid. They are telling people to point out Wakefield did not "publish" a "study" but "issued" a "paper" and therefore Wakefield's medical licensed was revoked on specious and incorrect grounds.

Whether their assertion is true or untrue is irrelevant. A jury of his peers gave him a fair "trial" and found either him or his "research" (or whatever anyone wants to call his research) lacking or both. His license was revoked as a result, and as much as people will say that the people who scrutinized him were "Big

Pharma" shills, no one has produced any overwhelmingly concrete and universally convincing evidence that these people are in fact "Big Pharma" shills, or that a "Big Pharma" conspiracy even exists (although the "evidence" they compiled may be convincing to *them*).

Wakefield seems to be an easy target for many to point at when criticizing what they deem to be a poor researcher. However, there are probably many researchers (both inside and outside the autism community) who produce shoddy results using shoddy methods, but who publish "cleaned up," "doctored," and "immaculate" results that look valid to honest reviewers.

It has been reported in the press many times that research into many different areas (not just autism) that *looked* good to reviewers was never duplicated. More often than not, such poor research *isn't* reported in the press. In either type of case, once the questionable methods and/or doubtful results are discovered, scientists are forced to withdraw their research.

Don't believe me? Google the words "research", "withdrawn," and "doctored" and you will find all kinds of articles about the likelihood of scientists to fake research. You will find out how it is done, and how they (at least for a while) get away with doing it.

Can researchers be trusted?

Certainly most can, but be careful, and recognize that when an argument breaks out, it is almost certain that a when a researcher is involved in the discussion, the researcher will almost always assert his or her own perspective rather than someone else's on whatever the subject at hand happens to be.

Further, be sure to double-check when someone quotes a study that has been done. For all anyone knows, that "study" could have been withdrawn.

J. Curiosity Seekers

These are probably the least informed out of anyone who enters a conversation. These people may wonder if they have autism, or they may wonder if their children have it. Their value to a discussion is that they may have read an article about autism, or observed someone with autism, or in some other way picked up some nugget of information about autism, but plumb them for more information, and their knowledge well quickly runs dry.

They may also be incredibly ignorant.

Curiosity seeker: "I read the autism is caused by refrigerators."

Informed person: "You mean refrigerator parenting?"

Curiosity seeker: "Er... I don't know. Refrigerators or something. Maybe it is the chemical they use in refrigerators. The coolant. Neon."

Informed person: "You mean freon?"

Curiosity seeker: "No. That's the gas they use in signs. I mean neon."

Informed person: "I think you might mean refrigerator parenting. And that's a disproved theory."

Curiosity seeker: "No, I mean neon."

Informed person: "Well, that hasn't been proven either."

Curiosity seeker: "No, it must be, because I read about it in [names a conspiracy theory blog]."

If these people happen to believe they are an "authority" on what limited knowledge they possess, the argument can get out of control.

Be kind to them, but fact-check anything they say, just to be safe.

K. People With An Agenda

These may be quacks who are looking to sell something, and scam artists who are looking to make money. One of their methods is to enter a conversation about autism and mention in passing whatever it is they are selling. This method is similar to the subtle insertion of products into movies or subliminal advertising elsewhere. They will rise to the forefront when the conversation turns directly to treatments, or when autistics are looking for ways to help themselves, or when caregivers are looking to help the autistics they care for. When people are desperate for solutions, they appear out of nowhere like saviors, but what they really are are predatory salespeople who are looking to make money off of people when they are least able to think clearly.

These people will appear nice and charming to the people they are trying to rook, and they have a way of making *real* helpers look like predators. I have seen some volcanic online and offline arguments erupt whenever quacks and scam artists enter a discussion.

Another kind of person with an agenda is an autism advocate. Still another, is an author. We will get to advocates and authors in a moment.

At the beginning of this book, we addressed trolls, who may of may not have an agenda. Way further down, we will get to them again.

L. Neurotypicals

Neurotypicals are defined by many autistics as people who are not autistic. In the general disability community, they may be defined as people without psychiatric impairments, or even people without physical disabilities, or both.

For many autistics, if one does not "have" autism, one cannot know what it is like to have it, ergo any comment a non-autistic makes about autism is largely speculative and therefore irrelevant. Some autistics will not entertain any comment from a neurotypical, no matter how insightful.

Neurotypicals can be:

- Pro-autistic
- Anti-autistic
- "Curebies"
- Sympathetic to the "plight" of autistic
- Unsympathetic to the "plight" of autistics.

Neurotypicals will be discussed in greater depth later on in this publication.

M. Advocates (A Whole Category Of Their Own)

Many autism advocates can be trusted, but many cannot. Those who cannot be trusted are the ones who advocate with a specific agenda in mind, or who may be covertly acting on behalf of an advocacy organization.

The autistic genome is being mapped, and the jury is mostly out as to *how* the gene variations autistics have occur. Because this research is incomplete, and because uncertainty as to the meaning and implications of this research exists, people can say almost anything they want about autism's origins, its presentation, its treatment, and even its "cure," and in most cases not be held accountable for making deliberately false statements when they can make their "errors" or misrepresentations seem accidental and unintentional.

An individual advocate acting on his or her own who is deemed to be unscrupulous may be trying to promote an agenda. Before believing anything they tell you, find out more about them. The advocate could be any one of the following:

- Diagnosed
- Self-diagnosed
- In the process of getting a diagnosis
- Seeking a diagnosis
- A wannabee
- Misdiagnosed
- A parent of an autistic
- A sibling of an autistic
- A relative of an autistic

- A spouse of an autistic
- A friend of an autistic
- A teacher
- A school administrator
- A school psychologist
- A medical practitioner
- A researcher
- A curiosity seeker
- Neurotypical
- A Quack
- Someone who is trying to sell you something

And they may be:

- A vaxer
- An anti-vaxer
- Pro-cure
- Anti-cure
- A proponent of quack therapies
- A proponent of conspiracy theories

If the advocate is autistic, they should be diagnosed with only *one* of the following, but many may deliberately mislead by claiming to be diagnosed with more than one of the following:

- Autism (DSM-IV TR)
- Asperger Syndrome (DSM-IV TR)
- Childhood Disintegrative Disorder (DSM-IV TR)
- Rett Syndrome (DSM-IV TR)
- Pervasive Developmental Disorder Not Otherwise Specified (DSM-IV TR)
- Autism Spectrum Disorder (from the DSM-V)
- The ICD-10's equivalents for these diagnoses

(It should be noted that in the DSM V Autism Spectrum Disorder is the *only* diagnosis an autistic person can have.)

Further questions to ask yourself regarding the *autistic* advocate you are listening to:

- Is the "autistic" advocate high-functioning or low-functioning?

- Is the "autistic" advocate capable of functioning adequately in society, incapable of functioning adequately in society, or educably mentally handicapped?

- If the "autistic" advocate is low-functioning or educably mentally handicapped, does this person have a spokesperson, agent, or manager, and if so, who is it?

- Does the "autistic" advocate have comorbid diagnoses?

- Does the "autistic" advocate have allergies?

- Does the "autistic" advocate have sensitivities

- Does the "autistic" advocate have synesthesia?

- Does the "autistic" advocate" have perseverative interests?"

- Does the "autistic" advocate want to be treated or not?

- Does the "autistic" advocate want to be cured or not?

Regarding the advocate (whether they are "autistic" or not):

- Does the advocate believe that autism is caused by vaccines?

- Does the advocate believe that autism is caused by thimerosal?

- Does the advocate believe that autism is caused by mercury poisoning?

- Does the advocate believe that autism is caused by dental fillings?

- Does the advocate believe that autism is caused by heavy metal poisoning?

- Does the advocate believe that autism is caused by "Big Pharma" "vaccinating" or injecting people with autism? (Please note that some people will use the term "vaccinate" and "inject" interchangeably in this context.)

- Does the advocate believe that autism is caused by government "vaccinating" or injecting people with autism? (Please note that some people will use the term "vaccinate" and "inject" interchangeably in this context.)

- Does the advocate believe that autism is caused by genetics?

- Does the advocate believe that autism is the result of recessive Neanderthal genes becoming active?

- Does the advocate believe that autistics manifest genes that will eventually become active for everyone when the next phase of human evolution is complete?

- Does the advocate believe that autism is caused by women having babies after the age of 35?

- Does the advocate believe that autism is caused by women having babies before the age of 35?

- Does the advocate believe that autism is caused by mothers being overweight?

☐ Does the advocate believe that autism is caused by mothers being too thin?

☐ Does the advocate believe that autism is caused by women with a D bra size of larger?

☐ Does the advocate believe that autism is caused by mothers avoiding breastfeeding?

☐ Does the advocate believe that autism is caused by breastfeeding?

☐ Does the advocate believe that autism is caused by refrigerator mother parenting?

☐ Does the advocate believe that autism is caused by men who are over 40 fathering children?

☐ Does the advocate believe that autism is caused by smart people procreating?

☐ Does the advocate believe that autism is caused by unintelligent people procreating?

☐ Does the advocate believe that autistics are alien-human hybrids?

☐ Does the advocate believe that autistics are "rainbow children," "crystal children," Or "indigo children"?

☐ Does the advocate believe that autism is caused by high fevers in children?

☐ Does the advocate believe that autism is caused by gluten?

☐ Does the advocate believe that autism is caused by celiac disease?

- Does the advocate believe that autism is caused by Low Levels Of Vitamin B-12 And Vitamin C?

- Does the advocate believe that autism is caused by fluoride?

- Does the advocate believe that autism is caused by genetically modified organisms?

- Does the advocate believe that autism is caused by electronic and battery operated devices like cell phones, televisions and other electronic gadgets?

- Does the advocate believe that autism is caused by electromagnetic radiation in the atmosphere?

- Does the advocate believe that autism is caused by demonic possession?

- Does the advocate believe that autism is a diagnosis?

- Does the advocate believe that autism is a mental disorder?

- Does the advocate believe that autism is a disorder?

- Does the advocate believe that autism is a disease?

- Does the advocate believe that autism is a health-related problem?

- Does the advocate believe that autism is a difference?

- Does the advocate believe that autistics are a minority group?

- Does the advocate believe autistics are a separate race?

Regarding the following therapies:

- Is the advocate for or against ABA therapy?

- Is the advocate for or against antiviral drugs?

- Is the advocate for or against auditory integration training?

- Is the advocate for or against chelation therapy?

- Is the advocate for or against coffee enemas?

- Is the advocate for or against electroshock therapy?

- Is the advocate for or against exorcism?

- Is the advocate for or against facilitated communication?

- Is the advocate for or against "floortime"?

- Is the advocate for or against gluten-free therapies?

- Is the advocate for or against homeopathy?

- Is the advocate for or against hyperbaric oxygen therapy?

- Is the advocate for or against intravenous immunoglobulin (IVIG)?

- Is the advocate for or against stem cell treatments?

Regarding the following issues (which will be discussed in more depth later):

- Is the advocate for or against intravenous immunoglobulin (IVIG)?

- Is the advocate for or against restraints?

- Is the advocate for or against institutionalization?

- Is the advocate for or against an autism registry?

- Is the advocate for or against the sterilization of autistics?

- Is the advocate for or against an in utero genetic test for autism?

- Is the advocate for or against weeding autistics out of the human genome through selective abortion?

- Is the advocate for or against abortion?

- Is the advocate for or against selective abortion?

- Is the advocate for or against the neurodiversity movement?

- Is the advocate for or against pushing the United Nations to grant autistics minority status?

- Is the advocate for or against the consolidation of the five DSM IV-TR autistic spectrum disorders into one designation in the DSM V?

- Is the advocate for or against autistics' participation in studies?

- Is the advocate for or against wars and drafts?

Another important question (which will be discussed later):

☐ Does the advocate like neurotypicals, hate neurotypicals, or hate neurotypicals but support the neurodiversity movement?

Some *very* important questions (which will be discussed later):

☐ Is the advocate morally conservative or liberal?

☐ What is the advocate's religion?

☐ What is the advocate's religious denomination?

☐ What are the advocate's political leanings?

☐ What is the authors opinion on Cassandra Affective Deprivation Disorder?

☐ What autistic movements has the advocate supported or not supported?

☐ What petitions has the advocate signed, not signed, or refused to sign?

☐ What autistic alliances are the advocate affiliated with?

☐ What autistic organizations does the advocate belong to?

☐ If the advocate belongs to an autistic organization, what is their position within that organization?

☐ What government organizations is the advocate affiliated with?

☐ Who are the advocate's friends in the online and offline autism world?

☐ Has the advocate been arrested for illegal activity that could be linked to their autistic political views?

These questions are a fraction of what you should ask yourself before you trust an advocate. If the advocate's opinions on something do not correlate to what you know, what you've read, or what you've have heard, they may be ignorant, pushing an agenda, or both, and they may be dangerous for that reason.

Who advocates are affiliated with is a particularly important item to focus on. The following is an excerpt from Autistic Authors, and Autistics, and Autism in Literature: A Commentary that illustrates how "autistic" authors gain status among their peers and among those who follow them. "Advocates" are similarly created by autistic advocacy organizations, and they are used by autistic advocacy organizations in a similar fashion:

> I have been watching autistic advocates online for a very long time now, and what I notice is that some of the larger (and most notorious) autistic organizations infiltrate the online media and get published by it the way a bunch of amateur chefs will befoul a ceiling with pasta. They know that if there are a lot of people throwing a lot of sticky stuff, there's a good chance that no matter how much might fall off the ceiling, *something* thrown by *someone* will stick.
>
> Autism self-advocacy organizations in particular might have *dozens* of their members writing for Examiner.com and Huffington Post. Some will purposely assail the opinions of their fellow members in a realistic looking but contrived argument meant to lead the readership to a consensus and a conclusion. Other times, these same people and their organization's fellow members/bloggers may write similar sounding pieces on a particular topic to make it appear that a majority of the "journalistic" opinion supports a certain viewpoint.
>
> It's all a coordinated effort, and it's all done to mislead.

The are many reasons autism self-advocacy organizations might have to mislead people:

1.They want to increase their rankings in search engines by having their organization mentioned as many times as possible on the web.

2.They want to promote their organizations to attract a larger membership.

3.They want to get people to sign a petition *en masse*.

4.They have a political agenda, such as trying to get legislation passed, and want to swamp the net with their agenda.

5.They want to incite the autism community at large to act on an issue in a manner that is ultimately favorable to them.

6.They want to attack a sector of the autism community and make it look like they hold the majority of the public support.

7.They want to make people believe that the members of their organization are noted and/or prominent journalists to raise the standing of the organization in the eyes of the media, potential new members, and also its enemies.

8.They want to make legislators believe that because of their supposed breadth of impact on the population at large, they are a viable political entity with significant influence.

9.By encouraging comments to their articles, they can gather intelligence about their supporters and dissenters, such as email addresses and IP addresses. (They can use this information later to either recruit people or bully them.)

10.By touting themselves as "authorities" in the areas they are talking about, there is an implied threat that if you disagree with them, there may be repercussions.

It's interesting to note that if you continually review the "board" profiles of some of the board of directors for many of these self-advocacy organizations, you will find that someone's profile might start out saying "Jane Doe is a self-diagnosed fast food restaurant employee who aspires to be an autistic author..." and over the course of months or years, this profile winds up changing little by little until it reads "Jane Doe is an autistic journalist who writes for Huffington Post...."

In the intervening time, if you listen to Jane Doe rant and rave in a chat room, or if you communicate with her via email, you will discover that not only has she been fired from that fast food restaurant job, but she has been fired from many other jobs as well, and all of her attempts to get diagnosed autistic have resulted in her being diagnosed with bipolar disorder. But all that isn't mentioned in the final biographical send up. When you go on the autistic self-advocacy organization's website, what you will read is "Jane Doe is an autistic journalist who writes for Huffington Post..."

I know someone who once wrote to each advisory board member of an organization individually, challenging the activities of some of its staff. The result was a denial and a shirking of responsibility by each advisory board member. The advisory board claimed they were not responsible for the activities of their staff outside the mandates of the organization. Regarding the resumes of the organization's staff, they claimed that they were not responsible for verifying the biographical or vocational information included therein, even when this information was posted on their website.

After this, the organization's staff stepped up their activities against the inquirer.

"Jane Doe is an autistic journalist..." sounds good to everyone who reads the biographical note, and for those people who wouldn't think to write for Examiner.com or Huffington Post, it sounds *really* good. The problem is, almost *anyone* can write for those two publications. If you don't believe me, fill out an application and give it a try. It's easy.

But it certainly sounds good for self-advocacy organizations to say they have a "journalist" on their board. And it certainly sounds good to someone reading the "journal" in question to read that the journalist whose work they're reading is a board member for an autistic self-advocacy organization.

People and organizations that engage in this behavior might see it as symbiosis. A person promotes himself a certain way, and an organization promotes the person the *same* way to the benefit of both the person and the organization.

But in a sense, it's mutual parasitism, with the person and the organization feeding off of one another so that each can be seen as being greater than what they are.

And as awestruck gullible readers, our organizational support and our donor dollars are the secondary food for these bugs.

The above quote makes a good transitional passage to our last "authority."

N. Authors

The questions I suggested we ask of advocates could be asked of almost anyone involved in an online argument, but they should be asked of authors too, mainly because the credence many authors gain is not always the result of their good work, but instead via the result of aggressive marketing.

Many authors seem to have an inflated opinion of themselves and their craft, and have a way of convincing others that they *are* authorities in the areas in which they write. If you want proof of that, just look at how many authors no one has ever heard before quote themselves -and are quoted by others- as being authorities in one area or another without being able to present suitable credentials to explain from whence comes their authority.

Heck, I'm an author, and I admit that there is plenty of stuff I don't know.

In reality, most authors are far from knowledgeable, far from skilled, and in regard to their assertions about -and depictions of- autism, far from right.

If you take a look at my blog www.thomasdtaylor.wordpress.com, you'll see that I have interviewed lots of authors and have even been interviewed by other people a few times myself. But those interviews have taken place for the benefit of our fans. We are just everyday people who go about our day to day existence like everyone else, with the only difference being that writing is our profession (although for some, it may merely be a pastime or a dalliance). And if those statements can be made about me and other authors, they can be made about autistic authors as well.

As far as fiction goes: What I have been noticing is that literature that is written by, for, or about autistics seems to be deviating down a dangerous path. It seems as though autism is being portrayed in literature less as a diagnosis, and more as a minority lifestyle. Sometimes it is even portrayed as a culture or cultural imperative. Much of what is written by "autistics" is actually being written by "self diagnosed" autistics, and no matter who is doing the writing (autistic author or self-diagnosed author), plots, characterization, and other elements, are many times being drawn and presented based on observation of "autistics" with unconfirmed diagnoses in informal venues rather than upon observations of real, diagnosed autistics in realistic or controlled settings.

The same observations apply to what I have seen of nonfiction "autistic" and non-autistic authors. The researching, the writing, and the publishing, may be questionable in many cases, as may be the author doing the work, and the author's motives.

Thus whenever an "author" enters a conversation and tries to weigh in on the topic of autism, that author should not be given too much credence unless his or her resume is established, and acceptable to others in the field of autism as well as to the parties concerned in the discussion, and even then, because someone's credentials cannot always be verified, it is impossible to know if authors -or anyone else- are as "great" as they make themselves out to be.

For a more extensive exposition on the subject of autistic authors, please see my book <u>Autistic Authors, and Autistics, and Autism in Literature: A Commentary</u>.

Factions Ad Nauseam: What Autistics Believe About Autistic Issues

Chunk II: Other Issues

It isn't just who you are and what you believe about autism, its origins, and its treatments that can make you a target in the autism world, it can also be that you are target for what you believe on other autistic issues, and issues outside of autism.

A. Restraints

Are restraints good or bad? Are they used unfairly? Is it right to use them for disciplinary purposes, or should they only be used when autistics are a danger to themselves or to others?

I could go on with more questions, and simply state that when people stand on different sides of the issue, there is the potential for rivalry. However, the issue of restraints is not always as clear-cut as it seems.

Let's say you have someone on the spectrum who is a selfish whiner. This person has no reservations about pushing the envelope to get what he wants, going so far as to stage meltdowns in public, or in the company of others. Sometimes, if a person like this doesn't get what they want, they will break things, throw things, hit people, threaten people, threaten to self-harm, use objects as weapons, etc.

This behavior seldom has anything to do with autism, particularly when, in the presence of people of authority whom they have never met before, these offenders mind their manners... until they believe they have sized-up the person in authority.

What does a caregiver do in that situation?

Do they give in?

Out of frustration, many do.

However, I've observed in one country with a national healthcare system that nurses and doctors have no patience for people like these and will calmly restrain such people with clinical detachment. They will sometimes do this against the wishes of the parents, and will have the parents removed from the facility if they object.

At this point, the restrained person has two options: Comply or continue to be restrained. Some comply. Others push the envelope even further, first struggling in their restraints, and/or calming down and waiting until they are released, and *then* attacking with all the force they can muster when the people who restrained the person least expect it.

That they can plot like this suggests that they can control their behavior. That they can control their behavior in such extreme conditions suggests that they can control their behavior in less extreme conditions. That they *choose* not control their behavior in less extreme conditions shows that unless something is done to prevent them from getting out of control in the future, their outbursts -timing, frequency, and severity will not change.

What is to be done?

While it is humiliating for someone to be restrained so much, so often, and so long -especially when it becomes necessary to relieve themselves- and while it sounds absolutely terrible, if the alternative is self-harm or their harming others, what other choices are there?

There *are* other choices, but those choices are almost always more extreme. These individuals could be placed in a permanent state of sedation, or made to undergo electroshock therapy in a medical specious (but not punitive) attempt to curb their outbursts, or, if it is ultimately shown that they are *not* in control of their behavior, given a lobotomy.

As you've seen, I've made a good argument *for* restraints as being a temporary solution to a difficult problem.

But in other instances -ones where autistics clearly *cannot control their behavior*, is it fair to restrain them? This is a difficult question to answer, and because it is a difficult question to answer, this is the argument the anti-restraint faction uses to combat those who are in favor of the use of restraints.

The problem with the anti-restraint argument is that is compares apples and oranges. There is a major difference between a willful troublemaker and someone who is so out of his or her mind that they have no concept of the danger they pose to themselves and others.

My opinion is that each situation needs to be looked at separately, and I have been blasted by many people on the other "sides" of the issue for having that position.

B. Institutionalization

Just like with restraints, sometimes institutionalization is seen as the only option for dealing with autistics who are either out of control (either by their own choice, or because they cannot help themselves), or who seem to be incapable of caring for themselves. The degree to which an autistic should be institutionalized is also the subject of much debate.

The waters are further muddied when one gets into the nuances of affectation:

1)   How disturbed is the individual being institutionalized? In other words, are they partly capable of functioning on their own? Or not at all?

2)   What degree of institutionalization is required? In other words, should it be...

☐   A day school?
☐   A residential school?
☐   A military school?
☐   A group home?
☐   Assisted living?
☐   Full-time observation and care?
☐   Juvenile boot camp?

- Juvenile detention?
- Jail?

Many on the spectrum will argue to one extreme or the other, but the primary consideration for many of these people who argue with each other seems to be the comfort of the person being institutionalized with hardly any consideration being given to *medical treatment and care*. One the one extreme side is "If the world isn't going to change to fit my needs, I should be able to retreat from it to a private place where I have people around me that will cater to my every whim." On the other side are people saying, "Under no circumstances should any autistic's personal freedoms be compromised, even if they are so disturbed as to gouge their eyes out. These people should be able to walk the earth as freely as any person who is not affected with autism, and non-autistics should accommodate them as they do anyone else with real or perceived handicaps."

As one can see, on the one side, institutionalization is conceptualized as a vacation resort, and on the other side, any institutionalization of any kind seems to be equated with incarceration.

Most autistics' opinions fall somewhere in the middle, with autistic people believing that institutionalization may be necessary in some circumstances, but whenever this happens, whatever facility houses these individuals must be run well, with the occupants being treated humanely.

But there is still room for arguments with the people who take the middle-of-the-road point of view. Under what criteria may a person be judged in need of institutionalization? What does a well-run institution look like? What is the definition of humane treatment?

People ignorant of some of the discussions about institutionalization would be surprised at some of the answers that are offered up.

Some believe that each institutionalized autistic ought to have one or two round-the-clock full time attendants, that he or she should be given any and all needed items and discretionary wants, that whatever was "denied" the autistic person in the real world be given to them in the institution.

This may *sound* reasonable, here are examples of just a few of the more questionable "needs" and "discretionary wants" some "autistics" believe they should be given: [The reader will note, incidentally, that in the previous sentence, the word "autistics" is in quotes. This is because some of the people clamoring for certain items and services may be self-diagnosed or misdiagnosed autistics, or possibly even wannabees.]

1)   Education. Sensible autistics will say that they need an EA or tutor to help them understand the curriculum. "Autistics" with less sense will say they should be given the grades without having to do any studying, and without having to attend any classes at all, because it was not *they* who decided they should go to school, but some nebulous body of people who arbitrarily decided that all children *must* get an education.

2)   Food. While their parents may have "denied" autistics food because they were allergic to it, or "denied" autistics the desired portion sizes because they were becoming obese, eating is in the minds of people making this argument pleasurable, and institutionalized autistics should be allowed to eat whatever they want, whenever they want, in whatever quantities they want. Similarly, they should no longer be "forced" to eat things they don't want to eat anymore, Whereas their parents or caregivers may have tried to get the to eat vegetables for their nutritional value, some autistics believe they should simply be allowed to take vitamins instead.

3)   Illegal drugs. A familiar refrain among marijuana addicts is that pot calms them down. At home, and on the street, some "autistics" complain, they can't use it legally, but if a doctor could write them a prescription for it...

4)   Sex. And not just heterosexual sex either. Never mind that society has its moral quibbles. Never mind that homosexuality, bisexuality, polyamory, swinging, pedophilia, bestiality, and other sexual proclivities are frowned upon by many, or are, in some places in the world, illegal. To deny this behavior to anyone -in some "autistic" people's opinions- goes against one's rights as a human. Therefore, an institution should be required -in these people's opinions- to provide people of the same sex, or opposite sex, or multiple partners, or children ,or dogs, or cats, or sheep, or horses, or elephants, for sex to those "autistic" adults who want them, -whether those adults of the opposite sex, or adults of the same sex, or multiple partners, or children, or animals, are consenting or not.

5)   Weapons. As we have read, institutions can be dangerous places, and to protect one from harm and death, anyone who is institutionalized should have weapons, some "autistics" believe. *Especially* "autistics,' if not *only* "autistics." And it isn't enough to simply provide "autistics" with weapons, but they should be trained in the use of them, and should be granted free reign to use them -if they in any way feel threatened- not only on other patients, but on the doctors and administrators who are looking after them.

6)   Video games and electronic gadgets. Having been denied these things in the home setting, perhaps because of the over-focus on violence, or gambling, or erotica (legal or illegal), or the fact that gaming or web-surfing consumes their time to the point where everything else related to living takes second place, some "autistics" believe that institutions provide them with what's been taken away.

Now a keen counterargument to all of this is that if "autistics" are intelligent enough to be able to make these arguments, they ought not to *need* institutionalization in the first place. However, it is also recognized that if "autistics" are trying to fight for such things as I have listed above, most people do not want people with those values running around freely in society, especially when they threaten to self-harm or harm others when they don't get what they want.

All arguments aside, this particular issue may be decided on the world stage, since some autistics have taken to suing their governments on the basis of national healthcare systems infringing on their "rights" as provided for in the United Nations Convention on the Rights of Persons With Disabilities. And they have been winning.

Everyone from criminal psychopaths to pedophiles are watching the outcomes of these trials to see what the results may be so that, if things look favorable to them, they can sue on their own behalf to receive the "needs" their "disorder" causes them to require. Many of these types of people see nothing wrong with what they are doing, and believe that institutions should be a sort of respite from real life where their deepest fantasies are realized.

While it is humane to ensure that these people are comfortable, and not mistreated, as their caregivers of some "autistics" will say, when something has been removed from these people's ownership, be it a privilege or a possession, it is, in the caretakers' judgments, for the good of the autistics, or for the good of the autistic peoples' mental and physical health, or for the protection of society.

[Again, I will remind the reader that the word "autistics" is in quotes above and below. This is because some of the people I am speaking about here may be self-diagnosed or misdiagnosed autistics, or possibly even wannabees.]

Now, it has taken a while, but we are finally at a juncture where parents and caregivers of autistics have begun to catch up with what their charges have been doing online. Some simply review internet histories. Others may have installed programs on their home computers which enable them to access their charges' online activity. It is the same in some institutions. This sleuthing has enabled parents and caregivers to find out where their charges have been surfing, to what web groups and forums they belong, and in some cases, parents and caregivers may even manage to penetrate email and other personal accounts.

What they have discovered in some cases is that the people they care for have been playing them for fools. In many cases, "autistics" are playing the disability card to get "accommodations" from schools, employers, and their caregivers. Imagine how upsetting it must be to discover that there are online forums where "autistics" talk about how to manipulate people to get what they want. Imagine how disheartening it must be to discover that they are laughing and jeering at the people who are trying to help them. That, worse, they may be patting each other on the back as they engage in bullying, manipulating, internet crimes, or even real-life crimes.

Some "autistics" find themselves being institutionalized in military academies, or boot camps, and they supposedly do not know why. To the external observer, it may seem that their parents and caregivers are being cruel, but when a parent discovers that these "autistics" laugh and jeer in public forums about hitting their caregivers "just for the fun of it" under the guise of having an autistic meltdown, caregivers realizes that they do not stand a chance against these people they care for. If the caregivers hit back, even in self-defense, unless they can prove to law enforcement authorities that the "autistic" people are faking it in some cases, they may be subject to arrest and prosecution.

Sometimes, it is hoped that re-programming in a military school or boot camp might help, and even if a stay in such a facility doesn't help, perhaps the threat of sending the child back would be scary enough to cause the "autistics" to modify their behavior.

Unfortunately, some *real* autistics who have *real* problems that cannot be helped by military schools or boot camps, find themselves in military academies and boot camps anyway. They may need psychological or psychiatric care, and never receive it. It is these people who autistic advocacy organizations talk about when speaking against the idea of military schools and boot camps, but ironically, some people in some of these autistic advocacy organizations are manipulators themselves, and might benefit from a stay in a military academy or boot camp.

Institutionalization can also be forced if it can be shown that autistics are physically unable to care for themselves, or if it can be shown that they are psychologically unfit to manage their own affairs. Part of the problem with online autistic advocacy organizations fighting for the rights of institutionalized "autistics" is that they have seen these "autistics" behaving normally online and possibly even in real life and so they know that these "autistics" do not deserve to be institutionalized. They seem to autistic advocacy organizations to be neither physically or psychologically unable to care for themselves. But this is one consequence of over-exaggerating the effects of a diagnosis in real-life situations. If you can behave close to normal online, but you keep up an illusion of helplessness among those who are supposed to be caring for you, you risk finding yourself institutionalized by your carers, with the caregivers fully believing that you are as incompetent as you pretend to be.

One consequence that is even worse than being institutionalized is the prospect of being held in a jail if the psychiatric facility you are supposed to be housed in is overflowing. It is actually quite a common practice that autistics do not go directly to a psychiatric facility, but instead find themselves on a "wait list", and housed in a jail until a place opens up for them. Alternatively, if they are already in a psychiatric facility, they may be moved to a jail for temporary housing if newer cases arrive that are deemed more important, or higher priority.

Autistics and "autistics" who find themselves in an actual jail may find themselves subject to any or all of the worst imaginable things that can happen in jail.

My opinion is that most of these problems would not occur if the online and offline autistic community policed itself and rejected fakers, posers, and make-believers entirely.

But the numbers of people who call themselves autistic can be advantageous to autistic advocacy organizations when they try to present autistics as a political force to be reckoned with, and so many times, these fakers, posers, and make-believers are allowed to go unchallenged. In many cases, these "autistics" are like dead people who somehow make voter registration lists and vote in elections. Their votes shouldn't count, but they do.

C. Autism Registries

Many autistic advocacy organizations are -unbelievable as it may seem- in *support* of autism registries, and encourage as many people as possible to have their doctors put them on them. If society is to understand just how many autistics there are in the world, it is argued, the registries are one way for them to see the numbers.

Other proponents of the registries see them as a way for autistics to get the services they need. If they are "officially" listed as autistic, their portion of the "swag" the government -be it city, county, township, state, or federal- chooses to give them will be assured.

The argument most often heard in favor of the registries *after* they are established, is that, given the violence perpetuated by many autistics and "autistics", it is good to know who and where they are at any given time, just like it is important to know the whereabouts of convicted sex offenders after their release from court proceedings or prison. These proponents hope that the information on registries will be shared with all law enforcement agencies, schools, and medical personnel internationally. That way, their movements can be tracked, and people who might fall in harm's way from the violent behaviors and strange proclivities of autistics and "autistics" can be warned about them.

Finally, (and as I said before) another use for the autism registries is that they can give a "true" accounting of how many autistics there really are. But this case isn't just being made by autistic advocacy organizations, but by organizations who are making the case for an in utero genetic test for autism. If they can take the numbers from the registries and use them to point out that the "autism epidemic" is raging out of control, they can point out that an in utero genetic test for autism is needed *now,* so that autistics can be aborted out of the human race before the human race becomes too sullied and unpure.

Many autistics who initially scrambled to get on these registries to "get what's due them" regret it now. They were not expecting that it was mostly medical care that was in store for them, but instead thought they would be getting other perks, such as adaptive technology, or food stamps, or discounts to recreational activities. This goes to show -in some people's minds- how little time autistics spend investigating newly proposed programs that are made up on their behalf. It actually bolsters the case -some people think -for autistics to be registered against their will.

So, in the autism world, you have some real autistics and also self-diagnosed autistics and wannabees trying to get on the registries, and you have real autistics and misdiagnosed autistics wanting to get off of them.

Too late for this latter group. The decision has been made, either by them or for them, and as unpleasant as it may be, there is not much they can do to eliminate these registries, primarily because no one is interested in hearing their protests, and because those non-autistics who do not understand autism very well are pleased that these "retards" [their word, not mine] are increasingly becoming accounted for.

D. Sterilization

"I want to be sterilized. I don't want to breed. I don't want a son or daughter that has what I have," a blog entry from an autistic who wants to be cured might say.

Most autistics do not feel this way, and torment those who *do* feel this way almost endlessly.

It is almost universally agreed upon by all autistics that *forced* sterilization is a violation of both reproductive rights, and human rights, but some are fighting to end *elective* sterilization procedures for autistics based upon the idea that, since autistics are a minority group, and not people affected by a disorder, sterilizing them is a hate crime, and also a crime akin to genocide.

It is a mixed bag as to what people who are not on the spectrum believe about sterilization, be it elective or forced. Setting aside religious beliefs and values, some believe that autism has not been proven to be genetic in origin, but is caused by vaccines, or mercury, or fluoride, or electromagnetic radiation, etc., and so trying to prevent the passing down of bad genes into the next generation is silly, due to it being an impossibility. Others, however, who do believe that autism is genetic in origin, or who believe that autistics are alien-human hybrids, want to prevent a lineage of mutants from overpopulating the gene pool.

Fortunately, this is one place where the United Nations Convention on the Rights of Persons with Disabilities *does* help autistics. Somewhere in its verbiage, it is indicated that disabled people should not be subjected to sterilization against their wishes. Countries who have ratified the Convention are to agree to that concept, ergo, in those countries, there is no sense in arguing the point, particularly if those countries *are* adhering to the Convention.

But most autistics are ignorant that the Convention even exists, and so they waste time arguing over sterilization instead of applying their efforts to other worthwhile causes.

Another argument revolving around the issue of sterilization is the expense that may occur when an "unfit" autistic parent has, or "unfit" autistic parents have, children. If, it is thought, the majority of autistics who are out in the world cannot take care of themselves, should they breed and produce children (either healthy or unhealthy, autistic or not autistic) that will probably need to be taken care of as well? Even some autistics who understand they would need subsidies to provide for their children still argue against sterilization, saying that society pays for multiple successive generations of "welfare bums," and so it would be discriminatory to prevent autistics from breeding *just* because they may be incapable of taking care of themselves or their children.

E. In Utero Genetic Tests For Autism

A genetic test for autism has not been developed as of the time of this writing, but researchers are *in the process* of developing it. Some are looking forward to the test hitting the market. Others are not.

Proponents might say:

"If you are able to determine that the baby in your womb is going to be autistic after it's born, you can prepare in advance for its arrival."

Other proponents might say:

"If you know your baby is going to be autistic, you can abort it before it's born and save yourself a lifetime of trouble and financial expense."

Detractors might say:

"The fact that a test like that *can* be used to abort autistics before they are born is reason enough not to allow the test to be created in the first place."

I decided to infiltrate a group of proponents and pretend that I agreed with their point of view, and what I found with that particular group is something akin to what has been alleged by detractors.

I was told (in essence):

"Look, autism is a crap-shoot anyway, isn't it? There's no way to prepare for it because you never know what you're going to get from one day to the next. And you don't know what the cost of it will be because it all depends on how badly the baby is going to be affected. But one thing we *can* say about the money part of it is, it will cost a *pile* of money more than you were expecting. More than you can *ever* save or prepare for in nine months. So we make the 'preparedness' argument to get people to shut up, and in the meantime, we pull the weeds out of the garden to make what's left grow stronger."

Me: "Sounds like eugenics to me,"

Them: "Was Hitler so daft to euthanize the retarded and the like before the war? I mean, he needed the beds, didn't he, for all the wounded that were going to be coming in. And the retarded and the deformed weren't doing anything for the country except being living money pits. Plus, they were kept in miserable conditions, so it was better for them if they were just dead, right?"

Of course, not all people in favor of an in utero genetic test for autism hold this view. Some really do want to prepare themselves, and in these cases, the preparedness is primarily emotional. They want to love that baby as much as possible, come hell or high water, and to make every possible preparation they can so that the baby can live in comfort, and receive the care it needs. Beginning to care for an autistic person even before he or she is born is one way of giving that child every chance in life once it *is* born, and to people with this philosophy, I say: "More power to you!"

Can you understand, though, why this issue is one that causes a lot of fights to break out in the autism community?

And it's mostly pointless anyway.

Why?

Because it has been proven that just because someone has the gene variations which many autistics have, it does not mean that those gene variations will actually *cause* autism in everyone who has them. Thus parents whose fetus has autistic genes and find out about it through an in utero genetic test for autism might wind up killing their baby for nothing.

But then again, if parents are deliberately choosing to kill their *potentially* autistic children, then maybe they are not good enough to people to be parenting autistic children anyway.

The biggest combatants to an in utero genetic test for autism are those who are trying to get autistics to be seen by the United Nations as a minority group. If they succeed, then a genetic test for autism, if it is used for the express purpose of a selective abortion, might be considered by some courts to be a tool used in committing genocide, Making use of it could be grounds to charge, prosecute, convict, and jail people for genocide. And they could possibly be put to death for genocide too.

F. Weeding Autistics Out Of The Human Genome Through Selective Abortion

This is the same thing as having an in utero genetic test for autism, right?

No.

Though an in utero genetic test for autism can be used for the purpose of weeding autistics out of the human genome via selective abortion, it can also be used for other purposes.

But people *right now*, are using abortion to weed autistics out of the human genome.

How can that be when there is no in utero genetic test for autism?

Well, one of the latest trends seems to be doing a test to see whether the fetus is a boy or a girl. If it's a boy, parents often elect to abort. The reasoning is that with autism being more prevalent in boys than in girls, one stands a fair chance of getting rid of a *potentially* autistic child if you abort the boy.

The actual "figures" vary, depending on which source you look at, but some estimates say autism is four to five times more likely to present itself in boys than in girls.

The problem with the idea of using selective abortion to prevent potentially autistic children from being born is that, as mentioned earlier, many kids who wind up being diagnosed autistic do not actually have autism, but are simply labeled as such for convenience, or with ulterior motives. Here we see *another* direct consequence of misdiagnoses: It's literally resulting in boys who would otherwise be born getting killed off.

Let's take a look at how this plays out in terms of actual numbers, and also look at how autistics feel when *they* look at the numbers.

Now, some autistics laugh at these "selective" abortions, because, with autism being as prevalent as 1 in 64 kids, if that figure stays current, it means the chances of killing off a potential autistic at all is 1 in 64 if you did *not* select for sex, and in 32 if you *did* select for sex. Thus when male babies are selected for termination, 31 out of every 32 abortions kill off non-autistic babies. So if anything, selective abortions (presently) reduce the number or non-autistics in the human population, and do not substantially decrease the numbers of autistics in the human population.

And if we remember that many autistics these days are misdiagnosed, it means that the number of people who have TRUE autism could be more like 1 in 100, or 1 in 200, 0r 1 in 500. No one really knows. But if it were true that only 1 in 500 people actually had autism, it would mean that if people were aborting males to avoid having a child with autism, they would have to kill 249 healthy babies first in order to kill that one baby who has autistic genes. And even if that baby were allowed to be born, the genes might be switched off and stay off anyway.

But many autistics and "autistics" laugh hard at non-autistics who are trying to abort autistics out of the human race. The wannabees and fakers often laugh the hardest. After all, even though they may bear some responsibility for the possible inflated numbers that make up the "autism crisis" they are already born. So it's great fun to see parents worry about bringing more autistic kids into the world, and to see them abort their own perfectly healthy children as they worry.

At the same time, these autistics and "autistics" understand that they only have so much time left to laugh. Once a genetic test for autism is developed, it will be more likely to pinpoint a child that *might* have autism when it is born and kill it off.

Going back to the idea that many autistics diagnosed today may be misdiagnosed, what these parents may be doing is weeding out potential kids with behavior problems who would otherwise wind up getting falsely diagnosed with autism, but not actually weeding out autistics.

Some say this is a good thing, since kids with behavioral problems can be pretty rude these days. Many autistics feel that it is misdiagnosed "autistic" people with behavioral problems that commit the deeds which wind up reflecting poorly on people who are truly autistic. It is thought, therefore, that it's good to weed such people out of the genome. [The hypocrisy of this thinking is obvious, but many of the autistics who think this way do not apologize for it. Society rejects behaviorally challenged people as much as they do autistics. Why should autistics be the only ones who are selected for termination. Why should autistics *not* be in favor of selective abortion for certain purposes when much of the rest of society *is* in favor of selective abortion.].

Bitter and sarcastic autistics will take their statements one step further: Since many studies show that behavior problems in children are the result of poor parenting, it would follow that parents of kids with behavioral problems should be weeded out of the human race. Perhaps they should be shot dead for raising such poorly disciplined children. Or maybe they should just be sterilized....

But murder is illegal, and abortion isn't. Thus the debate continues.

Again, the biggest combatants to selective abortion are those who are trying to get autistics to be seen by the United Nations as a minority group. If they succeed, then selective abortion of this kind will be considered genocide, for which people can be prosecuted, jailed, and possibly put to death for murder.

G. Abortion

People may wonder why this should even need to be explained? If you are against selective abortions, you are against *all* abortions, right?

Wrong.

Many autistics feel that abortion is permissible under *any* circumstance...except if you are aborting "autistic" fetuses.

Other autistics believe that a mother's right to choose takes precedence over the rights of the fetus no matter what, in which case, it is acceptable to abort even fetuses that may be autistic.

H. Selective Abortion

Well, if you are against selective abortions that result in the death of autistics, you are against selective abortions, right?

Once again...

For some that is true, but...

If you abort because you don't want kids, that's selective.

If you abort because you want a boy instead of a girl or vice versa, that's selective.

If you abort because fertility drugs cause you to have five fetuses and you only want to keep two, that's selective.

If you abort because the fetus looks to be deformed, that's selective.

If you abort because the fetus is the result of a rape, or incest, that's selective.

If you abort just for the hell of it, that's selective.

In short, to these people, *every* abortion is selective, and it's perfectly fine for *anyone* (including autistics) to abort for *any* reason...as long as it's not for the purpose of weeding out autistics from the human genome.

A General Note On Abortion

I have seen many a "war of words" break out between autistics over the issue of abortion, mostly over abortion's moral, ethical, and religious implications. But in regards to abortion of autistics specifically, usually Down syndrome is dragged into the discussion somewhere, and when that happens, the conversation can go at least two separate ways, one of the results being an instant resolution to the argument, and another resulting in an epic battle that never ends.

Conversation A:

Autistic #1: "There is already a genetic test for Down syndrome. Isn't it hypocritical to say that it's acceptable to abort a fetus because you don't want a kid with Down syndrome and at the same time say it's wrong to abort a fetus that might turn out to be autistic?"

Autistic #2: "I guess you're right. There ought not to be any selective abortions for any reasons, or at least where disabilities are concerned."

Conversation B:

Autistic #1: "There is already a genetic test for Down syndrome. Isn't it hypocritical to say that it's acceptable to abort a fetus because you don't want a kid with Down syndrome and at the same time say it's wrong to abort a fetus that might turn out to be autistic?"

Autistic #2: "No. Don't compare apples and oranges. Down syndrome and autism aren't the same. Who the fuck wants a retard in the family?"

Autistic #1: "But thanks to science, if they catch it early, they can fix it so that the effects of Down syndrome are much less than they ever used to be."

Autistic #2: "Doesn't matter. They're still retards. Get rid of them."

But *both* sides, when defending themselves against people who want to abort autistics, will say that there is no need to use selective abortions on autistics, because, as it has been shown with people who have Down syndrome, science and medicine has moderated the symptoms and presentation of Down syndrome to the point where most people with Down syndrome are no longer a burden on society, and if breakthroughs can happen for people with Down syndrome, maybe similar breakthroughs will happen for people with autism, so it's best to wait on developing a genetic test, or, if it is developed, not to use it for the purpose of selective abortion, but for putting effective measures into place for moderating the symptoms of autism.

But there is a third conversation about abortion of autistics that sometimes crops up, and it is one that usually has a parent taking the lead. It usually sounds something like this:

Conversation C:

Parent: "Do any of you autistic assholes and neurodiversity nutheads know what it's like not to get any sleep for decades when you have an autistic that gets up at all hours of the night and roams the house doing dumb things like sticking their hands into plugged in toasters and trying to pour water into the grille of your console television set?

"Would any of you people like to come over and change my thirty-three year old's poopy diaper? Or maybe you just want to bitch me out because I 'inhumanely' feed him his pureed meals through a straw so that he can avoid chewing up plastic spoons?

"You want to pay his medical bills, you jobless freaks?

"You're all going to take care of him after I die, I presume? Are *you* setting up a trust fund for him?

"Do you know how much better my life would have been had he never been born? And considering that he seems to have no presence of mind whatsoever, don't you think it would have been better *for his own* sake if he had never been born?"

Autistic(s): "But we're not as dysfunctional as he is. If you abort him, it sets a precedent, and paves the way for future people like *ourselves* to be aborted. That's not fair. And so, unfortunately, for us to live, people like your son have to live too, regardless of the inconveniences to yourself and the trauma to him. People like you must see yourselves and your child differently than you do. You should see yourselves as sacrificial lambs for *our* sakes, and be pleased with your role when it is painted in that light. It is selfish to to feel any other way, and I and my friends are going to report you to Facebook for hate speech.

"P.S. If you've got a problem with your son sticking his hand in the toaster, unplug the toaster and hide it from him. If you've got a problem with him pouring water into the back of your TV set, get rid of the TV set. If you've got a problem with him loading up his diapers, hire a nurse. If you've got a problem feeding him, hire another nurse for that too. And if you can't afford two nurses, work harder so you *can* afford them. *You* decided to bring the kid into this world. *You* do what is necessary to take care of him, you selfish, inhumane, uncaring creep. *I* certainly wouldn't want *you* for a father."

I could, of course, list out every single type of argument I have heard regarding abortion, selective abortion, and an in utero genetic test for autism, as well as arguments for or against abortion from the perspective of every faction in this book and all the factions not listed in this book, but you can imagine that it would take a lifetime to do it, and still I would not be done, because the reasons people have for arguing with one another are infinite after all.

I. Neurodiversity

As mentioned earlier, the neurodiversity movement as I understand it believes in universal acceptance of *everyone*, no matter what their psychiatric diagnosis might be. It also accepts people who do *not* have a diagnosis, be it psychiatric or (sometimes) physical. People who do not have a diagnosis are called neurotypicals or "NTs." NTs are within the main bell curve of society and are commonly considered "the norm." Many in the autism movement, however, have usurped the meaning of the word "neurotypical" to mean *people without an autism diagnosis*. Some have also co-opted the term "neurodiversity" to mean a group of people not prejudiced against others with psychiatric disorders that is composed *only* of autistics.

The definition of neurotypical changes from person to person. People who use the term loosely seem to include people with physical disabilities in the definition, forgetting that "neuro" is meant to indicate "brain function," although it can be stated that some physical disorders may be the result of disorderly activity in the brain.

Despite the movement's insistence on open-mindedness and free-thinking, there seems to be a lot of infighting in the neurodiversity movement:

-Two people in agreement about how neurodiversity is defined can be friends.

-Two people in disagreement about how neurodiversity is defined can fight back and forth until they stop being friends with one another or, if they are on social media sites, block one another. [Ask them why each has shut the other one out, and they will each accuse the other of being "closed-minded."]

-Many autistic advocacy organizations who carry the banner of neurodiversity before them argue with each other because some autistic advocacy organizations are more "liberal-minded" or "closed minded" about neurotypicals than they "should be."

-Those "autistic" neurodiversity activists who don't actually have a diagnosis will sometimes push for inclusion of their *real* diagnosis in the neurodiversity movement, much to the irk and confusion of authentically diagnosed autistic neurodiversity activists who believe *only* autistics should be included in the neurodiversity movement. Thus they bicker with one another.

-And there can be a plethora of other reasons for fighting as well.

The views expressed by some neurodiversity groups are sometimes vehemently and vindictively stated in a manner similar to the way of speaking found in some "white power"/"black power" movements, and some factions of the neurodiversity movement will engage in subterfuge to achieve their goals.

How can this be? Isn't neurodiversity supposed to be about awareness and acceptance? And what "goals" could the neurodiversity movement have other than promoting understanding about people with psychiatric disorders?

Well, it's not always about awareness and acceptance. There are few people in civilized internet-using countries who *don't* know what a psychiatric disorder is. Likewise, there are few people in those countries who *don't* know that it is wrong to persecute people who are diagnosed with psychiatric disorders. So really, no neurodiversity movement is actually needed. Unless you are trying to get something *else* out of it.

What could that something else be?

-Money. "Donate to the cause" often translates into "Donate to me, personally, so I can blow your money on my personal wants, needs,and desires," or "Donate to my organization, so we can split your money up amongst us all, pocket it, and go home."

-Notoriety. The people and organizations that make the most noise are usually the ones that become well-known, even if they are good for nothing. These people and organizations *want* to be known as the ones you don't screw with if you know what's good for you.

-Career opportunities. I have seen many private bullies - who outwardly smile and simper- get picked out of a crowd and mentored by people in higher positions of authority and put to use.

-Media recognition. Sling as much shit into the fan as you can and sooner or later, the media takes notice and asks what you are doing. If you have a good radio voice, or look good on camera, or if an organization can produce such a person to speak on their behalf, you or the organization are quotable.

-Political power. A person or organization will often become a "source of reliable information" to politicians just because she/he/it is the *only* one that dared to vocalize opinions on an issue, no matter how misguided those opinions may be.

-Fame and acclaim. Whenever someone speaks on a topic, it puts them at the center of attention. This is why many times causes will attract certain people to be their spokespeople. Some people, especially some neurodiversity activists, *enjoy* being the center of attention. While this assertion seems specious given that most autistics are asocial, one must remember that not all "autistics" are autistics. Spokespeople *can* be diagnosed, but they can also be self-diagnosed, in the process of getting a diagnosis, seeking a diagnosis, wannabees, or fakers and posers.

While many neurodiversity activists are earnest and trustworthy, getting into a conversation with them is sometimes like walking into a giant hornets' nest, where every one of those bugs can sting a person many times over and still not tire out. This is particularly disconcerting to autistics when the "bugs" that do the stinging don't even have autism, but are just pretending to have it.

How would you like it if you were autistic, and protesting against something one of these known fakers was saying, and they were able to get people to publicly rally against you by saying: "Look at that heckler! I bet s/he doesn't even *have* autism!"

Happens all the time, which is why more and more autistics seem to be parting company with the neurodiversity movement as time goes on.

J. Minority Status

I just know I am going to wind up sounding like a conspiracy theorist as I talk about autistic self advocates' drive to gain minority status with the United Nations. However, all I am doing is passing on what I've heard. It makes no difference to me *what* they're trying to do, because the United Nations would never seriously consider anything these people have to say anyway.

But they want to be declared a minority. In their minds, being a minority means:

> 1) They would no longer be forced to go undergo medical treatments or procedures against their will, (including sterilization and taking their medication.) [Technically this is already covered to n extent by the United Nations Convention on the Rights of Persons With Disabilities in countries which ratified the Convention, but most people do not know this.]

> 2) They would no longer be forced to go to "special schools" or "endure the humiliation and indignity of" IEPs, or "special programs" when in school, but *could* sue schools for not getting a Free Appropriate Public Education (FAPE) due to "cultural bias" in the classroom, in textbooks, and due to poor test item construction. [In other words, instead of getting FAPE under the context of accommodations for their disability, they would now be able to argue that they have no chance of succeeding based on existing cultural bias within the entire educational system. Additionally, if their "culture" is of the kind that "requires" them to surf the net in class, play online games in school, etc., they could sue any school or district that denies them the ability to do that, too.]

> 3) They could bypass many college and university admissions requirements and gain admission under affirmative action laws.

> 4) If they are denied a job, they could sue on the basis of discrimination under affirmative action laws.

> 5) If their parents try to force them to do something they don't want to do, they could sue their own parents under

the argument that their parents are "discriminating" against them.

6) If they in any way physically, verbally, or emotionally abuse someone as the result of their autism (e.g. meltdown, or just because they feel like it) they would be immune from restraint, institutionalization, prosecution, or incarceration as the result of their behaviors because taking any of these actions would infringe upon their "rights" as a "cultural minority."

7) If someone says or writes something bad about autism spectrum disorders, they could sue for slander or libel.

8) They can sue law enforcement authorities if they feel arresting officers have "targeted" them for behavior that "must" be allowed for their "cultural minority" or if the law enforcement authorities are engaged in "racial profiling."

9) If they are convicted of a crime that they feel goes against their "cultural minority" they could sue for "wrongful prosecution" or "malicious prosecution."

One example of how numbers seven and eight would work... If an autistic person's perseverative interest is flying planes, and he manages to get into a cockpit of a jumbo jet and steal one, and is caught and arrested, he can say (these people think) that perseverative interests are one of the attributes people of his "cultural minority" have, ergo he should not have been arrested and ought not to be prosecuted.

Drop in *any* crime, including robbery, rape, and murder, and the same concept would apply in these people's minds.

To continue, in the minds of people seeking minority status, autism being designated as a minority means:

10) It would prevent institutionalization for reasons of mental instability or defect because autism would no longer be a mental disorder or a psychiatric diagnosis.

11) It would prevent any federal, state, county, township, city, or other law-making, or law-enforcement entity from barring an autistic from doing things other people may freely do, such as gambling, driving, owning credit cards, using alcohol, etc., even if the autistic in question has no demonstrable presence of mind.

12) It would prevent any military in any country from drafting an autistic into military service should the need arise if doing so goes against "autistic culture," [and if that were the case, autistics *might* then serve in alternative service, such as the kind the Amish served in as Conscientious Objectors during the Vietnam war, but only if *that* didn't go against their culture either.] but at the same time, if an autistic wanted to join the military, the military would be compelled to evaluate the autistic's candidacy just as they would any other potential candidate, always leaving out disqualification due to any mental and/or physical incapacity that may be symptomatic of their autism.

13) For diagnosed, autistics, it would allow prosecution of self-diagnosed and wannabee autistics who attempt to fraudulently take advantage of the "rights" afforded to diagnosed autistics.

14) Autistics -no matter how severely they are affected by their autism- would be allowed to run for public office, serve in law enforcement, serve in the military, etc.

The list goes on, and I won't bore the reader by adding more to it.

Lawyers reading the list will probably see many reasons why the beliefs imparted here would more likely than not fail to hold up if they were challenged in court, but obtaining minority status via the UN is what some autistics are hoping to do.

Of course, if autistics were given minority status, the implementation would be difficult. An autistic who has obtained minority status would have it all his or her life (and most likely would retain it even if they were somehow cured), but their children, if they were born non-autistic, would not have minority status at all. Thus *every single person in the world* would need to be tested and evaluated for autism for all of the people in this "minority" to be discovered and given their status.

Now, if you pretend to be ignorant, and ask some of the people spearheading this campaign if any of those fourteen points (and others) are what they are pushing for, they will deny it.

"That's ridiculous," they will say. "No citizen should expect special treatments like the kind you're talking about."

Put in private, they use the above fourteen points and more as selling points to potential supporters.

What is important to remember is that many of those who have started this campaign are not actually diagnosed with autism. They are self-diagnosed or misdiagnosed autistics, or they are wannabees, which only goes to show that some people who claim to be autistic but really are not don't care *who* they affect with their words, actions, deeds, and campaigns, even if the people they are hurting are autistic.

K. Consolidating Five ASDs From The DSM IV-TR Into "Autism Spectrum Disorders" In The DSM V

For those who still don't know that the DSM V exists, this is not an issue. For those marginally less ignorant, it's not an issue either:

> "So they've consolidated five descriptors into one. Big deal."

The problem is that only the most informed know that pretty much anyone with mild symptoms are to be booted from the Autism Spectrum Disorder [299.00 9F84.0)] category and lumped into Social (Pragmatic) Communication Disorder [315.39 (F80.89)].

It makes a difference for people with a legitimate diagnosis either way because accommodations for people with ASD may be different for those with Social Pragmatic Communication Disorder.

It also forces self-diagnosed autistics, misdiagnosed autistics, wannabees, and fakers to try harder to be autistic, because most of the qualities they felt caused them to be "autistic" in the first place are now classified under Social (Pragmatic) Communication Disorder 315.39 (F80.89).

So, if you "come out" and say something along the lines of "I support the DSM V," you are likely to get one of three popular responses more than any other:

1)   "What's the DSM V?

2)   "So what? What's the difference anyway?"

3)   "You're cold-hearted. You'd leave so many of us out in the cold without accommodations and without recourse to get them. Get a life you ignorant scum!"

There has been talk among autistics of trying to overturn and reverse the revisions to the DSM, but there had been talk about trying to prevent the revision of the DSM in the first place and nothing came of it. It didn't seem like anyone could get organized *before* the revision, and it doesn't seem like anyone can get organized now that the revision has taken place. More and more, talk seems to be centered around the idea that maybe the people who keep revising the DSM will see they are wrong, and correct their mistakes when it's time for the DSM VI to come out. Or else maybe they will do a DSM V-TR ["TR" stands for "text revised"] version, (as it was done for the DSM IV) and introduce the hoped for corrections there.

L. Autistics' Participation In Studies

Here is a (paraphrased) taunt I heard used against an autistic person who elected to participate in a study:

The taunt: "Here little lamb, come to the slaughter,"

The defense: "I know what I'm doing."

Another (paraphrased) statement I heard was from a self-diagnosed Aspie.

The criticism: "You idiot! The more people like *you* participate in studies, the closer doctors will come to realizing people like *me* are having them on."

The defense: "I'm diagnosed. You're self-diagnosed. Shut up and get a *real* diagnosis and join your *own* study!"

Here is a popular accusation against willing study participants:

Accuser: "You're prostituting yourself out for the free medical care,"

The defense: "Maybe so. But if I am, it's my right."

And here is a popular attack used against parents of autistics:

Attacker: "You're letting doctors use your son as a guinea pig,"

The defense: "Maybe in the process of this study, they will figure out how to make my son be less incompetent."

If autistics could get their United Nations minority status approved -it is thought- research and medical studies where the participant is unwilling would be considered a crime akin to Josef Mengele's experiments on Jews during the Holocaust. They forget, however, that countries which have ratified the United Nation's Convention on the Rights of Person's With Disabilities already protects people with disabilities from being subject to such experimentation against their will.

It has been pointed out that most autistics (and even most people in the countries which have ratified the Convention on the Rights of Person's With Disabilities) don't know about the Convention, nor do they know that they cannot be compelled to undergo studies against their will. However, who is to say that anyone will be any less ignorant about what rights autistics will be given if autistics are granted minority status?

As for autistics who volunteer themselves for these studies, they are often seen as selfish people who are willing to sell out *all* autistics for any possible perks that may be gained from participating in the study.

Compassion for the persons who enroll autistics in these studies against their will may be in order. Parents and caregivers who are desperate for help too often don't get any, and they hope that by offering the autistics they care for to these studies that something might be found to prevent future parents and caregivers from having to experience the hardships they have endured. And of course, if some of the autistics in question have *severe* presentations of autism, their hopes for those particular autistic people may be legitimately compassionate.

It should be stated here that there are autistics who self-harm to the point of severe impairment. Head banging, cutting, pulling out hair, even -I have heard- gouging their eyes out.

If some scientific research resulted in a treatment that could moderate behaviors like that, wouldn't that treatment be beneficial to the affected autistics?

"Accommodate them better and they won't do that," autistic advocacy organizations are quick to say, and it *sounds* plausible to most people's ears. If accommodations yield the desired results, why enroll autistics in stressful studies against their will? But these autistic advocacy organizations have no proof to back up their claims, and, to get proof that would be accepted by most people, the organizations would, ironically, have to provide the people they are trying to get through to with study results. Such a study would have to be conducted with autistics as the test subjects, and these autistics would have to be ones so severely affected by autism that they would have to be enrolled in the study against their will.

M. Wars And Drafts

Really, these should be two separate categories, but they do go together in a way.

A common question arises in times of crisis: "Do we go to war, or do we not go to war?"

The stance on this issue varies from person to person. It can stay the same over the course of one's lifetime, it can change over the course of one's lifetime, or it can change with each conflict.

For me personally, it depends on the conflict. I have been in support of military action in some cases, and against it in others.

Autistics have equally diverse opinions about war, but when the subject is a potential draft, conversations can be pretty heated. Many autistics want to serve in the military but cannot because the presentation of their diagnosis is severe enough to disqualify them from service. Others don't believe they should serve in the military at all *because* of their diagnoses. Still others believe they could be useful to the military because of their interest in technology, or in politics, or whatever their perseverative interest happens to be...but not autistics have a perseverative interest that might be useful to the military.

It's an issue that has lots of nuances, but the gist of the one that causes "wars" between autistic people is when autistics don't believe in wars -or more specifically, police actions- but hypocritically believe they should be protected from warlike persecution themselves.

Example: During the Rwandan genocide, a certain group of autistics thought that genocide was Rwanda's internal affair and the world should stay out of it. But guess what? The group that was saying this was the same group that was fighting for autistics to gain minority status with the UN.

When someone asked the group leader:

"Don't you think it's hypocritical that you don't care about what happens to another minority even as you are fighting to gain protection from the UN against genocide through eugenics?"

The reply from the group leader was profane. Not only was the person who asked the question banned from the group, but the group tried to get their social media account suspended.

And, not surprisingly, when someone else took issue with another part of the group's stance, the same thing happened.

Questioner: "If we went to war and there was a draft, would you go?"

Group Leader: "No. Autistics shouldn't have to serve."

Questioner: "So if a bunch of people decided to kill off autistics in some part of the world besides yours, you wouldn't go to fight on their behalf?"

I suppose we cannot blame the group too much though. There were protestors who were against both wars in the Persian Gulf who chanted "Hell no! We won't go! We won't fight for Texaco!" and then drove from the rallies in their gas guzzling cars to their houses with well-manicured lawns, lawns which had been cut by gas movers, and edged and weed-whacked with the same.

People don't always think about what they say or do, and that includes people on the autism spectrum.

N. Neurotypicals and Neurodiversity

Some neurodiversity activists like neurotypicals. Others dislike them. But most recognize that in order to succeed in life, ignorance of what autism is needs to be countered with honest efforts to inform.

But some neurodiverse people use neurodiversity as a platform to campaign for selfish wants, rather than the needs that most autistics may have. The common justification for this selfishness is usually that it is the most intelligent autistics who wind up speaking for those affected with autism, and just like an army travels on its stomach, these intelligent autistics need to have their "needs" satisfied so they can be the most effective at advocating that they can be.

Thus neurodiversity activists can be regarded either as autism's soldiers, or a quasi-political class.

What they really are is a combination of both.

Supposedly working independently of one another, in reality, many autistic advocacy organizations have moved their way into the neurodiversity arena and are now cooperating and collaborating ring masters of the advocacy circus. When an autistic advocacy organization issues a blanket statement that most on the spectrum feel to be wrong -such as the idea that autistics need to be seen as members of a cultural minority instead of people with a disorder or disability- and the rest of the heads of the neurodiversity movement parrot this concept to the public, it's plain that the neurodiversity movement has been corrupted if not taken over.

In response to this assertion, autistic advocacy organizations and autistic advocates will say that many neurodiversity activists have very high intelligence quotients, and this is justification enough for them to make pronouncements on behalf of *all* autistics without even consulting them. They have been heard to say things like this:

> "They don't know what's good for them. When we vaccinate babies, the babies don't know why they are getting jabbed with needles. But it's to save them greater trauma and discomfort later on in their lives. So it is with the decisions we're making for severely affected autistics. They are our babies. The neurodiversity movement is taking care of these babies because they are incapable of knowing what's best for themselves."

But when push comes to shove, if the neurodiversity movement is all about awareness, and maybe fighting for the rights of people with neurological disorders, then why go to the extreme solutions first? And is going to extreme solutions first what is "best" for autistics who cannot speak for themselves? Is it really necessary, for example, to have autistics designated a minority group by the United Nations? Why not just try a little harder to educate people about what autism is, and try to reduce prejudice against autism and autistics that way?

> "Because NTs don't get it. That's why. They're too dumb. They don't have our superior brainpower. Their brains are not cross-wired as ours are to make the connections we can. They just don't understand. So you have to push the envelope with them, and pull the wool over their eyes as you do it, so they won't realize the concessions they've made until it's too late to reverse what you've done. Someday, for every autistic committed to an institution, there will be NTs, and a bunch of doctors who will get jailed for putting him there. On what grounds? Hate crime"

But if NTs are the "typical" ones, and autistics are the "atypical" ones, shouldn't autistics try a little harder on their end to fit in with the rest of society?

> "That's like telling someone who is gay to become heterosexual. You're asking autistics to do something they are incapable of doing. Autistics should not have to conform to societal norms because society as it exists now is *not* set up for autistics to succeed within it. Society must be changed."

But if you change society for the benefit of autistics, won't that make it harder for NTs to succeed?

> "Who cares? Turnabout is fair play. They've screwed us over for years. It's time for us to do a little bit of the screwing. So fuck them!"

Provoke many of these neurodiversity activists and you will discover that there are a lot of bad feelings towards NTs.

You will see passive aggression against them. Sometimes outright anger and rage.

As far as NTs go, while there are a few who have entrenched prejudices, or else firm convictions based upon their experiences with autistics, most tend to be neutral in their opinions, simply because they haven't previously had much cause to think about autism.

But if their first point of contact happens to be an angry autistic neurodiversity activist with an ax to grind, one can imagine what kinds of opinions might be formed about autistics and autism, and why they might keep those opinions for a very long time.

People tend to remember fearful experiences more than happy ones. Ask Americans where they were when 9/11 happened, and most can tell you. But I doubt anyone can think of a *happy* event that would be as ingrained in the American psyche as 9/11 that would enable someone to even ask the question, "Where were you when [happy event] happened?" And if a person *could* find a happy event to use as an example, I doubt most people could say where they were when the event happened.

So as much as autistics like to say they are constantly persecuted by NTs, the reality is, autistic people within the neurodiversity movement are very guilty of using the movement to persecute NTs.

Factions Ad Nauseam: What Autistics Believe About OTHER Issues, Autistic And Non-Autistic:

A. Morals

It would seem that nothing more needs to be said about morals as they pertain to autistics than this: The spectrum of morals of people with autism mirror the spectrum of morals of people who do not have autism.

However, the difference between some people on the spectrum and most NTs, is that people on the spectrum are more likely to assert that they have a right to practice their beliefs publicly even when they are illegal.

Let's remember that if (for the sake of argument) 1 in 64 people are on the autism spectrum (as some people say), 63 out of 64 people are *not* on the autism spectrum. But how often do we see such a high percentage of NT people say it's their right to [insert immoral, illegal activity here] because they are [insert some personal attribute here as a reason]?

NTs may engage in all manner of activities that society may not approve of, but it seems to me that they are much more secretive about doing them, whereas many autistics can be very vocal about being deprived of the ability to do what they want. Common things some autistics complain about not being able to do, or blatantly say they do for the express purpose of defying the law:

1) Hacking into websites
2) Illegally downloading copyrighted material from the net
3) Downloading illegal porn
4) Engaging in what the DSM describes as "deviant" sexual behaviors
5) Shoplifting
6) Committing acts of theft/burglary/grand theft auto/grand theft train
7) Committing acts of violence
8) Committing acts of rape, incest, or child molestation
9) Using/smuggling/selling illegal drugs
10) Committing acts of arson

Recently, Temple Grandin's mother, Eustacia Cutler, wrote and article that tried to explain why some autistic men seem to have a sexual preoccupation with children and child pornography. It was an article that needn't have been written if no such preoccupation existed, or if it existed on a level equal with that of men in the rest of society, else why did she feel the need to write about *autistic* men, and not just "men"?

Most autistics reject Cutler's assertions, but some may view her comments as vindication, and this latter group of autistics may see her view as a "resource" they can quote as they try to gain their "rights" to satisfy their sexual urges (which they claim to be their autistic perseverative interests).

Thus when morals are discussed in the autism community, some participants in those discussions may find themselves exposed to facets of arguments they have never seen before, and the ensuing exchanges can be charged at the least, and explosive and potentially violent to boot.

Manipulative tactics are also thrown into the mix, which only increases tensions.

Someone might say, for example, "A study by Temple Grandin's mother, Eustacia Cutler, *proved*, that autistics-" when in fact, Cutler did not conduct a study, she merely wrote an opinion piece. Further, as she offered an opinion, and not a fact, nothing was *proved*. But so desperate are some people to grasp at any straw to support their assertions, that they will deceive if they think they can get away with it. If it is discovered by the opposition that a simple online search debunks their assertions, they will simply argue their points more forcefully, and use some other tactic to try to "win" the argument.

Such tactics will be discussed later in this publication.

I would be remiss if I didn't say a little bit about morally conservative autistics.

This group of people often seem to get the worst of it when an argument breaks out. Either they are accused of being "rigid in their thinking" (which would be consistent with one of the DSM IV-TR's descriptors for autism, or told that their views are prejudiced, short-sighted, stifling, restrictive, and oppressive.

Never mind that if child molestation were to become legal -as some autistic pedophiles want- that nearly every mother and father on the planet would want to keep their kid under lock and key, or within sight at all times in order to protect that child, it is, in some people's minds, prejudiced, short-sighted, stifling, restrictive, and oppressive that autistics who want to molest are legally prohibited from doing so.

Does anyone have a problem seeing why some autistics *need* to be institutionalized, and why other autistics are fighting so hard *against* institutionalization? Does anyone see why *some* autistics are trying to gain minority status to preserve their "right" to engage in their "perseverative interests," while other people are fighting so hard *against* giving minority status to autistics?

At any rate, it should be understood that in the autistic community, "moral conservatives" and "liberals" may be of a different sort than the types of conservatives and liberals we see in the rest of society.

B. Religion

Arguments about religion arise from time to time anywhere, and just as we see NTs arguing about religion, autistics will do it too. However, my observation is that autistics tend to argue *less* about spirituality *in general* than NTs do.

My further observation is that autistics are fairly open-minded about other people's religious values, and/or about whether or not a person believes in God. It doesn't seem like religion is a major point of contention to autistics, or, at least not as much as it is to NTs.

However, if a person's religious beliefs come to have a bearing on autistic issues, then there seems to be problems.

The way this works in practice is quite complex.

Those autistics who are capable of participating in conversations seem to know that taking issue with another person's religious beliefs is socially unacceptable, despite the assertions of many psychologists and psychiatrists that autistics don't understand social nuances and conventions. But autistics can and will take sides and fight vehemently when one's religion or beliefs seem to support a stance one way or another about autism.

When it comes to arguing over diseases people are born with, some people (particularly Christians) will argue that God had a plan for the unborn, and to abort such children before they are born is an affront to God. But others will argue that Jesus cured people with afflictions and affectations. "Curebies" usually take the "Jesus cured the diseased" side of the argument, while anti-cure people take the other.

The discussion can head anywhere from there, with people either sticking to the point or attacking one another. It almost becomes an eventuality that a person's religion winds up being assaulted or impugned. In those instances, the *only* way for someone to win against a religious person is to either convince them that God does not exist, or to convince them that their religious beliefs are fundamentally flawed, a near impossibility in both cases. A stalemate is the next best "win" against a religious person.

However, the goal for either side may not be to "win" the argument, but for either side to shut the other side up, because, despite the refusal of either side to admit it, both sides may have valid and convincing arguments. Leaners and fence-sitters may be inclined to pick a side after an argument of this kind takes place...but not if one side or both gets censored. Then their choice is made for them.

And that is really what most autistic factions are about: Doing anything necessary to ensuring that *their* view is the predominate one. As indicated earlier on in the text, methods by which this may be done will be spoken about later on.

C. Religious Denomination

We just got done talking about religion. Was there anything else that needed to be said?

Yes, because if people cannot win an argument with over-arching generalizations, they will try to win by focusing on minutia.

Anti-genetic selection via abortion person: "Abortion is murder."

Pro- genetic selection via abortion person: "No it's not. A fetus isn't a human being."

Anti: "What religion are you?"

Pro: "Lutheran. Why?"

Anti: "Lutherans believe abortion is murder."

Pro: "Not all Lutherans do. ELCA Lutherans believing abortion is acceptable under certain circumstances."

Anti: "Yeah? Well, I'm LCMS. LCMS Lutherans believe that abortion is murder. We also do not recognize ELCA as being Lutheran, especially since they have now joined up with Episcopalians and taken on some Episcopalian views as their own.

When we remember that any one faith can have multiple denominations, we can see how hairy things get on what some may feel are straight forward issues. About the only relief we have as far as denominations go, is that we forgo the "*My* God trumps *your* God" argument. Now it is *only* "*My* denomination trumps *your* denomination."

D. Political Leanings

Most people have political convictions, and those autistics who can understand politics have theirs. The amount of bickering that most autistics engage in over politics is probably no greater than the bickering seen between people who do not have autism.

However, there are some issues specifically pertaining to autism that can cause bitter fighting in the autism world. Most of these issues are in regards to "rights" and getting more of them.

Most developed countries already have anti-discrimination laws that work in favor of people with disabilities. There are laws to make accommodations for people with disabilities as well. For every disability that exists, however, there will be gaps in coverage, and it is generally a good thing when lawmakers are made aware of these gaps. Autistic advocacy groups generally work with all political parties to rectify any situation that needs to be addressed.

However, autistic advocacy groups often petition government and other entities for new "rights" on behalf of people with autism without consulting the autistics they claim to serve.

One major example of this happening is when some autistic advocacy organizations unwisely supported the creation of autism registries.

I've written before in this book about autism registries, but there are some things about them that deserve repeating here, and I will also be adding a few words here about them in this section.

As I have said before, very few autistics want to see themselves on an autism registry.

Parents and caregivers think it is a great idea because, they believe, it solidifies their ability to get services for the autistics they care for. How being on a list makes a difference in getting services has never really been explained to me satisfactorily. Currently, a doctor's note is usually sufficient to get a needed service, but in areas where lists exist, now some agencies are using the lists as proof that someone has autism evidently.

Another supposed advantage to being on the list is that (perhaps) law enforcement officials will check that list before detaining/dealing with suspects, and then use their training in autism spectrum disorders (if they have any) to deal with their detainee differently, taking into account the detainee's autism.

But for those autistics who are functional on their own, how would it be for them to go through life being "registered" somewhere? To them, it is no different than being on a sex offender registry, except in their cases, no crimes have been permitted.

And this brings up another reason for the registry: There have been a number of crimes committed by autistics, and because the media often sends up these crimes with an accompanying "the suspect, who has autism" or "the suspect, who has Asperger syndrome," people on the spectrum have come to be seen as criminals, so for those who now see autistics as criminals, it is "good" for a registry to exist, so they can "protect their loved ones" and especially children, from autistics.

Autistics who are upset over all of this say none of this would have happened if the autistic advocacy organizations would have fought *against* the creation of autism registries.

As for some of the autistic advocacy organizations themselves, they either deliberately ignore their critics, or they make blanket, unsubstantiated statements like "The overwhelming majority of autistics are *for* autism registries."

They make similar blanket statement about many issues where they go against the opinions of the majority of autistics.

Why?

Why would they betray their own "kind" in this manner?

Well, follow the logic:

1)   Many of the board members and members of some of these autistic advocacy organizations don't have autism. They admit privately to not having it, or admit privately to being self-diagnosed, or admit privately to be in the process of "diagnosis shopping' -meaning hopping around from doctor to doctor until they get the diagnosis they are looking for.

2)   Knowing full well that some doctors can be badgered and bullied into giving an autism diagnosis where none really exists, many self-diagnosed autistics and wannabees stand a good chance of getting "diagnosed" autistic someday.

3)   When their diagnoses come through, they want to have "perks" waiting and prepared for them. So it pays to establish these registries in advance.

Until this point in history, it was advantageous for a person to claim to be autistic when one really wasn't autistic at all, because society was more than willing to cut people with autism slack, or make special accommodations for them. But as people's medical privacy continues to erode, and as national healthcare systems continue to be modified, as the US one is currently, it will be much harder for self-diagnosed people, wannabees, and diagnosis shoppers to claim to be autistic when the government will be scrutinizing everyone so closely.

So some people figure it's best to try to get on that registry *now*, because once you are on it, it's very hard to get yourself removed.

Online, people can still claim to be whatever they wish, but even online autistic rights groups do have personal meet-ups, and if there is the merest chance, that a friend or a relative of a self-diagnosed, wannabee, or diagnosis shopping autistic spills the beans on them, they're cooked. But once someone is on the registry, there is very little anyone online or in real life can say that will get someone removed (some of these people think).

Another reason for people running autistic advocacy groups to get on autism registries is because the need for autistic rights groups is diminishing in light of national healthcare systems increasingly becoming more hands on (some say intrusive) in people's lives. It has already been determined by most governments who is getting what in terms of medical care, and while people can petition for more, it is doubtful they will receive much given that there is only a finite amount of funds available which must be distributed to everyone. But if a person can get into the existing pool, at least they can get a cut of "what's due them," even if they aren't really autistic.

It's not like anyone will be getting hurt in the long term, some of these people rationalize. Because funding is based on need, by more people getting into the pool, it is likely that funding will be increased as the need continues to rise.

What these autistic rights groups also fail to understand, is that every time funding increases -or a law is passed- while that funding may allow for greater freedoms -or the law may give someone greater rights (or validate their right to have them)- the same funding can limit someone else's funding -and the same law can limit someone else's, rights and freedoms. Some colleges and universities are trying to do away with affirmative action admissions guidelines because they are beginning to feel that these guidelines restrict their ability to admit better candidates to their schools. Something similar could happen with funding -and rights- for autistics, if autistic advocacy organizations push the envelope too far.

At any rate, getting back to politics and political leanings proper, the other thing autistic advocacy groups will do (and some will do this even if they have 501c3 status or are seeking 501c3 status, which prohibits them from telling their constituency how to vote on candidates and political issues), is try to get their constituency to vote for or against a candidate based on only *autistic* issues. The candidate could have other beliefs antithetical to most autistic voters, but autistics are encouraged to ignore those beliefs on issues -no matter what harm may be done should the candidate win and make it into office- and vote *only* on what that candidate promises to do for autistics.

Many lower functioning autistics who have obtained voting cards will march in line and vote as they are told by autistic advocacy organizations to vote, not realizing that in so doing, they are voting for someone who may not be good for them generally speaking, despite having a stance favorable to autistics on autistic issues.

Thus you will see intense fighting going on.

Person #1: "Don't do what the autism organization says. Vote the *opposite* way! Voting for *their* candidate means you won't be able to get food stamps anymore."

Person #2: "I don't understand the food stamps thing, but the people at the autism advocacy organization are nice to me, and they seem pretty smart too, so I'm going to do what *they* say."

Person #1: "You don't understand. They're trying to get that politician to-"

Person #2: "Don't talk mean to me. You act like I'm stupid. The autism advocacy organization doesn't treat me like I'm stupid. I trust them, and not you. They wouldn't tell me to do anything that would cause me more harm than good."

Person #1: "But-"

Person #2: "You know what you sound like? You sound like my parents did when they didn't want me to get a driver's license. Just because I can't concentrate doesn't mean I shouldn't have the right to drive. So what if I can't drive well? Other people should have to make way for me because I have a disability. In fact, that's *another* thing the advocacy group is pushing for: Drivers' licenses for everyone on the spectrum. They want to make it illegal for parents and doctors to go to the Department of Motor Vehicles to prove that someone like me is incapable of driving. I think that's a good thing because then I finally *could* get my license."

Fortunately, many autistics do not have much interest in politics in the first place. And while some autistics are inclined to agree with the pronouncements from certain autistic advocacy organizations, not as many autistics as one would think actually register to vote, and even fewer actually *do* vote.

Thus all the bickering about politics may be for nothing anyway.

E. Cassandra Affective Deprivation Disorder

If I understand it, according to this theory, which is attributed to Maxine Aston, a person becomes affected by those who surround them, and so, if a person is married to an autistic, or in a relationship with an autistic, the likelihood is (supposedly) that the person who is not autistic will become negatively affected by the demands placed upon them by their autistic partner.

As much as autistics would like to deny that they can be quite demanding of people, the lack of many autistics having long-lasting friendships and relationships argues against their assertions.

But bring this up to an autistic who believes otherwise, and you will find yourself on the receiving end of a great amount of animosity.

With that said, it needs to be stated that it takes two to tango, as the saying goes, and one of the things people entering any kind of relationship (romantic or otherwise) fail to do is acknowledge the warning signals they may be getting from the people they are about to take into their lives.

People tend to want to give others the benefit of the doubt, and want to believe the best about other people, and so when something doesn't feel quite right about the person they are interacting with, they tell themselves that it is their feelings that are in error. It is usually when their doubts become so overwhelming that they begin to distance themselves from the other person, at which point, finding faults with that person makes it easier to make the break.

Yet people should acknowledge that it is both parties who are equally to blame, whether one of those parties is on the spectrum or not.

Thus it should be remembered that the Cassandra Affective Deprivation Disorder works both ways, and not just one way.

F. Autistic Movements

Many autistic movements are political movements in the strictest sense, but there are other movements as well that may or may not bear on actual politics. Some of these movements have been identified, such as the one that is trying to get autistics declared a minority by the United Nations.

Others (to name a few) are:

-The pro-Autism Speaks movement
-The anti-Autism Speaks movement
-The pro-Age of Autism movement
-The anti-Age of Autism movement
-The Pro-Jenny McCarthy movement
-The anti-Jenny McCarthy movement
-The pro-Tony Attwood movement
-The anti Tony-Attwood movement

I could delineate the politics of all of these movements, and given that this is a book about autistic political factions, I should, but I won't.

Some descriptions seem self-explanatory. Others, a little less so. But by not explaining the sides of all of these movements, it encourages you to investigate for yourself what each movement might be, and what the arguments are that each side takes. Then you can see for yourself how complex some of these movements can be.

Suffice it to say, where one stands in each of these movements can make a person or break a person, depending on how much power or influence a particular movement's members may have over someone at any given time.

G. Petitions

As I wrote in the Midnight In Chicago blog (see "Thomas's Ten Rules for Letter Writing in Advocacy: Part III") at www.midnightinchicago.wordpress.com:

> Many people are under the misperception that petitions work best to motivate politicians and corporations to do something. My feeling is that although there are exceptions, for the most part, nothing is further from the truth. The absolute truth is that the importance of a petition varies with the cause and depends on who signs the petition.
>
> Let's say your street needs to be paved. If you run around the neighborhood and collect signatures from your neighbors and send it to city council, you are likely to have that petition be read and responded to. This is because your alderman or alderwoman knows who lives in his/her district and can verify who signed the petition and when. The alderman or alderwoman can even visit your street and see what, if anything, needs to be done.
>
> But if you get your neighbors to sign a petition to end "canned hunting" [the shooting of animals in enclosures] in your country, whatever lawmaker you send it to, isn't going to pay much attention to it unless you live in his or her district, and even then, politicians are very aware that petitions can be forged, with a few people writing in names and addresses and using many

different handwriting styles to make it look like there were more than just a few people signing.

Put simply: If voter registration lists can be forged, so can petitions.

The only way I can see that a petition can really work on a national level if you get "important" people to sign it. If you got the CEOs of major corporations to sign your petition, and if those signatures had contact information accompanying them, it would cause legislators to take a second look, not because the people are "important" but because it is unlikely that a petition with those signatures would be forged.

Online petitions are even more useless in my opinion. You can sign some of them as many times as you want with as many false names as you want. If others only allow people with one email address to sign, you can use different email addresses. If they allow only one signature per IP address, you can go to the library or a friend's house and sign from there.

Nevertheless, if you participate in the autism community, you will sooner or later encounter someone who wants you to sign a petition. Autistics should be aware that once they have put their signature to a petition, they have declared their position on the particular issue the petition has been created to address. If that petition is readable online, other people may see what your position is, and attack you for having it.

And given the uselessness of most petitions, autistics would do well to consider that maybe the person, people, or organization behind the petition created it *specifically* as a means to find out what your stance is regarding an issue.

Or even to acquire personal information about you.

Such personal information can be used against you in the future, if not to work against your interests somehow, then to defraud you.

Of course this assumes that the creators of the petition have ill intent. Most people who create a petition have honest intent, and possess no ill will toward the people who sign the petition. Nevertheless, third parties will sometimes do internet searchers to see what you've signed, just so they have something to blast you with out of left field if they need to.

Worse is when a person signs a petition without having any real knowledge of the issue, and having the signature come back to haunt them later in a seemingly baffling way.

Person #1: "Do you know what I just did?"

Person #2: "I saw you signed that petition to appoint XXXX to XXXX legal advisory team."

Person #1: "Yep. I think she'd make a great XXXX. She's always being nice to people in the autism forums."

Person #2: "She doesn't give a shit about autistics. All she is trying to do is get marijuana made legal. She was canvassing the autism forums to see who supports her, and *you* supported her, dumbass."

Person #1: "I never saw her doing that. Maybe you're just saying that because you don't like her stance on medical marijuana. Or maybe you just don't like her."

Person #2: "We're not talking about the legalization of *medical* marijuana. We are talking about the legalization of marijuana for recreational use, or *any* use."

Person #1: "Well I never saw her trying to ask anyone about marijuana."

Person #2: "Well, start scrolling through the posts in some of the forums you go through. It's the main issue for her in nearly every damned one of them."

Person #1: "She seems so nice though. Always speaking in support of autistic causes."

Person #2: "That's because she wants the support of people dumb enough to sign her petition. She also supports the right to choose. And she supports the pro-life movement. She supports ending corporal punishment in the schools who still have them, but supports the rights of teachers to administer corporal punishment in schools. You've been *had*, you idiot. And worse, you've made *all* of us autistics look stupid by supporting her candidacy for the position on XXXX."

Person #1: "But *she's* autistic."

Person #2: "No she isn't. Here is a screenshot where she says she was diagnosed sociopathic but is just calling herself autistic because people have a negative association with the word 'sociopath.'"

Person #1: "I've never seen that screenshot before. It's probably something made up, that's meant to defame her."

Person #2: "You know what? I hope her petition is a success, and she makes not just pot legal, but *all* illegal drugs legal, and then you take some of those illegal drugs *croak!*""

Since people who are meant to receive petitions seldom act on them, it is hardly worth mentioning the topic of petitions at all, except that, in the autism community, people who sign them can wind up getting targeted for stating their position one way or the other. Alternatively, some people who create the petitions are doing so with intent to deceive or influence. Fights often break out after people realize they have become the human equivalent of cows enticed to the slaughter.

Refusing to sign a petition can make things worse as well. It may be seen as refusing to align oneself with a cause, or of working against a cause, so autistics may be doomed as far as petitions go no matter what they do.

H. Alliances

The word "alliance" connotes the idea of a "faction", but an alliance in the autism community is more descriptive of

- an allegiance of two or more people
- an allegiance to a group of people
- an allegiance between groups of people
- an allegiance to an autistic advocacy organization
- an allegiance between autistic advocacy organizations
- an allegiance to a specific cause
- an allegiance between causes

than it is membership in a faction.

An alliance can range from a loose affiliation to a close-knit bond. While most autistic alliances are as innocent and ordinary as alliances outside the autism community, some are structured very much like cults, with many rings of membership -the least important members being on the orbiting rings, the more important members being in the inner circles, and the controllers residing within the nucleus.

When alliances are structured like cults, getting into the inner circles and close to the nucleus usually means proving oneself through acts of loyalty to alliances over a long period of time. The main ways in which this can be done are by:

1)	Keeping the alliance's confidences and
2)	Doing whatever one is told to do

The higher one advances in the alliance, the more responsibility one will be given. At the same time, greater tests of loyalty may be asked for, and these tests may straddle moral and ethical boundaries.

Testing members in this way does two things:

1)	It increasingly conditions people to rely on the alliance for orders whilst eliminating free thinking, and

2)   It erodes morals, values, and ethics previously held dear by members aspiring to higher positions.

Once the alliance members are in this manner turned into drones, they may then be programed like robots to defend the alliance to insensible limits. This method of conditioning works particularly well with vulnerable people, and with people with suggestible brain sets.

People who fail to meet the requirements of those who reside in the nucleus of the alliance will usually be ejected, but sometimes, members are ejected -and then taken back into the fold simply to manipulate them.

Those that are permanently ejected from the alliance, and those who leave on their own, are sometimes shunned in public, stalked in real life, or cyberbullied or cybermobbed online, the intent of the intimidation being to prevent them from revealing the alliance's secrets to others.

It is usually with distance from such cult-like alliances that people begin to realize how much they have been controlled and manipulated, and considerable mental trauma may occur at such times.

Unfortunately, as much as they try to relate their experiences to others, the tales they tell seem so wild and unbelievable that they are usually ignored. Adding to the problem are people from the alliance sent to disgrace or humiliate, the tattle-teller in order to destroy that person's credibility.

These types of methods are often employed by some of the autistic advocacy organizations too, but there are also dangerous mobs of people which may or may not be allied or affiliated with an organization that will employ similar tactics.

People within alliances act almost like contractors, who assume most of the risks and get very little payoff (save recognition and praise) for their efforts. They are seen as disposable, and will be thrown out of an alliance if it looks like the goal, mission, or reputation of the alliance is imperiled by negative public opinion. At times like these, an alliance may deny anything the ejected member says, even though the ejected member may be speaking unadulterated truth about the alliance.

I. Organizations And Organizational Affiliations

There are many different organizations within the autism community. Some are charitable in nature. Others are not. Some from the United States hold 501(c)3 status. Some do not. Those based in other countries may or may not be accredited in *their* countries of origin.

Every single organization differs from one another. Sometimes the gulf between them is so large as to incite fighting between them. Pro-vaccine organizations will often squabble with anti-vaccine organizations, for example.

Interestingly, the larger and longer-lasting fights seem to be the ones that develop over how organizations conduct themselves, and how their conduct reflects on autistics. To have 501(c)3 status, for example, means that an organization is recognized by the US Internal Revenue Service (IRS) as being tax exempt. Such organizations cannot support political candidates and there are limits placed upon lobbying as well.

Yet this has not stopped representatives and high ranking members of some autistic advocacy organizations from firmly speaking in support of certain political candidates.

Is that ethical?

Those who believe it is unethical often take issue not just with a representative from the organization in question, but also the organization to which the person belongs, particularly if the individual is a high ranking member (such as a board member) of that organization.

In addition to what I have described above, and in addition the unsavory, cult-like methods described in the section on alliances, organizations may behave in other ways that are inappropriate (and these ways shall be described in detail later on in this book) which results in attacks from individuals who disagree with their actions.

In the US, people who think they have a legitimate grievances against an organization will go as far to report a 501(c)3 organization's alleged inappropriate activities to the IRS using Form 13909 [Tax-Exempt Organization Complaint (Referral) Form], and they will supplement that form with supporting documentation if they can obtain it. They may also contact their state's regulatory agencies and file a complaint with them if they are able to.

As much as reporting the perceived "bad" activities of a tax-exempt organization is a good thing, when an organization does not meet the criteria for filing a complaint against it, some people will do it out of spite just to cause trouble, providing false information in their complaint. They may elect to take this course of action for spurious reasons (e.g. perhaps the organization's values and mission is antithetical to their own). Some rival organizations will also engage in spiteful reporting in an effort to get their competition shut down.

Sometimes, when two sides engage in such activities against one another, both sides will accuse the other of engaging in these activities while claiming innocence to engaging in the questionable behavior themselves.

While most of the more familiar national and international charities and autistic advocacy organizations are above board, and completely moral and ethical in terms of how they function, there are a few autistic advocacy organizations that are exceptions to the rule. Well-informed autistics and non-autistics know which ones are which.

J. Positions Within An Organization

In unethical organizations, or in organizations that behave unethically, people who hold the highest positions in those organizations are seen as being the ones most capable of changing an organization's status, or stopping the unethical behavior. Some will work to do so, and infighting will result. Others will do nothing, their principals in firm alignment with the unethical mandates or behaviors of the organization, in which case they will sometimes be subject to attacks from their detractors.

Generally speaking, whether you are ethical or unethical, the more power you hold, the more you will be resented by people who do not hold the power. Also generally speaking, the less power you hold, the less likely you are to be heard by those in power, and the less likely your opinion is to be taken seriously by those in power.

In one case, a person wrote each and every board member of an autistic advocacy organization about an important issue, and got no replies from most of them, and (essentially) form letters from the rest. The issue remained unresolved.

Reputable people in the autism community are clearly in agreement with the letter-writer about the issue, yet the organization's board members remain steadfastly determined not to address the issue, probably because in so doing, they would destroy their organization's reputation in the process, and the organization would have to fold. Given that the organization's board members reap certain benefits from their authoritative positions, it is not likely they will reconsider their decision not to act any time soon. The organization's board members have, from time to time, hounded the original letter -writer, however.

It is important to remember that not every position within an organization is important. The old adage "Keep your friends close and your enemies closer" has worked well for the autism community. By appointing trouble-makers to manufactured positions and assigning them make-work tasks, these trouble-makers can walk around with a sense of importance...and they are less likely to attack the organization to which they belong.

In still other cases, people who may be slightly mentally impaired might be given token positions as a sort of window display to the public that an organization which claims to support the autism rights movement actually does (when in fact the organization's purpose may be entirely the opposite). These same mentally impaired individuals can also be made to do less than ethical things, and then thrown to the wolves afterward without significantly impairing an organization's operations.

When a person suddenly finds themselves on the outside of an organization looking in, they will often attack that organization, but their attacks are usually combated by the organization using prepared material designed to paint the attacker in the worst possible light. An organization's lower membership, which may be ignorant of the organization's behavioral atrocities, may be called in to defend the organization, and they usually do so with zeal.

Some parents and caregivers, who may be wiser than their autistic children -and even adult autistic children- will fight with the organizations to which their children belong, intuiting that their children may be brainwashed into believing some of the things they wouldn't normally believe, or coerced into doing things they wouldn't normally do. In such cases, sometimes organizations will fight the parents.

There is a case I am reminded of... A 16 year old boy allegedly ran away from home with a woman nearly twice his age. He is alleged to have taken 5,000 English pounds of his family's computer equipment with him when he left. He went on to found an autistic advocacy group whose members defend him -and his much older wife- to this day against his parents and anyone else who assails him. He is also stood up for by other autistic advocacy groups who use him as an example of how autistics should overcome the oppression allegedly perpetrated against them by their parents.

To many autistic advocacy organizations, except for any potential monetary income or financial wherewithal that may be gained from an autistic person's parents, parents are the enemy, because they have the advantage of having an external perspective to the type of brainwashing and conditioning that these organizations engage in. With that external perspective, parents have the potential to destroy the plans, machinations, and membership of groups with questionable agenda, and groups which use questionable means to control their membership.

There are many other reasons why one's organizational membership may cause for bickering, but we will leave the discussion here, the examples presented being sufficient to elucidate the point.

K. Government Organizational Affiliations

There has been at least one autistic advocacy organization whose founder has served in an appointed position on a government panel. In the opinion of most, this was another make-work "keep your friends close and your enemies closer" appointment. The organization is felt by some to for be radical. People may have wondered: Wouldn't it be better to keep the founder pacified and quelled on a government panel instead of going unleashed and unpredictable in civilian society?

As it happened, the move -if it was a move- may have worked. The organization did not seem to be as politically active during the appointment as it was before the appointment. Yet that could also be because the organization itself was hoping that its political agendas could be realized via its founder having a government appointment.

But even if there are not many members from an organization on government panels, some people and organizations do have direct or indirect government ties, and are praised, or fall under attack, merely for that reason, or both.

Anti-vaxers who believe that "Big Pharma" and "Big Government" are interlinked, may be wary of any people or organizations that have ties to the United Nations, and/or to the governments of individual countries. Other types of conspiracy theorists feel similarly.

Generally, people or organizations who either have the ability, or are perceived to have the ability, to influence government, are not trusted because the possibility exists that they will either -by accident or by design- influence government in a way that is counterproductive to most autistics, or else there is a possibility that they may become turncoats, dropping the needs of the autistic community altogether in favor of acquiring power, be that power political, or some other kind of power granted to them by politicians.

This distrust -or outright fear- of government, (which is most of the time irrational) stems from the fact that poor government policies are remembered, while good ones are forgotten. People do not often talk about times of prosperity or good health when relating personal stories. Rather, they are inclined to talk about times of hardship and great pain. And so for those who believe themselves to be hurt by government, when they see someone or some organization attach themselves to a government official or entity, those people and those organizations may become distrusted, feared or, even "potential enemies" or "enemies" as well.

Even if the individual or organization is actually working *against* government policy, or is trying to *change* government policy *for the better*, they may still be thought of as "the enemy" by virtue of the fact that they are required to interact with the enemy. In other words, in some peoples' opinions, it is hard to be within the vicinity of corruption without getting corrupted.

Making things even worse is when people do indeed succumb to the temptation of power and abandon those who they represent. They wind up embodying the stereotype, and making it worse for those earnest people who may come after them to take their place.

And so, when one mentions a government program, a government official, or a governing body, there is always the possibility that an argument will break out (even if past government programs have worked for autistics, even if past governing officials have done worked hard for autistics, even if past governing bodies have served autistics well) and when it does, politics, morals, ethics, values, religion, and other issues will almost always be dragged into the argument too.

L. Friends

"Friend" means something different to each individual, and perhaps no place is that more true than in the autism community. For some autistics, who do not know -and will never know- what true friendship is, a "friend" to them is someone who has "liked" something on their Facebook page, or who says "Hi!" to them in the halls at school, or on the street, just to be friend-ly and polite.

To others, a friend is someone who is "nice" as opposed to anyone who is "mean." But "nice" and "mean" to an autistic may mean something else to people who are not autistic. Who is the "nice" person in the following conversation, and who is the "mean" one?

Person #1: "Marijuana is a good thing to smoke, especially if you are autistic and pregnant. It calms you down and it probably relaxes the baby inside of you as well."

Person #2: "There is no scientific evidence to support that fact."

Person #1: "No evidence is needed for something that feels so right in the gut. Love is where your heart is, and if your heart says smoking weed is good for your pregnancy, than you love yourself, and you love your baby."

Person #2: "I see on your Facebook page that you advocate pot for all kinds of other reasons as well, and on a pro-choice page, you state that if pot kills a fetus, what's the difference? It's not a baby yet."

Person #1: "You, of course, are a right wing conservative religious zealot. That makes you a narrow-minded bully."

Person #2: "It's convenient to cite someone who disagrees with your views as a bully in a forum where many of the people are functionally illiterate and classified as slow learners. When you try to garner the support of such a population to validate their viewpoint, it's manipulative, don't you think?"

Person #1: "He called you all functionally illiterate and slow!"

Chorus of spectators: "He's MEAN!"

Person #1: "Now if you'll all just donate a few dollars to my Paypal account, I'll use this money to help unborn babies by making them and their mommies feel better."

Here we can clearly see that person #1 is a manipulator who is exploiting lower functioning autistics to his advantage, but is ultimately regarded by the lower functioning autistics to be a friend because he's able to make the more logical and well-intentioned person look "mean."

This happens all the time.

There is person out there who claims to have been born dead, and who, by her own admission many years ago is a diagnosed psychopath (though now she claims to be autistic). She runs one of the largest groups on Facebook, and at any given time, she can sway most of its membership to attack other people, either on social media sites, or in real life, or both. There is another person who consistently bullies people online and in real life, but runs an anti-bully campaign -perhaps in order to make him *appear* to be an anti-bully crusader- and there are a group of people who believe one or the other or both people are honest.

There are literally scores of people who may have been terribly hurt and scared by the aforementioned individuals, but the overwhelming majority of people may have been duped by them, and may believe them to be honest and sincere in their endeavors. Many of these "friends" support the manipulators to the hilt, and they will vigorously defend them against any attack.

Whom a person in the autism community is friends with is very important. Alliances are forged against people who have certain friends, and these alliances may be very strong and very powerful. This is why some bullies have managed to stay in the autism community for more than a decade. These "allies" who may have either been brainwashed, or who may have the same morals and ethics that they do, have protected them at all costs, and have ruined or tried to ruin those who have tried to expose them for what they are.

And while it is true that those who have been hurt by others form groups of their own, because these individuals are not natural leaders, and are not by nature vindictive or manipulative, they tend to become wallflowers, or they disappear from the net after a while.

Parents have their own groups of friends, and they fight among themselves, and sometimes also with autistics. They fight over treatments, beliefs about the origins of autism, over what an organization might be doing. You name it.

There is a lot of fighting between friends in the autism community.

M. Arrests And Illegal Activities

Some autistics would have you believe that their illegal activities are actually perseverative interests that ought to be made legal, and their arrests are the result of simple misunderstandings with police officers. They explain their point of view with such convincing arguments that a person is almost inclined to believe them...until one considers that if someone is intelligent enough to be that convincing, they should be intelligent enough to understand what is legal and what is illegal, and they should be intelligent enough to figure out a way to control their own impulses.

There is no scientific study that shows a link between autism and criminal behavior, but the media may have many believing otherwise. Too often, when we read a newspaper, we will see a column detailing a crime, and we will see "The suspect, who had autism..." but when we see such an article, we should ask ourselves how often we see an article which says "The suspect, who had obsessive compulsive disorder..." or "The suspect, who has colitis..." It seems neither the media nor the general public have a problem with autism being identified as a possible reason the crime was committed, but how would the public feel if it was written that: "The shooter, who was African American..." or "The shooter, who was homosexual..." or "The shooter who was sexually molested in their childhood...?"

But I digress...

Because autism is still very much misunderstood, people who have it are sometimes vilified in the media for having it.

Yet many of the people who hold positions high up in advocacy organizations do have criminal records, and some quite extensive. In 2013, one was convicted of possessing child pornography. This individual actively involved himself in two autism advocacy organizations.

And of course, the gullible will defend these criminals to the hilt if these criminals are "nice, and view those who take issue with criminals as "mean."

Inmates in prisons also prey on autistics via money-making scams. Some have access to social media from prison, and will try to engage autistics via letter-writing. Once the letter-writing is well-underway and trust has been established, then comes the appeal for money. The person who sends the money has no idea, of course, that they are sending money to inmates. But they are.

Autistic politics can actually aid and abet criminal behavior. There was a time when the inmate scam was discovered, and a number of forum owners banded together to spread the word about the scam. In rival forums where they were merely members, they tried to inform the rest of the membership of those forums about the scam. These people were not only prohibited from telling the memberships about the scam by administrators, but also banned from those forums. Thus, over simple and silly rivalry, thousands upon thousands of autistics where put at risk, and many of these at-risk autistics may have given their money -and possibly even their personal information- to inmates in prison.

Other types of exploitation exist. At the time of this writing, I happen to administer one of the biggest online Asperger women's forums on the net, and I have seen "autistic" men try to establish friendships with naïve autistic women in attempt to get either sex or money from them. Such men are reported to the authorities and banned from the forum by the forum's chief administrator and group owner, but it happens surprisingly often.

The criminals themselves tend to be very charismatic, and very convincing in their stories and appeals. The avatars they use are usually false of course, as are their names and the personal information they provide about themselves. Judging from their account activity, they tend to join a forum, watch for a while, identify their targets, and then alter their existing personae to one that will appeal to that target.

Criminals who lead autism organizations, or who hold leadership positions within them behave similarly, albeit on a much larger scale.

Because many autistic people take what people say at face value, they are easily duped and swindled.

Try to point out to people -even very intelligent people- that these individuals may have criminal pasts, and they won't believe you, even if you produce newspaper articles with mugshots, or sex offender registry profiles, or court transcripts, for the ones you *can* identify. People will say the media is biased, sex offender profiles can be photo-shopped, documents can be forged And when you tell them how to find the information themselves, they will tell you that they trust the people you are accusing implicitly, and even entertaining your point to the least degree would be an act of disloyalty. And besides, even if they *are* ex-convicts, everyone deserves a second chance, right? To which people may respond "Including people who have been convicted of fraud? Theft? Sex crimes?"

If those people who disbelieved you later get scammed, they will come back to attack you, ruthlessly, and with malice, saying that somehow you "set them up" for the exploitation. They will say that merely by suggesting that the people they had pledged their allegiance to were criminals, those criminals were *forced* to take defensive measures. They will ask you why you couldn't have shown more compassion to the ex-convicts.

> **Person #1:** "Don't you have any idea how hard it is to tow the line in real life once you have been in jail for a while? These ex-cons are delicate! You have to be gentle with them."

> **Person #2:** "And what about the autistics you are supposed to be serving? Are we to be callous towards *them* as we are being nice to the criminals?

> **Person #1:** "If you would just be nice to both, *no one* would get out of line.

> **Person #2:** "Are you supporting these criminals because you have a criminal record yourself?"

> **Person #1:** "How did you know that?"

> **Person #2:** "I-"

Person #1: "*Fuck* you anyway! I served my time for what I did. The past is the past. And unlike others, I *do* tow the line, so you've got no reason to accuse *me* of being a scammer."

There was one time when a group of people tried to set up an organization ostensibly to detect corrupt autism organizations, or fraudulent activity within autism organizations, but luckily, when three of the people in that group were shown to have criminal records, the group shut itself down. What would have happened had the group stayed open? Would they have identified the honest autism advocates and organizations as being corrupt ones that were engaging in fraud? Would they have identified the corrupt organizations that were engaging in fraud as being honest?

Who knows?

What is known is that there are advocates out there who have convictions for anything from petty thefts and assaults, to breaking and entering, and possession of child pornography. Many of these people have extensive followers and supporters, all of whom will fervently defend those they follow tooth and nail.

Worst of all is that many people who spot these criminals are no longer interested in warning the autistic community about them because of the flack they get for doing it. These people are increasingly coming to feel that it might be best for autistics -even lower functioning ones- to become victims and deal with the consequences themselves.

If they are able to.

And so now, when the internet is more of a dangerous place to surf than ever -especially for people on he autism spectrum- those who are in the greatest position to prevent others from getting hurt, are beginning to bow out.

Methods Of Attack

Depending on what they believe, people who are diagnosed, self-diagnosed, in the process of getting a diagnosis, seeking a diagnosis, wannabees, misdiagnosed, a parent of an autistic, a sibling of an autistic, a relative of an autistic, a spouse of an autistic, a friend of an autistic, a teacher, a school administrator, a school psychologist, a medical practitioner, a researcher, a curiosity seeker, a neurotypical, a quack, or even someone who is trying to sell something, may ally themselves for or against people, autism charities, organizations, and self-advocacy groups. They may also ally themselves with, or fight against, certain government organizations.

Autism charities, autism organizations, and autistic self-advocacy groups may or may not incorporate any of the beliefs and values listed previously in this book, and they may or may not incorporate any of the beliefs and values that are *not* listed in this book. These charities, groups, and organizations may or not be as firm or as fickle about their beliefs and values as its membership. Thus at any given time, support by people ebbs and flows, and alliances shift.

If people who are diagnosed, self-diagnosed, in the process of getting a diagnosis, seeking a diagnosis, wannabees, misdiagnosed, a parent of an autistic, a sibling of an autistic, a relative of an autistic, a spouse of an autistic, a friend of an autistic, a teacher, a school administrator, a school psychologist, a medical practitioner, a researcher, a curiosity seeker, a neurotypical, a quack, or someone who is trying to sell something, have an agenda, the degree to which they will push that agenda, and the lengths they will go to achieve the desired outcome varies.

Some are fine with fostering discussions, creating think tanks, signing petitions, initiating letter writing campaigns, etc. Others will infiltrate organizations, rise to board membership level -or even leadership level- and then attempt to destroy those organizations. Still others will engage in online trolling or offline harassment, using covert and overt methods. They may do things to their target like:

- Troll them
- File false reports with social media sites for violation of services
- Steal their online accounts

- Cyberstalk them
- Cybermob them
- Astroturf them
- Crank call them at home
- Crank call them at work
- Vandalize their cars and homes
- File false police reports against them
- Make false reports to child protection organizations
- Make false allegations against people to their employers
- Steal their identities
- Stalk their children
- Etc.

A. Trolling

Trolling is something that happens most often online, but can happen to a lesser extent offline.

I will address offline trolls momentarily.

Online, people who troll may *appear* to be asserting their side of the issue, but may have an entirely different agenda altogether. Sometimes, their intent is to hijack a discussion for the express purpose of debunking the credible research of honest and well-meaning individuals. They do not care who is negatively affected by their words and actions, and they do not care about personal consequences of their actions.

Initially, they may "play devils advocate" but rather than sticking to the point, they use any opportunity to go off on tangents, and if they can make "digs" at their opposition on a personal level, they will do so.

If they cannot win the argument, they will assail the credentials of the person they are attacking directly, never accepting the person's word as truthful, but demanding additional proof, such as documentation. If documentation is provided, they will state that such documentation can be forged. The ignorant will see these trolls as crusaders, and buy into any frivolous or specious argument they make. Often the intent of requesting personal information is to steal their target's identity either with the intention of stealing their accounts, or stealing their identity offline. Alternatively, they may reproduce the information elsewhere in whole or in part, but out of context, with intent to do damage to the individual, his or her family, or his or her business.

If a troll can effectively make himself or herself out to be a hero, and the legitimate person out to be a fraud, the resulting consequences for the legitimate person can be far-reaching.

It should be pointed out that women are as guilty of trolling as men. Women will fall back on the "you are being abusive to me" statement if they find themselves losing the battle to debunk their target, and people may see the legitimate person as an abuser if he or she persists in defending himself or herself. People may also see the legitimate person as an abuser if he is a male, and a "bitch" if she is a female.

If a troll is banned from a forum as the result of their behavior, a friend of the troll is often called into the fray, and the friend assumes the role of trying to harass the target. If this friend is banned, a third friend may be called in who will say that their target is bullying a whole population of people as evidenced by his or her ability to get so many people banned.

There is very little a person can do when targeted in this manner if the trolls are determined to debunk the legitimate person. However, it often catches up with trolls in the end when they cross someone whom they didn't know is highly respected in the autism community, or when people see them attacking multiple targets on multiple forums over an extensive period of time.

There are trolls with a reputation who have existed online for some time. They are allowed to stay in online venues because the owners of these venues are largely unable to determine who is legitimate and who the trolls are, and as long as these trolls do not violate terms of service, they are allowed to keep their accounts.

The harm here extends beyond the targeting of specific individuals, because people who are new to the autism world may find themselves falling under the influence of these trolls, who will provide them with false and potentially harmful information about autism, while keeping them from learning true facts, true research, from authentic and trusted sources.

Offline, trolls will enter a real-life conversation and try to sidetrack it with small talk, or, if the conversation cannot be sidetracked, will throw into the conversation an assertion that will have to be counter-argued. In the course of that counterargument, they will throw in yet another argument that needs to be counter-argued until the original topic is forgotten. Once again, a person's credentials might be asked for, and then taken issue with once provided.

It is particularly damning if the troll is successful in flustering the legitimate person in front of a live audience, because there are observers to the conversation who can and will take their observations elsewhere. Once the gossip begins to spread, it will also de-evolve into pure fiction, so that by the time word of the event reaches someone of importance to the person who is attacked, the reputation of the attacked person may be damaged beyond repair.

Perhaps the only way for an earnest, honest, and trustworthy person to withstand this assault is to stay quiet, and/or withdraw from the conversation, but doing that may be taken by observes as a concession to defeat.

Trolls are very effective at what they do. Fortunately, intelligent people are not fooled by their antics.

Unfortunately, people who are a little bit slow in thought and mind *might* be fooled by trolls, which is why volunteer trolls are often used like sharpshooters by self-diagnosed individuals, misdiagnosed individuals, wannabees, autistic advocates and autistic advocacy organizations when they are trying to destroy someone or some group that they consider themselves at war with. Sometimes parents, relatives, spouses, teachers and administrators troll too. In short, anyone can be a troll.

What trolls would do well to remember, however, is that if someone else is "using" them, they are often considered expendable.

B. Filing False Reports With Social Media Sites For Violation Of Services

If trolls cannot win against you by gathering public support against your opinion, they will simply try to prevent you from having an opinion at all.

One way to do this is to file false reports against you with the social media services you are a member of. Most reports and citations are not reviewed by people, but by "bots." Thus it is possible for a "bot" to automatically take action against a person's account, even if that action is entirely unwarranted. Burden of proof that no transgression has taken place falls upon the accused and/or disciplined person. If a person is so lucky as to be allowed to dispute the report, and if the person wins the attempt to have his or her account privileges restored, it is only to find out that the accusers have been given the benefit of the doubt about *motives* for filing the report, and have not been disciplined at all.

The accusers wait a little while, and then file false reports at some later time.

If the number of occurrences reaches a certain level, sometimes the account is terminated automatically, without giving the account owner any recourse to dispute the reports filed against them.

This practice is not only used by some trolls, but by some other individuals, some autism advocates and some autism organizations as well.

C. Stealing Online Accounts

Stealing online accounts is not always a matter of one single person cracking someone's password as the result of trial and error. Groups of people with an ill agenda have members that are technically savvy and can implant viruses on a person's machine which will enable them to hack and steal personal information. While some are not so bold as to steal other people's identities, they will steal people's online social media accounts.

Once obtained, they will scour the account information for more personal information and steal any other accounts they can gain access to. Additionally, they may keep the stolen accounts for a while, and deliberately spam or troll other users to ensure that the real account owner's reputation is tarnished or utterly trashed. When they are finished with the accounts, they either abandon them, or delete them.

These cyber-attacks can be very sophisticated, often requiring more than one person to pull them off. They may also require a lot of planning and coordination, and attackers may need to have hacking programs, or the ability to write hacking programs, at one's disposal.

But if these people get caught, they often fall back on their autism as either a defense, or an excuse:

1) I'm autistic. What you're talking about is too sophisticated for me to pull off, let alone understand.

2) Autism made me do it. Hacking is my perseverative interest.

Increasingly, lawmakers and law enforcement authorities are not being fooled by the "autism made me do it" defense. This may actually be a bad thing, however, because real autistics, with real compulsions which cause them to accidentally or deliberately break the law, wind up being treated the same way the account hijackers -who may not be autistic at all- are treated if they are caught.

But many hijackers don't care. They just do what they do, and do not care who gets injured in the crossfire.

D. Cyberstalking

Haven't we just covered that? If someone has trolled another person, and stolen their accounts, doesn't that seem to be cyberstalking?

In part, yes.

But they can do much more, too.

☐ They do net research in the extreme, digging up as much information about their targets as they can.

- They take the worst of what they find and use it against their target.

- They try to find where their target lives and works, whether or not their target has children, and if they do have children, they stalk the children too (both online and offline).

If false linkages are made along the way between their real target and someone else with a similar name, they may not care. In that case, everyone gets targeted, and the victim and unintended victim wind up having to sort things out.

They will set up multiple accounts with multiple usernames for themselves which they can use to attack their victims. These multiple accounts are also there in case one or more of their accounts gets reported and deleted. If that happens, they will have many others they can use to continue their attack.

They may ask others to do their research as well, creating false stories about their victims that are so atrocious, that their assistants will feel compelled to help them. Because these assistants are less skilled than the stalker, the information they come up with in their research is likely to be fragmented, but enough for them to believe the stalker they are working for is telling the truth.

How can such a person even get support from anyone, given their stalking behavior is so obvious?

The adage "birds of a feather flock together" is only part of the explanation. I have observed that many cyberstalkers – who are mostly just social misfits, or else people with behavioral problems –are learners. They have been told most of their lives by bullies and earnest people alike what is "wrong" with them, and they have memorized what things are "the right things to do." Hiding behind their computer screens, they only show the "good" and "right" side of themselves to their potential assistants, and not the "bad" and "wrong." And so they wind up looking "good," "honest," and "earnest" not just to the people who become their assistants, but to other people, who have no idea about the more unsavory activity they may be engaging in.

For the record, I seldom see real-life autistics stalking people online with the zeal that fakers do, and I do *not* often see them conniving behind each other's backs. I do *not* often see them ganging up on people and picking on them until their victims are near-suicidal. The real-life autistics that I know are mostly employed in good jobs, are financially solvent -or have little debt- are involved in friendships and amorous relationships, are not prone to all the "deviant" sexual proclivities described by many of those misdiagnosed and self-diagnosed people in the online forums. They are upstanding citizens, do not have a criminal record, and have saved for their retirement.

Then again, I know mostly high-functioning autistics or those who have *real* diagnoses. I also do not keep company with the less savory elements of the autism world.

And by the way, it goes without saying that most low-functioning autistics do not have the mental faculties to engage in online and offline intimidation to the degree higher-functioning autistics and "autistics" do.

E. Cybermobbing

One form of revenge in cyberspace is called cybermobbing. It is when two or more people pair up to retaliate against someone for a perceived injustice against themselves or someone else, or even to pick on someone whom they believe has done a social or societal wrong.

In the world of autism, this can get pretty nasty, and can be done for reasons which may seem, for lack of a better word - idiotic- to the casual observer.

On example: There are certain autistic advocacy organizations that are widely known to have unsavory characters on their boards, or in other authoritative positions. These leaders can get up to some questionable activities from time to time. When people question these activities, the accused organizations hardly need to cybermob the "whistle blowers." Generally, and organization and its leadership can take a lot of "hits" without significant repercussions ensuing. After all, there are plenty of oblivious people who are blindly loyal to the organization, and who truly believe that said organization and it's board members, leaders, and membership can do no wrong.

Nevertheless, when it is pointed out someone in a leadership role in one of those organizations has a lengthy criminal record, or may be engaged in immoral activity (e.g., writes stories involving the sexual or physical abuse of mentally impaired children) or may not have the credentials they say they have (e.g. giving themselves a title -such as "Doctor"- that they may not possess) out of nowhere appear people who attempt to utterly destroy the reputations of the accusers. Even when the accusers produce screenshots, chat transcripts, and other documentation showing the damning evidence, and even when the accusers produce documentation in which the accused admit to the allegations, the cybermobbers accuse the accusers of fabricating everything. They do whatever it takes to save their "heroes" even if doing so means their heroes may ultimately harm the autistic community at large.

They will even cover up allegations that have already been proved.

When a board member from a well-known autism organization was *accused* of possessing child pornography, neither the organization to which the person belonged, nor the organizations with which the person associated with, made an announcement to their membership until word got out, and then it was only a small announcement in a web forum. When this same person was *convicted* of possessing child pornography, no announcement was made by those organization at all to my knowledge. But when people found out about the conviction, and spoke about it, many were immediately mobbed by groups of people who supported the convicted person. To this day, that person's books sell in various venues, and they are purchased by unsuspecting people.

And they will continue to be unsuspecting as long as cybermobbers continue to harass and intimidate concerned people in the know into silence.

Some people have taken issue with Dr. Tony Attwood because they did not agree with his supposed views about how some intimate partners of people on the autism spectrum experience Cassandra Affective Deprivation Disorder. Despite

Attwood's attempt to explain and clarify his position on the relationship between ASDs and Cassandra Affective Deprivation Disorder, some cybermobbers have persisted with their campaign against Attwood's supporters.

Oddly, the behavior of some of these people rather proved the Cassandra theory that some autistics can negatively affect other people.

Sometimes, there doesn't need to be a major autistic issue that causes a group to decide to cybermob. Sometimes the issue is a distorted worldview on the part of the attackers. One fictitious example follows.

Note: In this example: **Person #1** might have been diagnosed Asperger syndrome by a school psychologist who overrode the diagnosis of Bipolar Disorder from a board certified medically licensed psychologist at a prestigious institution, and **Person #2** may be self-diagnosed with Asperger Syndrome.

> **Person #1:** "My teacher gave me detention because I punched a kid in class. She doesn't understand that when someone affects my sensitivities, I over-react."

> **Person #2:** "That's terrible. Did you try to explain it to her?"

> **Person #1:** "Yes. It was the girl in front of me whom I hit. The sheen from her hair affects my ability to see anything. I have light sensitivity, you know. So I told her to wash her hair less so her hair wouldn't shine so much. I tried explaining this to her numerous times, and then she finally told me that she wasn't going to wash her hair any less, and if I didn't like it, I could ask the teacher if I could sit somewhere else...so I hit her."

> **Person #2:** "Sounds like the girl deserved it. And the teacher gave you detention for *that*?"

> **Person #1:** "Yeah."

Person #2: "What a *bitch*! Let's see if we can round up a few of our buddies, find her online accounts, and set her straight on the accommodations people with autism need. If that doesn't work we'll humiliate her in front of all her social media friends. That'll be *her* punishment."

F. Astroturfing

You offer an opinion and suddenly, in comes what seems to be a disproportionate number of people with the opposite opinion. They may initially appear to be neutral, but as time goes on, they begin to turn against your opinion. Not only do they voice their opinion in whatever forum you are having the discussion in, but soon their opinion appears in other forums, blogs, podcasts, YouTube videos, petitions, and Tweets. You can hardly believe that there are so many people in support of something that most people you know disagree with, but there you are. Loads of people are against your opinion, and not only that, but they begin to trash you personally for having that opinion. Before you know it, all your accounts are spoofed. Some are hijacked. And now it is *you*, and not the original issue, that is the subject of the attack.

Would it surprise you to know that you, and not necessarily the issue, were the target all along?

The people who engage in this behavior are sometimes in someone else's paid employ, and what they are doing is called astroturfing. While the term "payment" is usually meant to mean financial compensation, there are many different kinds of payments, and these payments, although not strictly financial, may yield financial results in the long term.

"Attack that person and I will promote you to a position of leadership in my nonprofit organization. We don't pay money, but if you go and speak for us on the lecture circuit someday, some of the people who host you might pay you."

Or...

"Speak against that person and our organization will promote your blog at some later time. We know you have paying advertisers on your blog, and with us driving more people to your blog, the potential for you to receive ad revenue from click-throughs to your advertisers increases."

Bartering may also be employed.

"If you promote our position on that blog, we will defend you somewhere else the next time you get attacked."

This is why it is important to take a close look at the issues first, and who is saying things about the issues online and/or publicly afterward, and in what numbers, and to try to discern their motivation for doing so. Trying to figure out a person or group's motives can sometimes be very hard to do, though.

It is common for public opinion about something to go against what has been proven through the scientific method, and this is because, generally speaking, the public is mostly uninformed about the specifics of issues. It is unreasonable for anyone to expect each and every person to know all of the studies you may cite, and what the conclusions were that were drawn from these studies, and what ramifications those conclusions may have for the population that was studied.

Yet, when an argument is presented logically, with facts given honestly and without prejudices, and sources properly cited, there ought to be less criticism against the argument from intelligent people, with those people taking issue less with the results than how the study was conducted.

But when a horde of people come into an argument and simply heckle the person trying to present the argument, or torpedo the argument with insufficient proof on their side, it's either indicative of a group of people with an ax to grind, a group of people with an agenda, or a group of people with a paid agenda.

Many people who have been in the autism community for a long time begin to know which people and which organizations pull the puppet strings. For those who are more casual about their involvement in the autism community, they may see nothing covert, and it is a tough sell to convince these people that people, advocates, and advocacy organizations that appear so benevolent on the outside could be so malevolent on the inside. The attackers will simply respond by being friendly and clueless. (*"Who* is astroturfing? *Us*? That's silly. Why would we attack our fellow autistics?") The friendliness and cluelessness may persist indefinitely... until the casual observers become the targets.

It may be best to let people be astroturfed, and it may be best to let casual observers be used and manipulated, because the more victims there are, the more people there are to eventually spread the word about the attackers at the appropriate moment.

Of course, if every victim who has ever been astroturfed ganged up on the astroturfers, the astroturfers would turn the tables on them and shout that *they* are the ones being cybermobbed and astroturfed.

And people would probably believe them.

G. Crank Calling Someone At Home

Given the prevalence of caller identification on most phones these days, one would hardly think that anyone would make crank calls anymore, but a determined person, or a determined group of people will make the calls, and they will do it using calling cards or pay phones to hide where they are calling from. Generally, when people use calling cards, it is harder, if not impossible, to trace the call back to the original source.

It is not unusual in the autism community for whole groups of people to work in concert to intimidate their target. Doing this means the attackers can work around the clock, and because the type of harassment inflicted on the victim by one caller may be different from the type of harassment inflicted on the victim by another caller, it also means they can inflict multiple types of abuse on their victim.

Crank calls to one's home are mostly meant to annoy or intimidate, and tacitly threaten...but they may also be used for intelligence gathering.

If callers can find out a little more about the person they are harassing, it gives them additional ammunition to covertly or overtly attack them elsewhere. And so even as callers are speaking, they may be listening for background noises. What television show is their target watching? Are there city sounds in the background, suburban, or country? Are there kids laughing? Crying? If so, what ages might they be, and what sex are they? Is there music playing, and if so, what kind? Rock? Country? Gospel? Is there a member of the opposite sex around?

They will also call at different times of the day to try and discover their target's routine. If they call enough, they can find out when a person gets up in the morning, what time they go to bed at night, when they eat, when they go to work, when they drive their kids to school, what time their kids get home from school.

When the crank calls start coming in, it is usually best not to engage the callers in conversation, however tempting it might be, but instead hang up on them. If a person has caller ID, letting the calls ring through to the answering machine is a good option, because the machine will record the number of times a crank call comes in and how often. If a person does not have an answering machine, it may be a good idea to let the phone ring. This may be difficult to do. What if an important call comes in and gets missed? People who are harassed by crack callers will have to do what's best for them. But the general idea would be to prevent the callers from achieving their goals, whatever their goals might be.

When children are home alone, they should be instructed in advance to hang up the phone if a caller is someone they don't recognize, or to say to anyone who *sounds* official, "My mother [or father] cannot come to the phone right now. Can I take a message?" It may be unwise to tell them *not* to pick up. What if their parent, or someone else of importance, is calling them?

Logs should be kept of all crank calls in case it is necessary to turn the matter over to the police at some later time, as should any crank messages that may be left on one's answering machine.

It all sounds drastic, but crank calling happens quite frequently in the autism community.

It should be remembered that taking these steps may not have the desired effect of discouraging the callers. In fact, the opposite may happen. The callers may redouble their efforts, making twice the number of calls -or more-, just to annoy their victim.

H. Crank Calling Someone At Work

In addition to harassment and intelligence gathering, crank callers may have an additional objective in mind when they call people at work: They may be trying to cause someone to lose their job.

Too many incoming calls to one's desk may be seen by a person's managers as interfering with work, thus the calls may be cause for a worker to be disciplined by their employer. If those incoming calls are identified as being crank, such calls may also raise doubt in the minds of the employer about what a person might have done to attract the wrath of the crank caller(s).

How a crank caller at work is handled can result in unfavorable opinions as well. Is the worker firm and decisive with the caller? Polite and diplomatic? Or does the worker let the caller run roughshod over them? Depending on the type of work environment a person is employed in, and what kind of people are managing the concern, any or all of the above responses -or any responses not listed here- may reflect negatively on a worker. Thus the holy grail for some crank callers is to create a rift between their target and their target's employer.

Aside from the possibility that one might lose one's job as the result of too many incoming calls, there is also the threat pertaining to intelligence gathering that we would do well to remember. In some workplaces, if a person is away from their desk or work station, and a call comes in, nearby workers are required to pick the call up. That gives the crank caller a chance to ask questions about their target, and if the person who takes the call is innocent-minded, helpful, or has some animosity toward the absent worker, the call taker may inadvertently or deliberately provide the information the crank caller is looking for.

I have known people and organizations to use multiple people to make coordinated crank calls against their targets in an attempt to gather information on them, which they later post publicly online using fake usernames and profiles. Doing such can endanger people's careers if the targets apply for jobs where it is standard policy for employers to do net searchers on all job applicants. Posting private information online can also damage existing and potential friendships, business relationships, and romances.

This is why it is important that people either keep their professional lives a secret (especially online), or, if this is impossible, try to do damage control as soon as the damage is spotted. Explaining to employers and colleagues about the stalking as soon as the stalking behavior begins is often a good course of action, for example. An employer may actually be able to assist someone who is being stalked through legal means, or alternatively, they may be able to put the victim in touch with someone who can help them.

I. Vandalizing Personal Property

Vandalism is probably seen by the vandal as a tactic to strike fear into the hearts of his or her victims. Homes, garages, vehicles, boats, and other possessions could wind up getting damaged or destroyed once a vandal commits himself or herself to action.

But as with other kinds of intimidation, it's probably done from a position of impotence.

I may be wrong in my thinking, but it seems to me that people who need to take extreme measures to get the advantage in a situation are ones who feel like they *need* to have the advantage in a situation. They may also be people who are incapable of gaining the advantage through accepted means, or are who are just plain wrong in their thinking in the first place.

Further, if the action -in this case vandalism- is an action meant to inflict inconvenience, pain, or injury (either literal or financial) on a person, or damage or destruction to a person's property, it seems as though a concession to defeat has already been made by the attacker. The attacker is in effect saying that he or she cannot beat their target through argumentation, or by persuasion, or via emotional appeal, or through any accepted means, but they *can* at least beat their opponent metaphorically speaking by beating up their opponent's property in the most literal sense.

Property in the context of this section can also include servants, animals, and pets, though strictly speaking, a servant isn't property. But, if a person has a live in maid or butler, for example, and that person's possessions are harmed to the extent that they feel compelled to leave their employment, that may be considered vandalism in a loose sense. There have been incidences where livestock was poisoned or mutilated (although I do not know of this happening in the autism world specifically), and where pets have been killed, poisoned, or otherwise harmed.

When harassment steps up to this level, the perpetrator has crossed into a whole new realm: one that needs to be attended to by law enforcement authorities.

The degree to which the police investigate will usually be based upon the type of incidents, and/or the frequency with which they happen. It is not likely the police will conduct a thorough investigation if someone finds that the air has been let out of their tires, for example. Any people in the neighborhood could be a suspect...and any people out of the neighborhood, too, for that matter. Kids will often get up to such pranks on the spur of the moment. But if this type of incident happened many times over a lengthy period of time, the police might be more inclined to find out who is responsible.

On the other hand, one brick thrown through a window might be enough for the police to come out on the very first call.

It all depends.

But one interesting thing to consider, is that no matter who the culprit is, if the vandal is engaged in vandalism, they *should* be regarded as dangerous, don't you think? After all, if they are willing to risk being caught, arrested, and charged by the police, and possibly convicted in court, sentenced, fined and/or jailed, or made to pay restitution in some other manner, then they must be serious about what they are doing, and if they are that serious, who knows what they might do to your children, your relatives, your servants, or your pets, if they could get access to them.

Who knows what they might do to *you*?

J. Filing False Police Reports

How a person interprets what is being done to them is excuse enough to avoid getting arrested for filing a false police report in some jurisdictions. And so, if you have *one* incident that *could* be construed as (for example) bullying if you played it up the right way, you could weave around that incident any kind of tale you wanted, saying that this was just one of a whole line of incidents, the rest of them being lost to cyberspace, or not having been witnessed by anyone. Though police are generally able to figure out what's a lie and what isn't, they may feel inclined to follow up on the complaint, in which case the intended target gets put on the spot.

When the police knock on a target's door, the target is not expecting it, and is both shocked and on the defensive, eager to prove his or her innocence. Police may see such a reaction as a sign of guilt, when in fact, there is no quilt to be felt, because there was no real crime being perpetrated in the first place. At this point, the target might be inclined to file a complaint of his or her own, and there may be just cause with plenty of evidence to back it up, but the target may reflect that such an action might be seen by the police as sour grapes, or else a further "admission" to doing something wrong.

The police leave, the target goes online, and discovers that his or her bullies are posting *everywhere* that they possibly can:

> "Police called! Bully is being investigated tonight. Will inform if arrested or let go with warning!"

Implicit in a statement like that is that the target is guilty. The people making the announcements know full well that it is *they themselves* who are the bullies, and that it is *they themselves* who are the harassers, and that their target is innocent. But their supporters don't really know who is at fault. And so what follows the bullies' initial post is sympathy from these unsuspecting supporters. Their statements usually read something like this:

> "So sorry to hear you are being bullied! I hope they take your bully to jail."

Or...

> "Vile scum! If the police don't make him face justice, *we* will!"

Or...

> "Send me a PM with their FB and Twitter account names. If we report them in unison, we can get their accounts suspended."

Feeling that the police are now on their side, the bullies' campaign ramps up even more, often to the point where a lawyer has to be called in by the targeted person to threaten legal action if the harassment doesn't stop.

Getting a lawyer involved may ultimately be the best course of action. When you are dealing with people who know how to manipulate police, chances are they have some experience with criminality. This means they are not people to be trifled with.

K. Filing False Reports To Child Protection Organizations

If they can't get to you directly, they will either try to get to you through your children, or they will try to get your children.

Well, it doesn't matter if they call a child protection organization on you. If you've got nothing to hide, you're safe, right?

Maybe.

It all depends on what an investigator has been told, what they perceive when they visit you, and what they think after they talk to your children.

Unfortunately, if you find yourself being bullied, and you have children who are under the age of 18, or if you have guardianship of someone over that age, it pays to investigate what you can legally do *if* an occurrence like this should happen. For example, do you even have to let a worker from a child protection organization in the door if they ask to be let in? The answer varies depending on where you live. So find out in advance, and have a plan ready for such an eventuality. Also have a plan for even worse eventualities, such as if they take your child, children, or one(s) you care for away from you.

You wouldn't think there would be a need to be so paranoid about preparing for every eventuality described in this book, but the people you may find yourself dealing with may only *claim* to be autistic when in fact they many have another disorder or many disorders which have nothing to do with autism, and everything to do with other kinds of aberrant mental behavior. Having those disorders may make them unpredictable, or downright dangerous. Or yes, they may be autistic, but may have comorbidities which cause them to think and/or behave aberrantly.

The interest of the people who make false reports against you can be multi-fold. They may want to shut you up, inconvenience you, terrorize you, send an implied threat that they could make your life very bad for you if you interfere with their agenda, and maybe...just maybe, they really do want to separate you from your children. Even if their ultimate goal is *not* to separate you from your children, since the possibility exists that you *might* wind up being separated, it indicates that they don't care if it happens or not.

This should give you a good idea about the kind of people you are dealing with, how dangerous they are, and why it is they should be caught up with and dealt with in the strictest legal way.

L. Making False Allegations Against You To Your Employer

You're stealing supplies out of the company's supply closet. You're selling illegal drugs in the company parking lot after working hours. You're an exotic dancer working in a club on weekends.

Actually, none of these things are true, but someone who is calling up your employer insists that everything they say about you *is* true.

- ☐ Or maybe they are claiming you are stalking them online, and they are sending manufactured screenshots to your boss to "prove" it.

- ☐ Or maybe they are saying that you are crank calling them, and that you are making their work and personal lives difficult with these incessant phone calls.

- ☐ Or perhaps they are saying to your boss, or your company's human resources department that they want you to stop following their children home from Sunday school.

- ☐ And to stop calling up their grandmother in the nursing home in the middle of the night.

- ☐ Or maybe they are trying to convince your employer that they are creditors looking for employment history, and they want to make arrangements to garnish your paycheck.

It's doubtful that your company will act on what they hear, or give out much information about you without getting proof of identity from the caller(s), but they may wonder just what kind of person you are that has a person or persons saying these things about you or stalking you.

And they may use these phone calls and "reports" as one of the backup reasons for firing you at a later date when they have cause to get rid of you.

Sometimes, callers *will* tell the truth -as *they* see it- about your behavior online, and send in screenshots their "evidence" via email to your employer. Of course, said evidence conveniently leaves out what *they* did to incite you, and if you go hunting for it online later on to prove your innocence, *their* portion of the exchange has already been deleted.

More and more, just for offering an opinion, be it online or in real life, you can wind up with people calling up your place of employment so that they can tell lies about you, spread rumors, and get the gossip mill started.

If you wind up losing your job, they don't care. It doesn't matter if your comments were well-meaning or not. It doesn't matter whether you are on the spectrum or not. It doesn't even matter if you are a single parent with a child with autism. If it takes you losing your job and you and your kid going on the public dole just to get you to shut up, they don't care.

They just don't care.

M. Identity Theft

If they can hack your computer, they can see what's in it, and if can see what's in it, they may use what they see against you, including credit card information, bank account numbers, and whatever else they can think of.

If they live near you, they may take to going through your trash, or even your mailbox to find anything that has personal information inside of it.

They may follow you surreptitiously when you go to the ATM and use their cell phone to snap a picture of your ATM card when you are not looking, and take video when you enter your pin. They may do the same with your credit card wherever you may use it.

So it pays to guard your identity as best you can.

N. Stalking Their Target's Children

Those who do this may have no interest in the target's children per se. Their goal may be to make someone believe that their children are endangered. It's an implied threat to their target that the stalkers can act if and when they need to.

Keeping in mind that stalking children is not only criminal-like behavior, but disturbing behavior, such stalking needs to be taken seriously.

Remember, the people engaging in this kind of activity may not be on the autism spectrum at all, but may have a completely different kind of diagnosis altogether. For all you know, they could be sociopaths, schizophrenic, or someone who is undiagnosed, but who has some kind of deviant interests.

Call the police immediately if you suspect your child is at risk.

O. Etc.

There are so many things people, groups, and organizations can do in their war against a target. The above are just a few of the examples I have seen or heard of. Interestingly, I have not seen as much of this behavior going on in other areas of the disability community. It seems to be most prevalent in the autism world.

Instruments Of Deception

We've talked about methods of attack. And in regard to instruments of deception (although this was not a specific category in this book up to this point) we've talked about how the phone, internet, and word of mouth can be used both to attack and to deceive.

There are many other instruments that can be used to pit one faction against another, but I feel the need to address three of them here: Books, blogs, and podcasts/audiobooks.

1) Books

For our purposes, we will restrict our discussion to nonfiction books. Readers looking for a more in depth discussion on autistic nonfiction and fiction should see Autistic Authors, and Autistics, and Autism in Literature: A Commentary.

Two quick words about fiction, however:

1)   Readers should keep in mind that some misdiagnosed and self-diagnosed autistics are publishing fiction in which autistic characters have an important role in them. Often, they are basing their autistic character's attributes on autism as they -the authors- "know" it. In other words, if these authors do not have autism, the "autism" they are portraying in their books may be in the most literal sense, fictitious.

2)   Autistics will publish fiction too, but, like I have noted before in this book, it is often said in the autism community that when you've seen one autistic, you've seen one autistic, and so autism represented in fiction by one autistic may only represent autism as it manifests itself in one autistic, and not autism as it manifests itself in other autistics, or even *most* autistics.

Yet people admire these "autistics" and autistics as authorities merely because they have written a book.

So it is with nonfiction books about autism.

Autistic nonfiction in books can be just as guilty as autistic fiction in misrepresenting autism. It can also push an agenda on its readers. Further, nonfiction in books can actually come across as more credible than any other mode of writing - such as blogging, journalism, and podcasting for the simple reason that emotional arguments are usually absent, and supporting documentation are usually substituted in their place in order to back up one's assertions.

Can the works cited be trusted in such circumstances? Yes and no. It depends on the works themselves, who wrote them, and how they are being used. Often times credible and respected sources may be cited, but comments from those sources may be cherry-picked to support a different kind of argument than the source documents make.

Adding to the overall problem is the proliferation of "autistic authors." Nowadays, in addition to the familiar publishing houses, there are publishing companies which publish books that only pertain to autism, and if people cannot get published in any of those places, they can self publish via vanity presses, or publish through something like CreateSpace (www.createspace.com). Additionally, or alternatively they can upload files for sale to Kindle users. Their books and Kindle files can then sell on Amazon.com (www.amazon.com) as well as other online and offline venues. And there are many other places people can host their self-published books as well.

And so, with so many options available to prospective authors, there has been an abundance of autism books available for readers to peruse.

With those books comes a whole new list of "sources" which may be quoted, and if any of these autistic or "autistic" authors have an agenda, or if they are poor researchers, or if they are simply making everything up, they hardly qualify as sources.

How does an unethical autistic or "autistic" author become a "respected" source when what they are peddling is the worst sort of tripe?

Well, as with blogging, many "authors" from one single organization with an agenda can now publish books on the same topic. If these authors publish their books in succession, each new author can quote the previous one, thereby giving credibility to a series of otherwise incredible "sources."

This is how "authorities" on autism are "made" in many instances. But keeping in mind that these "authorities" may be no more knowledgeable about the subjects they are writing about than the readers who buy their books, it is important to research the authors themselves and find out more about them. As I said earlier in this book, the same questions that I suggested readers ask about advocates should be asked about autistic authors and "autistic" authors.

You will find many different agendas pushed through nonfiction, and you will find many specious sources to back up the theses of the authors.

One of the more popular specious sources backs up the repeatedly disproved idea that vaccines cause autism.

Andrew Wakefield and his study are most often quoted as "sources," but many times absent from books that push the vaccines-cause-autism agenda are counterarguments, such as the fact that Wakefield was sanctioned, his medical license was revoked, and his research was disproved.

It would behoove readers of autistic nonfiction to be less trusting than they are. There are of course many trustworthy authors of nonfiction that has autism as its main topic. Dr. Tony Attwood, M.S. Garnett, Simon Baron-Cohen, Michelle Dawson, Dr. Peter Szatmari, and Dr. Laurent Mottron (M.D., Ph.D.) are just a few names that can be trusted, for example. But for each of those names, there may be dozens that cannot be trusted at all.

Just because someone publishes a book, appears at a convention, releases self-help audio tapes, is interviewed on podcasts, etc., doesn't mean they are a reputable author of nonfiction. Only the research they use to back up their argument matters. If the research is shoddy, or if it is used unethically, or if it used contrary to how it was intended, don't trust it as a "source."

The other thing readers should do is to educate themselves about autism research and autism researchers generally. I mentioned a name that is familiar to me, but perhaps not familiar to you: Dr. Laurent Mottron (M.D., Ph.D.). Who is he?

Among other things, he is:

1.Head Research Chair in Autism Cognitive Neuroscience at the University of Montreal

2.Scientific Director of the Centre for Excellence in Pervasive and Developmental Problems, University of Montreal

3.Tenured Professor, Department of Psychiatry, University of Montreal

What has he done?
Well.... Look it up!

People who are trying to deceive others, and push an agenda, are banking that you won't "look it up," and are hoping you trust what they are talking about, and see them as authorities.

Many of them are as far from being authorities as you can imagine.

2) Blogs

Have you ever noticed that some really terrible products have been hawked in commercial ads by celebrities? Unethical authors/journalists/bloggers do the same. "Look at me!" They will say. "Pay attention to me, and not so much in the believability of what I am telling you."

There are only a select few people who can get away with tacking their resume after their names. Three common examples are doctors (M.D.s), doctors (Ph.D.s), and people we commonly know to be associated with a certain profession, title, diagnosis, or combination thereof. Examples: Country Musician Taylor Swift, President Barack Obama, Autistic Author Temple Grandin.

The media can be guilty for assigning labels to people who cannot and should not be labeled, and to people who do not want to be labeled. Donna Williams is much more than an author, and she is much more than autistic. Williams is an artist, a lecturer, and friend to many. Communicate with her and she will tell you that she is a person who has autism, not the embodiment of autism itself. Yet to the media, she is oftentimes, and more often than not "Autistic Author Donna Williams."

It seems that in this generation, more people than ever have taken to creating their own image and then spend a great deal of time trying to get people to buy into that image. I believe that even though this is a very common practice, it may still be an unethical thing to do, because if you are not who you say you are, and if you have not accomplished what you say you have, what you are doing by promoting an "image" of yourself is inciting people to buy into an illusion.

When I publish *one* way, I do not claim to be publishing *another* way.

For example:

1. As of the date of publication for this book, I have published eight books of fiction, but I am not writing fiction here in *this* book.

2.I may have edited someone else's books and supplied a few words for those books here and there, but I am *not* the author of *those* books.

3.I may have written editorial commentaries on various blogs, but those blogs were *not* newspapers, and I am *not* an editorial columnist.

Autistic bloggers are not exempt from committing acts of deception. They will spend a great deal of time trying to create an image for themselves, and even more time trying to get people to buy into that image. And one way that makes them succeed in this deception, is when they pass off one type of media as another.

There are many different forms of publishing, and all forms are valid. While I have personal feelings about which forms of publishing are better than others, it is not my purpose specifically to lambaste the forms I consider less than stellar. My purpose is to point out that a particular form of publishing cannot be greater than what it is no matter how hard it tries.

There are two online blog sites which ostensibly seem to be online newspapers. These are <u>Huffington Post</u> and <u>Examiner.com</u>.

<u>Huffington Post</u> and <u>Examiner.com</u> encourage people to write about particular topics in a journalistic fashion (as far as I can tell) but nowhere do they say –nor should they say- that their bloggers are professional journalists. To the extent that some of the bloggers write like professional journalists, and sound like professional journalists, they are journalists of a kind, but most of them are only amateur journalists because they are not writing for legitimate newspapers or magazines, and/or they do not have degrees in journalism.

To be a true journalist requires years in the making.

Someone who writes for <u>The Washington Post</u> is like a cup of coffee where the beans have been hand picked, slow roasted, ground, and brewed. Someone who writes for Huffington Post is more like instant coffee. Still coffee, still consumable, but not as good.

This is not to slam any blogger or journalist, or to write poorly about them. Nor is this a slam against Huffington Post or Examiner.com. They are what they are, and they do provide a useful service to their readership. I've read blog articles on both sites, and have learned much about many of the subjects being written about there.

But my opinion about those two publications and those who publish on them is –to my way of thinking- a valid opinion.

Another opinion I have is that it seems like people in the autism world who write on those sites call themselves journalists, or, even worse "autistic journalists."

Now granted, if Huffington Post and Examiner.com are journals, then the people who write for them are journalists. But if you ask *me* what a journalist actually is –and if you ask almost anyone else- the answer would be that a journalist is someone who writes for a publication that is indisputably a journal. Publications like The Washington Post, The New York Times, The Wall Street Journal, Time Magazine, Newsweek, and even Good Housekeeping and Rolling Stone Magazine are all journals.

Those publications have a history. They are commonly seen as respected publications, and those people who publish in them are commonly seen as journalists.

Now, it is theoretically possible for a blog to call itself a journal, I suppose. But if I am publishing in a blog as a journalist, ought I not to have the same qualifications as a journalist who writes for a recognized *traditional* journal? And if a blog that purports to be a journal does not have qualified journalists writing for it, can we say that such a blog upholds itself to a similar standard of integrity that other journals have? We can't say that, because other journals have staff with higher qualifications.

But if these arguments don't sway you, the legal system's view of blogs surely will. At the time of this writing, in most countries, if not in all countries, courts do not recognize blogs as journals, nor do they respect the right of blogs and bloggers to protect the names of anonymous sources.

All these words that I have written up until now have been written for the purpose of making a single point: Though journalists can be bloggers, not all bloggers can be journalists. Ergo, when a blogger presents themselves as a *journalist*, try to find out what their qualifications as a *journalist* actually are, and don't be so quick to call them a journalist if all they are doing is writing for something like Examiner.com or Huffington Post.

To call oneself a journalist when one has no established qualifications is "bad", but to tack the "autistic" qualifier onto title is worse in my opinion, and potentially more misleading.

Assuming the "autistic journalist" actually has autism and is *not* self-diagnosed, why should the fact that someone has autism make them *qualified* to write about autism and bill themselves as an autistic journalist?

On the surface, it makes perfect sense. A person has autism. They know what it is to live with autism. They are therefore qualified to write about autism.

But what if the journalist didn't have autism? What if the journalist had alcoholism? How would it sound to your ears if you read

"The following article is from alcoholic journalist John Doe."

Or

"Journalist Richard Roe has been an alcoholic all his life…"

Or

"Today's news comes from Jane Doe, who provides a view of the world through a drunkard's eye."

Would we take any of those authors seriously? Perhaps, if they were talking about alcoholism we would, but it still sounds…well…kind of silly.

Why then, do we take "autistic journalists" seriously?

I will grudgingly admit that sometimes when people with autism write about autism, their diagnosis gives them some degree of authority on the subject, but my firm belief is that just having autism does not necessarily qualify someone to write about the topic.

In the first place, most people who write blogs are just that: Bloggers. This holds true whether they have a diagnosis or not. And because they are blogging, rather than writing as journalists, what they write should be taken in by us the same way we would consume fast food: It's pleasing, it tastes good, but it's not necessarily what's best for us.

In the second place, one's qualifications need to be taken into consideration as well.

In <u>Autistic Authors, and Autistics, and Autism in Literature: A Commentary</u> I have stated *ad nauseam* that I have listed out a bunch of things I've done which I feel qualify me to talk about publishing. I have *not* listed out my diplomas, degrees, and awards. Hardly necessary, in my opinion. I never said I was a journalist. All I said was that I was an author, and I can say that because I have now written and published nine books -not including this one- some short stories, and some other things of note.

But if I wanted to say I was a journalist, I would first have to produce some evidence that I write or wrote for an actual journal, and, barring that, prove that I have a degree in journalism from an accredited college or university.

Here I will get into legal trouble if I start listing out the names of colleges and universities specifically, but let me just say that an accredited school is one that can be said to be recognized by certain organizations as being legitimate, and that has academic programs that meet certain standards. These programs have classes that are taught by qualified educators with proven credentials.

In the past decade or so, new "colleges" and "universities" have sprung up which look like accredited colleges and universities, and have programs like accredited colleges and universities, but do not meet the standards that are met by accredited colleges and universities. Try to transfer your credits from one of these places to an accredited college or university and you will not succeed.

In recent years, the line has been blurred between accredited and unaccredited schools even further, because the unaccredited schools have colluded together to form their own accreditation programs and organizations. Thus these new colleges and universities can *claim* to be accredited, but still can be substandard in comparison with historically proven accredited colleges and universities.

So, if a person says they have a degree in journalism from XXXX college or university, the degree they are waving in your face might not be worth the paper it's written on. That is something you have to investigate as a reader.

But even if you have done the homework, and discovered that the person whose writing you're reading is autistic, and has a journalism degree from an accredited university, can you trust that what this person is writing is completely truthful?

The answer to that question in these cases is almost *always* no for two reasons:

1.Nothing that anyone writes is written without some kind of slant, no matter how unbiased they say they are or believe themselves to be, and

2.Sometimes people have a specific agenda.

Now, if you have been keeping track, I have made six points throughout this section:

1.Journalists can be bloggers, but not all bloggers are journalists.

2.Blogs can be journals, but most blogs aren't journals.

3.Many who call themselves journalists do not write for true journals and do not have journalistic credentials.

4.Some who call themselves "autistic journalists" are using the "autistic" descriptor to mislead people into believing they are more qualified to speak on the subject of autism that they are.

5.The academic qualifications that an "autistic journalist" may present to you may be suspect.

6.Many "autistic journalists" have agendas and ulterior motives for writing what they write.

And all of these six points, plus the questions I've asked, lead me to ask you: With so much doubt revolving around "autistic journalists", why would you want to risk reading what they have to say about autism? If you want material that is more trustworthy, your best bet is to read the actual research that has been done regarding autism. Or read the material published by recognized and respected autistics who have already established their credentials and demonstrated their integrity.

Mostly, trust your gut.

If something doesn't feel right, it probably isn't.

3) Podcasts And Audiobooks

The public's gullibility has not lessened as quickly as technology has matured. People are not savvy enough to understand that something produced in someone's basement could sound and/or look very professional, but may really be a production that is meant to deceive. This is why I urge caution to anyone who normally trusts a podcast or a an audio book without first stopping to check who made the production, and without first stopping to investigate why the production was made.

As someone who has written and co-written many podcasts for Midnight In Chicago, I have taken great care to make them fact-based, with sources quoted and cited so listeners can review anything I say. The website where the podcasts are posted, www.podomatic.com, has terms of use that must be adhered to, but MIC founder Elyse Bruce and I have put rules of our own into effect that go beyond those on www.podomatic.com. At www.autism.podomatic.com, you will find cheerful podcasters, but you will *not* find ones who will try to hypnotize you, or try to subtly or subliminally influence you.

In other words, while we try to sound pleasant, we do not use tones in our voices or other gimmicks to try to get you to believe something that you would not so easily believe if you were just reading it.

Audio books can have an even more powerfully influential effect on you that podcasts do. If you are listening to an audio book that is nonfiction, chances are you will be listening to one voice -without background noise or foley- for the entire recording. Listen long enough and you may find yourself falling into a state of mind that is more suggestible than if you were having a give and take conversation with people.

If you don't believe me, try to think back to times in history when whole nations were rallied to a cause. Where people have been rallied most effectively, it was usually in a situation where they were enclosed in a building or stadium, and where one lone speaker spoke on and on for a very long period of time, slowly bringing everyone to a consensus. People would become more rapt with each passing minute until finally, the final words were given, and whether those words were "The Final Solution" (Holocaust) or "Kamikaze! Kamikaze! Kamikaze!" or what have you, the people approved!

Books afford you the opportunity to go back and re-read what you have read. While you may be able to re-listen with audio books and podcasts, you may not be so inclined, because

> 1.It is instinctual in us not to interrupt people while they are still talking

> 2.We are trained not to ask questions until people are finished speaking

> 3.It may simply be inconvenient to rewind or replay a portion of a recording

In audio books and podcasts, a person's voice, or the speed at which they speak, can distract us and keep us from thinking logically, but with a book, there is nothing but words on a page. If we do not understand a word in a recording, we may not have time to dig out a dictionary to find out what it means, but when we are reading a book, time affords us the opportunity to get out a dictionary and educate ourselves.

Two Other Instruments of Deception

1) Videos And TV Appearances

Most video cameras these days produce very good digital recordings, and devices to capture audio can be purchased for $250.00 that will provide professional grade sound.

Using simple movie making programs, people can now edit footage, provide stunning graphics, and they can post these productions to YouTube and other online venues. They can also show these movies in public venues.

When we purchase something, the old saying "Let the buyer beware" always applies. Sometimes the most flashy automobiles are the ones that are the least durable, and are the worst lemons. We should feel the same way about videos that we watch for free.

A video is window dressing for whatever message is trying to be imparted. If you watch a television commercial for a product, listen to what is said verses what is being shown. Is the commercial actually telling you anything substantive about the product, or is the video enticing you to make an impulse buy based on what you see? Turn off the audio the next time the commercial comes on, and chances are, the images by themselves won't be very compelling either.

People and organizations that are trying to "sell" you on an argument about autism might not be able to convince you if they simply sat you down and had a conversation with you, but if they can appeal to your emotions using images, and other propaganda, they might succeed.

Some autistic advocacy organizations are well-known for producing videos. This is because those organizations know that people who do not have the equipment and/or the knowledge necessary to record, and then edit and assemble film or videotape footage may associate a "Golly! Gee whiz! I'm impressed!" feeling with the production. Or those organizations know people might think, "If they can produce such high quality videos, they must be a BIG organization."

If it is an individual producing the video, a person might think "Wow! They must be very successful and influential to be able to have the money to pay for such a high quality production."

But most of these videos are written, filmed, edited, directed, and produced by an unremarkable group of average everyday Joes.

We should not hold one individual or organization in higher esteem because of a video production any more than we would some person or some organization who has *not* produced a video.

When we see people or organizations interviewed on TV, we might be very impressed, but we would do well to reflect that getting ourselves in the newspaper or on TV is actually not that hard. The more you submit material to a newspaper, the more likely it is that something you've submitted will be published. For every letter to the editor I have published in a newspaper, I must have sent in a dozen or so that never made the cut. Likewise, for every television and radio interview I have done, there were many interviews that I was slated to do, but wasn't able to do, because I wound up being dropped from the show, usually because something more newsworthy took my spot.

If a person or organization garners enough attention, they may be seen by some reporters as the go-to person or organization for a comment, or used as a consultant. They may use the person or organization in favor of others who are dying to voice their opinion. It should be remembered that just because a person or organization is used as a consultant doesn't mean what the consultant says is correct. It may mean that the reporter has gotten lazy, and is using a preferred source rather than finding new sources that may be better informed.

But what you will see on websites of individuals and organizations are links to radio and TV interviews, YouTube videos and whatnot. If these people and organizations are legitimate, that's great, but they could just be trying to impress people with what they've "done" verses who they are, and who they are may be very ignorant representatives of the autism world.

Learned people will look to studies, research, and doctors for their answers about autism. Television interviews and YouTube videos ought to be the last thing people look at, as they are meant to "wow" people and get "ratings" (for the TV station in the former case and for the person or organization posting the video in the latter case).

When arguments take place over autism, you will often see people and organizations dragged into it either as "sources" for their argument, or as "body guards" to assaults against them. It's the adult version of

"I have a big brother and he can beat you up!"

Vs.

"Oh yeah! Well, I have a *bigger* big brother and he can beat up *your* big brother!"

Ignore it when you see this happening. The credentials of the sources may be nothing of consequences. Pure showmanship. The only sources that matter are licensed board certified medical professionals, published research, and peer-reviewed studies.

2. Conventions

"I'm going to go to a convention and hear XXXX speak!"

To which I say "So what?"

I have spoken at conventions.

Further, I regularly speak with people who have spoken at conventions, both online and offline. These people are *not* far and few between as one might expect, and the reason is because conventions are not interested in who is right or wrong. They are interested in selling tickets to the people who go to see the speakers. And so they get who they can and showcase them as though they are product, when in fact, what they may be, are ignoramuses.

You might look at a person's or organization's online resume and see that they have spoken here and spoken there, and it may look very impressive, but ask yourself this: What are they actually saying? What do they actually believe in?

Review the questions I posted for advocates and ask these questions of the people that are speaking at conventions. If they do not come up to your level of measurement, ignore them.

The only sources that matter are licensed board certified medical professionals, published research, and peer-reviewed studies.

Why Does All This Happen? What Kind Of People Do this?

As I mentioned in <u>Autistic Authors</u>, and as I have mentioned in *this* book, autism presents itself differently in each person who is diagnosed with it, and I cannot in good conscience write a book about autistics "exactly" as they are for that reason. Right now, I doubt I could even write a book about the *similarities* autistic have, because, thanks to misdiagnosed, self-diagnosed, and wannabee "autistics" intermixing with the diagnosed autistic population, it has become almost impossible to discern what is *autistic* and what isn't.

Thus writing about autism politics and autistic political factions has been equally difficult.

I am not sure where all this controversy began, but as I have pointed out earlier, I can at least trace it back to the disintegration of the Aspergia message board.

Most reminiscences about Aspergia are fond and favorable, with some former members recalling feelings of genuine sadness and sorrow when Edan closed the board and chat, as though a real place was being shuttered. Most blame trolls and fakers for the ultimate demise.

Now, we have a proliferation of message boards, chats and meeting places, with the most successful ones being places where there are few if any rules, and "anything goes." The most popular place that I can think of right now has an entire section devoted to adult topics. Whether those topics are legal or illegal, they can be talked about at length to the content of any of the board's members who want to participate. Sex, drug use, criminal behavior, are all acceptable topics for discussion. To date, two of that boards members have gone on killing sprees.

Why do we have a proliferation of places for autistics to go on the net?

I have two working theories.

Working Theory #1:

Autistics -*true **diagnosed*** autistics, are **!!!FED UP!!!** with what they see in the major forums, and many of them want to create what they believe to be the *perfect* place to meet and associate with other *true **diagnosed*** autistics. If they can find a place they like, they will stay there, but if they cannot find that place, then they will make one of their own.

A second component of this theory is that people who are self-diagnosed, in the process of getting a diagnosis, seeking a diagnosis, wannabees, misdiagnosed, a parent of an autistic, a sibling of an autistic, a relative of an autistic, a spouse of an autistic, a friend of an autistic, a teacher, a school administrator, a school psychologist, a medical practitioner, a researcher, a curiosity seeker, a neurotypical, a quack, or even someone who is trying to sell something, create groups of their own where *they* can feel good about themselves and the people *they* interact with.

But for some of the people in this category, there may be an additional purpose for setting up their own groups. It seems that there is a need to validate their beliefs, their habits, their wants, their needs, just as much as there is a need to find and congregate with people who are like them.

This is why we have forums for "autistic" cannabis users. This is why we have forums for "autistics" who are Satan worshipers. This is why, for every type of sexual proclivity you can imagine, there is probably a forum for "autistics" where such proclivities can be discussed.

Parents create their own forums to discuss their autistic children. Spouses create forums to discuss their autistic spouses. Relatives create forums where they can discuss their autistic relatives. Teachers create forums to discuss teaching autistics. Doctors create forums where they can discuss autism spectrum disorders. People create forums to sell trinkets, books, and services. Autism charities create forums, as do autistic organizations, and self-advocacy groups.

Working Theory #2:

People want to be in control of their own forums so they can eject or ban people they don't like. Alternatively, they want to be able to have a place where they feel free from the types of intimidation and threatening behavior that I have outlined in this book.

People want to be *safe* in other words.

Despite many autistic advocacy organizations attempts to bring everyone together under one unified group, more and more people are going their own way, mainly because whatever autistic advocacy groups are promising, they aren't what autistics, or even "autistics" are looking for.

In a very real sense, for perhaps the first tine in the history of autism spectrum disorders, autistics are developing a sense of self, even as they attempt to integrate themselves into close, tight-knit communities of their own manufacture.

The attempts by autistics to find themselves and create their own environments, however is still under threat. It seems that no matter what group is created, there is contention, because people with an agenda just cannot stay away from people who want to have peaceful communication and congregation.

Hardly anyone in the autism community can talk to anyone anymore, either in real life or online.

I fell witness to an interesting conversation the other day. Someone whom I have known, in person, for nearly a decade -a diagnosed autistic person who has a diagnosed autistic child (both of whom were diagnosed by a licensed board certified doctor specializing in autism spectrum disorders via an exhaustive process that lasted years), and who has extensive experience in the area of autism spectrum disorders in and out of the school system, and in and out of autism organizations, and with researchers and doctors- was trying to offer an opinion about the behavior of a supposed "autistic" individual in an online forum. I will produce here a conversation that was representative of the incident. It should be understood that **Person #3** represents my friend.

Person #1 (Mom Of An Aspie): I'm looking for information about Asperger Syndrome. My daughter is diagnosed AS seven years ago at the age of ten by a school psychologist. She is 17 years old now. It almost seems like since the moment she was diagnosed, she began talking rudely to me and my husband. To be honest, she uses profanity, makes snarky comments, gives us the finger, and sometimes throws things at us, usually in response to us pointing out that she forgot to button a button, or that she left a towel lying on the floor in the bathroom. Is this a trait of Asperger Syndrome? Is this is what's called "having meltdowns?" And what can I do to resolve the situation? I really need your help. We live in the US, but are in an area without too many resources for people on the autism spectrum, so I would really appreciate any advice you could provide.

Person#2 (A Self-Diagnosed Aspie): Talking in blunt terms is a well-known trait of Asperger Syndrome. That your daughter started being "rude" as you call it, shortly after her diagnosis was the direct result of her getting her diagnosis. She probably did some research and found out that Aspies behave awkwardly in social situations, and she decided to "let it all hang out" as it were, and be herself.

      When you tell her to do unreasonable things, like change her way of expressing herself by buttoning a button she'd rather leave unbuttoned, or by picking up a dirty towel (all Aspies have OCD comorbidities and do not like germs), you are really piling it on and upsetting her.

      When you persist in trying to force her to comply with these unreasonable demands, you cause her to get upset, and she responds by telling you how she feels. You may consider this "rude," but this is the way *all* Aspies express themselves when they are under the type of pressure you put them under. When she really gets upset and throws things...yes...it's what's called having a meltdown.

Person #3: (My Friend): Actually, rudeness or bluntness is not an AS trait according to the psychiatric criteria as the previous poster has stated. You might want to go and check the American Psychiatric Association's Diagnostic and Statistical Manual – IV, Text Revision (DSM-IV-TR) People with Asperger Syndrome *do* have impairments in communication, but they are usually a delay -or lack- of development of spoken language, an inability to sustain a conversation, stereotyped language, and a lack of ability to engage in make believe play.

Your daughter's behavior sounds more like a behavioral issue to me. Given that some on the spectrum have a mental age lower than her physical age, it could be possible that she is responding to you like a much younger child would, but as I said, the degree of rudeness she responds with sounds atypical of people on the spectrum.

Not all Aspies have an OCD comorbid diagnosis as the previous poster suggests. Only some do. So in regards to your daughter, OCD may not play any part in her behavior at all.

You mentioned she was diagnosed by a school psychologist. Did that school psychologist diagnose any comorbidities, such as OCD? And did your daughter have any other diagnoses or comorbidities before she was diagnosed with AS that were diagnosed by someone other than your school psychologist?

Incidentally, though there is no real agreed upon definition of what a "meltdown" is, a meltdown is commonly thought to be when an autistic has a reaction to something and that reaction cannot be controlled. Not by them, and not by anyone else. A *tantrum*, on the other hand, may be an occurrence similar to what you see in children, where they are looking to provoke, and where they are making their feelings known via their words and behaviors, and where they have control or partial control over their behaviors. Ask yourself what is happening when your daughter is swearing or throwing things. If she seems to know what she is doing, it could be that she is having a tantrum, rather than a meltdown.

Person #1 (Mom Of An Aspie): She was diagnosed bipolar by a psychiatrist after extensive evaluation. When the school psychologist diagnosed AS, the psychiatrist said the school psychologist was wrong. When that happened, my husband pulled my daughter out of therapy altogether, which the school psychologist said was a good thing, as it would interfere with the IEP and therapeutic programs they were going to put in place for her at the school. The school psychologist ruled out bipolar by the way, and he didn't say anything about OCD.

Person #3 (My Friend): It could be your daughter's psychiatrist was correct. Some school districts have been known to deliberately misdiagnose students to secure funding for special accommodations. You may want to take her to a third party...another psychiatrist, for an evaluation. Just my opinion.

Person #2: (Self-Diagnosed Aspie): Person #3, are you diagnosed, because you don't seem to know what you're talking about.

Person #3 (My Friend): I'm diagnosed.

Person #2: (Self-Diagnosed Aspie): Bullshit. I'm a diagnosed Aspie, and if you knew anything about ASDs, you'd know that they came out with the DSM V because everything in the DSM-IV as it pertained to AS was wrong. It is in the DSM V where they talk about bluntness.

Person #3 (My Friend): I used the DSM-IV-TR in my reply because Person #1's daughter is diagnosed with AS, a diagnosis eliminated from the DSM V. Nevertheless, the DSM V makes no reference to autistics using blunt language. My opinion is that her daughter's behavior is probably behavioral. Neither the DSM IV-TR or the DSM V say that OCD is a comorbidity of *all* AS people either, BTW.

Person #2: (Self-Diagnosed Aspie): Do you have a child with AS?

Person #3 (My Friend): I have a daughter with AS. She's 24, and teaches elementary school students.

Person #2: (Self-Diagnosed Aspie): It's a miracle she survived your shitty parenting. As for her job, most Aspies aren't able to work. Sounds like your daughter was misdiagnosed. Or else you are lying. It's clear to me that you have no experience with AS whatsoever.

To Person #1, I wouldn't listen to the witch who is trying to tell you she knows everything about AS. She's *not* AS and doesn't know what it's like to have it. If *I* sound rude to your ears, it's because I am dealing with this troll. In fact, if you want to know what a meltdown looks like, you are witnessing it occurring before your very eyes. And here is the perfect example of how it is your daughter can get irritated with *you*. I am trying the best way I know how to show you how AS works, and here is this ignorant person trying to say that *she* knows how it works. So I get upset.

Your daughter is getting upset at you because she is trying to explain to you how *her* AS is working. She just cannot find the words. So from now on, just don't ride her on things like you have been. If she wants to dress without a button buttoned, respect that that is her choice. If she leaves a towel on the floor, it's no big deal for *you* to pick it up. She probably has OCD.

Fail to to what I've told you, and you'll wind up just as ignorant and stupid as Person #3, and your daughter will continue to hate you just like I hate Person #3. Personally, I hope Person #3 dies. I'd kill her myself if I knew her address.

Person #3 (My Friend): Actually, the best thing to do is listen to neither one of us, and take her to a doctor who is trained in the area of autism spectrum disorders. That doctor will be most qualified to determine whether or not your daughter is on the spectrum, and if autism spectrum disorder is ruled out, you can then try to find out *for sure*, what your daughter's true diagnosis is.

It pays to take this step now, because the course of her life is going to change once she leaves school. It's better that she knows what disorder she has (if any) now, so she can learn how to deal with it, rather than have it hold her back.

Person #4: (An Autistic Self Advocacy Organization Leader): Hello. I couldn't help seeing the exchange that has happened here. I am from the XXXX, an organization by autistics, for autistics. Everyone in our organization is either diagnosed or in the process of getting a diagnosis. We are considered *the* online authority in the autistic rights movement.

In the interest of giving you the *correct* information you are seeking, I'd have to say that everything Person #2 told you was correct, though it could have been stated better. Person #3, on the other hand, is a known troll who incites arguments wherever she goes. That she has provoked Person #2 to the point where he is experiencing a meltdown -and it *is* a meltdown he is having- proves this.

It has been shown repeatedly in other venues that Person #3 is *not* diagnosed, that she does *not* have a daughter, and her knowledge of autism spectrum disorders is poor at best.

Most of her posts are deliberately meant to deceive.

My organization has worked hard and tirelessly to getting her banned from the net. There is a petition you can sign if you feel she has in any way misled you with her irresponsible advice. We intend to submit it to all social media with the intent of getting all of her online accounts banned completely once and for all, and her IP addresses blacklisted.

Her behavior should not be allowed to continue under any circumstance.

Person #1 (Mom Of An Aspie): Thank you Person Number 4. I think I *will* sign the petition, and if you wouldn't mind, I would like to donate to your organization. Thank you, Person #2, for your sage advice. Your manner of speaking is similar to my daughter's which is why I am inclined to believe that *you* are an Aspie, and Person 3# is a fraud.

And as for you, Person #3: You can go to hell for endangering my daughter's life, you fucking BITCH!

This happens all the time.

We've certainly come a long way from Aspergia, haven't we?

But maybe not so far.

It could be argued that the proliferation of message boards began shortly after Aspergia ended.

Many people back then said that even the Edan-approved successor boards did not have quite the same "feel" as Aspergia., possibly because of the trolls and fakers becoming more populous on them then they were on www.aspergia.com. Even to this day, there are arguments about what caused the ultimate demise of Aspergia, and people will argue over whether or not present day autistics are Aspergians or not.

People who populated the original board and used its chat oftentimes do refer to themselves as "Aspergians." It is a made up name that is fast growing into popular acceptance by many people with Asperger Syndrome who were never members of the board at all. Some people do not even know there *was* an Aspergia, or else they are only familiar with the successor boards. There has, therefore, been some resentment by actual former members of the Aspergia board toward people who call themselves Aspergians, but who were never members of the board.

To make matters more confusing is the Aspergia "hierarchy." Are you a "true" Aspergian *only* if you were a member of the original Aspergia board? Or could you be an Aspergian if you were never a member of Edan's board, but were a member of one of Edan's approved successor boards after www.aspergia.com's closure?

Most confusing of all was the rivalry between some Aspergia successor boards, and, in one instance, a "coup" where a successor board owner claimed the board had been "stolen" by an administrator!

It all makes for an interesting study in "autistic culture" if such a culture can be said to exist, although if you have ever participated in some of the disputes, you will have found that they can get quite combative.

At any rate, all of the Edan-authorized groups are gone now except the Fellowship of the Aspergian Miracle series of boards.

What you will find out about some of the most militant people and "activists" if you go deep into the forum threads, chat-rooms and conversations, or if you have private correspondence with them, is the truth. Many of these trolls and troublemakers were bullied when they were children. Many were often disciplined by their parents and relatives in ways they didn't like. Many were fired from their jobs. Some were institutionalized for a time. Some have been, and are, on the government dole. Some have poor work histories and criminal records.

Through the illustrious and ubiquitous internet, however, they have been given a voice, and if they can crowd their way into a conversation, or shout from the electronic hilltops, they will.

Online, some may have multiple user names with multiple accounts set up under each of them. Some may have pay pal buttons set up under each of those accounts to collect money for many different causes.

Now, if you have read this far, you may be thinking that some of the beliefs and behaviors displayed by some autistics seem very similar to those often displayed by supremacist groups.

Unfortunately, your intuition has not failed you. There are indeed people and groups who do believe that autistics are superior to all of mankind, and that it is the destiny of those with autism to rule the world. It sounds completely ridiculous on the surface, but when one considers that there are many famous people with autism, and that rumors of Thomas Edison, Henry Ford, and Albert Einstein's supposed autism abound, one can see how some autistics would believe themselves to come from superior genetic stock. [Remember now, in the minds of these people, there need not be a direct familial relationship between themselves and the famous people, it only matters that these famous people may possess the same gene variants.]

There are forums rife with hate speech against neurotypicals, and talk of how society should be structured and regimented a certain way, with autistics in control "for the betterment of mankind." Given that some of the people spouting this garbage hold college degrees, their language may sound compelling if not convincing, and the manner in which they draw you around to their way of thinking may be quite scholarly. Yet do not be fooled. These pronouncements sound startlingly similar to Adolf Hitler's Nazi propaganda.

The intrigue becomes more entangled when a member of one "faction" claims to be a member of another "faction" to torpedo an agenda. Many pro-vaxers, for example, will claim to be anti-vaxers, and deliberately troll online forums as anti-vaxers to get all anti-vaxers thrown off of those forums. Taking this one step further, a pro-vaxer might, as a "journalist," take the side of an anti-vaxer and deliberately write inflammatory stories, or stories with spurious content in an effort to make anti-vaxers look mentally unstable and uneducated.

The fact is, without having circulated in many different sectors of the online and offline autism community for an extended period of time, a person would be hard-pressed to know who is, or who is not, a reliable and trustworthy "autistic," and whether or not the "autistic's" motives are earnest and legitimate.

Here I am presented with a dilemma. Should I or shouldn't I list out the people and organizations which I believe to be suspect?

The answer to that question must be no.

Readers need to determine for themselves which people and organizations they deem "good" or "bad." For me to cite people and organizations specifically would provide an editorial slant which might influence people positively or negatively, but which might have negative repercussions for them either way. All I can do is explain some of the "politics" and "political factions" in the autism world, and hopefully this will arm readers with what they need to weed the wheat from the chaff.

In some cases, I have been a passive observer to the scheming and conniving that go on. In others, I have made a show of actively involving myself in their plans, but then bowing out on some pretense or other at the last moment. But it's interesting what you will find out when you are part of the "inner sanctum," so to speak. For one thing, once you are admitted into the confidence of the more deviant people and organizations, what you will find out is that people claiming to be autistic on the net readily admit that they are not autistic and have never been diagnosed. In fact, privately, they characterize themselves as "social rejects" who fit in really well with autistics because "autistics are rejects too."

Pathetic as this may seem, it has its humorous side, because the autistics they believe they fit in with may not be professionally diagnosed either.

When going through teacher training a long time back, I had the benefit of teaching learning disabled and special education students in many different schools. I asked the special education teachers back then what the diagnoses were of the kids I would be working with.

A typical reply was usually:

> "Oh, that one's been diagnosed by the school psychologist with ADHD. That one has Asperger syndrome. That one has NVLD. That one has OCD and Anxiety disorder. But you can't go by a school psychologist's diagnoses. We just label them with something so we can get the state funds to educate them they way they need to. Most of these kids are either slow learners, or kids with behavioral problems which can be conveniently pigeonholed into something in the DSM.

But remember, there are five or six different diagnoses in the DSM that could fit each and every one of them, and only a rigorous diagnostic analysis could find the diagnosis that is right for them."

All these kids have grown up to believe they have a kind of autism spectrum disorder when they may not have one at all.

Yet another common element among these people is that they *may* have other diagnoses. Usually these are behavioral disorders. Specifically: conduct disorder, bipolar disorder, Operational Defiant Disorder. They may also have been diagnosed with schizophrenia, and have learning impairments.

There was also one irony I encountered during my incognito sojourn into the grotty corners of the net, and that is that these supposed autistics, who were kind to me, Thomas Taylor, on Facebook and on similar social media sites, were the ones inciting the incognito me to work *against* Thomas Taylor.

I have seen people admit in private online forums that they do not have autism and were never suspected of having it, but in the more public online autism forums, persist in claiming to have autism. These people will ruthlessly harass real autistics, going so far as to hijack their accounts, call up their places of business to sabotage their jobs, crank call them at home, file bogus complaints against them with the police department, and, if they meet in person, engage in physical altercations with them.

My opinion is that when someone uses another person's diagnosis in order to get something from unsuspecting people, what they are really doing is stealing a diagnosis so that they can con other people for selfish and greedy purposes.

Yes, But Why Do They Behave This Way?

Unless we can get into the minds of these people, there is no way of knowing. Some are deliberately malicious, malevolent, and vindictive. Others have "excuses."

The "Bad Childhood" Excuse

We must admit that terrible things can happen in a person's childhood that will traumatize people and stay with people for life. However, I have noticed that much of the "trauma" *some* people claim to have gone through isn't trauma at all. It's just everyday real life experiences that are no different than those experienced by other people.

That some people are less able to cope with day to day existence is true, and we must be compassionate towards those people. But I'm not talking about those people particularly. I am talking instead about people who, due to no medical or personal motivation, but pure selfishness, choose to be lazy, choose to be uneducated, choose to be jobless, choose to be rude or belligerent toward other people, choose to be unethical or immoral, choose to do things that are not law abiding, and...when their own behavior gets them into a jam...choose to act in a manner that will victimize other people.

Unless we have been locked in a cell all of our lives, we cannot help but see that the world at large follows certain laws and lives according to certain morals, values, and ethics. That the majority of the world's citizenry walks freely down the street and has not spent time in jail is a testament to the fact that these laws are *not* restrictive, that they *are* easily understood, and they *are* easily obeyed.

But they are apparently restrictive to *some*.

The same applies to morals, values, and ethics.

No matter who takes care of us after we are born, be it a parent or some case worker at an orphanage, our caretakers impart their morals, values, and ethics to us. Even if the intent of the caretaker is to be completely "neutral" about morals, values, and ethics, this neutrality in itself is something that will get picked up and incorporated into the mind of the person who is being cared for by virtue of being exposed to it. I believe this process persists, no matter what stage we are in life. Throughout life, our conscious selves behave like sponges, absorbing much of what we are exposed to.

The reciprocal event is to expel those morals, values, and ethics which we reject while retaining those which best fit our psyches.

It seems there is a segment of the population, however, that will argue that because of something they have suffered, be it a single traumatic event, or an entire childhood filled with traumatic events, they are entitled to shirk the laws, morals, values, and ethics that everyone else have, and live an existence that resembles anarchism.

Many times there is no traumatic event or traumatic childhood, and in reality, the "suffering" than a person claims to have experienced, was just and proper discipline for misbehavior.

Perhaps the child was lazy, rude, defiant, etc., and all these attributes due to choice, not a diagnosis. Perhaps the child was repeatedly disciplined when the desired behavior was not demonstrated. One can see that years of this discipline could be interpreted by someone as being "abuse" but this interpretation is more indicative of a very insecure ego -one that doesn't want to admit that it's at fault.

While we can have sympathy for an insecure person like this, the world cannot stop turning for them. People like these are a liability to other people who have managed to get their ducks in a row. Tough as it is to have to say this, people are usually avoided, shunned, divorced, fired, fined, arrested, and jailed, for a reason. If any of these things have happened, they have happened because the person and/or entity doing the dumping or disciplining has not only identified an issue that needs to be addressed, but the issue is so overwhelmingly prevalent that they have felt compelled to act.

I have read cover to cover an e-book by a self-diagnosed person -and "autistic advocate"- who claims victimhood throughout his life. An absent mother, and an incident of sexual abuse, I think, are clearly traumatic. But I have no sympathy at all for the excuses he makes for his subsequent behaviors. His father, being placed in the position of having to care for him and maintain a career, moves him from place to place around the country as job opportunities present themselves, but the author runs away quite often, and for petty reasons. He doesn't like his father's girlfriend. He doesn't like the fact that he has to do work around the house. People in school don't understand him. He's jealous that his sister got to stay with his mother. Taking his chances, he prefers living on the street rather than living with the exact same kinds of problems and responsibilities that most other kids live with.

I find kids who struggled to live through such troubling times to be more inspirational than this author, who suggests that every negative event in his adult personal or professional life has its roots in his childhood, and that most of his childhood was abusive. While other kids in his situation obey the law, go to school, do their chores, etc., this author writes about running away, hitchhiking, shoplifting, etc.

There is an incident where he is "on the road" and picked up by a man who hints at wanting sex, which the author refuses to provide. While the moment is very scary, I cannot help but think that the author put himself in harm's way by hitchhiking in the first place. Complicating matters further is that the author writes as though even as an adult, he should get sympathy from us, not only because of the trifling discipline he experienced as a child, but also because of this hitchhiking experience. To be honest, I have a hard time giving it to him, especially since he, as an adult, blames a lot of *current* common day to day events in his life for his failures.

As adults, we must at some point take responsibility for ourselves instead of making excuses. As much as the author I have just mentioned has indeed experienced traumatic events, I've read and heard of other people having far worse experiences, and who overcame their pasts to become very successful, and without help from anyone.

Not everyone can recover so easily, I understand, but there seems to be a large number of people claiming to be on the spectrum who seem to dwell perpetually in a muck and mire of inaction and inactivity due to the "abuse" (read "life") that has befallen them. Is this autism? Not according to the DSM or ICD.

At any rate, the "I've had an abusive childhood, and that's why I should be allowed to skirt the law and act immorally and unethically now" argument doesn't fly with me, but I have seen it used as justification for people behaving badly online and offline in the autism world.

The "I'm Disabled" Excuse

If a person has a disability, it is understandable and proper that society should make allowances for that person.

Making the life of a disabled person easier for them has the additional benefit of making life easier for those who are *not* disabled. If disabled people can care for themselves, people who *aren't* disabled can spend less time caring for them.

However, there are many self-diagnosed autistics, who have had a diagnosis of autism ruled out many times, who insist that they should receive special treatment due to their supposed "autism."

These people clamor for special treatment in school, jobs that they are not qualified to have out of school, and services they are not entitled to have. They may cite their "disability" as the reason for these perks, when in fact the only "disability" they may have is a poor attitude.

It is interesting to note how, one the one hand, people of this type will say that autism isn't a disability, but a difference, when they are fighting discrimination, but they will hypocritically cite their autism as a disability when trying to attain products and services they feel they are entitled to.

Perhaps for lazy people like these, it's the only way for them to get ahead. Having squandered their educations, and having failed to make it into college, having ruined their employment opportunities by willfully behaving in an antisocial manner, they now have no choice but to edge around -and sneak ahead of- people who have worked to get where they are, and edge around -and sneak ahead of- people with *real* disabilities, in order to survive. Some of them will even go so far as to trounce a disabled person -or a whole group of them- if they see some advantage in it.

I can remember what my teachers in elementary school used to tell us. "If someone asks to borrow a pen, or a pencil, or a piece of paper, or a ruler, don't give it to them. There are two reasons for doing this: 1) When you grow up, no one is going to help you out when you need something. 2) And you should never have to inconvenience yourself to help other people who are perfectly capable of helping themselves."

I and some of my classmates followed this rule. Others did not for fear of being "not liked" by their peers. Still others disobeyed the rule to deliberately sabotage their classmates. By encouraging their classmates to be ill-prepared, in other words, it increased the likelihood that the unpreparedness would hamstring them further on when it mattered. For instance, what if they were trying to get a job and the candidate they were competing with had forgotten a pen or a pencil, or even a resume? Maybe that would be all it took for that unprepared person to *not* get the job.

One of the ways many self-diagnosed people will try to convince themselves that what they are doing is right, is to force other people to believe that they are handicapped, that they need a hand, and that, since they are denied that help now and were denied that help in the past, they are justified in taking unlawful, immoral, and unethical actions to get what they need. In reality, this group of people is no different than kids who forgot to bring a pencil to class.

Another attribute of people such as these is that what these people think they "need" is really just what they "want." Going back to that unnamed book I was talking about in the previous section, the author kept talking about "needing" to get out, "needing" to go away, etc. But as we read about his homelessness, and his trials and tribulations on the road, what we think is that what the author *needed* was to mind his father, study in school, do his chores, learn responsibility, learn how to manage money, learn how to accept his faults, and learn how to commit to a person, situation, or action.

As an adult, that author has had multiple marriages, multiple unpaid debts, multiple jobs, multiple moves, some criminal convictions, and he still blames both his childhood and his undiagnosed "disability" for his problems.

Not to mention, bad fortune.

The "Bad Fortune" Excuse

This excuse is rooted in the Biblical and societal sin of covetousness, and pertains to rank, position, and fame. It seems to me that when a person holds a position, or gets a promotion, or gets recognition that someone else wants, the someone doing the wanting gets jealous. While it often happens that good fortune is responsible for social and vocational success, oftentimes it is who you know, what you know, where you learned what you know, and how hard you work with who and what you know that brings you success.

If a factory floor manager sees that one worker is more productive than another, that manager may give the better worker a compliment, a raise, or a promotion. If you or I see this, and aspire to get the benefits this other worker has gotten, chances are we will emulate the worker. We will adopt his attitude as our own, boost our quality to match his, boost our output to *beat* his, etc.

But if we are lazy, we will ascribe the recognition, raise, or promotion to favoritism, luck, or good fortune, and we will ascribe our own lack of success to the "fact" that the boss hates us, or the "fact" that the boss has "unreasonable standards," or the "fact" that we have bad luck. Never mind that we cannot get into our boss's brain to know what he's thinking. Never mind that everyone else in the plant is subject to the exact same standards that we are, and that it is perfectly obvious that the praised and promoted fellow beat those standards. It couldn't possibly be that we are lazy, or that the quality of our craftsmanship is poor, or that our output is below target, could it? It couldn't be that *we* have a poor attitude, a personality that is in some way lacking, etc., right?

We make all manner of excuses for ourselves when we don't want to admit that we have to work on bettering ourselves. But some people will take things in the wrong direction, and will try to acquire what other people have either by stealing it overtly or covertly, or by trying to convince others that they have been the victim of a string of bad luck.

And if none of that works, sometimes they will simply try to destroy whoever it is they feel the "lucky" one is.

There Is One Other Possible Explanation For Much Of This Strife...

In everything that I have mentioned, I have left out the fact that many autistics and non-autistics alike are medicated. Not being a physician, I thought it wise not to comment one way or the other on meds, but it should be acknowledged that many people can have an adverse reaction to them, whether they are taking just one drug or many.

Medication can moderate a thought process or a behavior, but it can also have the effect of worsening a thought process or behavior.

Some autistics and non-autistics are so heavily medicated that their *true* personalities are not present. So it would be unfair to attribute someone's "bad" personality, or "poor" behaviors to a *person* when the *true* person may be caught inside a fog of meds.

But these people may be partly responsible for the problems online and offline because of the way they think and behave. Subtract them from the equation and the autism world *might* not be as confrontational as it seems, although my instinct is that there would still be a disproportionate amount of arguing, bickering and manipulation going on in comparison with other segments of the disability community.

One Other Thing...

Successful Fakers May Hurt Our Perception Of Autistics Without Meaning To

As we all know, not all autistic wannabees and posers are bad people who are detrimental to autistics. Many are well-mannered, good intentioned, philanthropic individuals who have attained high and admirable status in society. Yet the problem with those people is that they too, may be a liability to autistics. Do autistics want society to place unrealistic expectations on them because they believe autism can be what fakers and wannabees have demonstrated by their supposed successes?

If society at large is to understand autism, they need to see it up close and personal, and without distraction, skew, or bent.

Autistics who are lower functioning might look to these successful fakers and posers and feel a sense of hopelessness. For this group of people, there may be no way -even if they have the accommodations they need- to live up to the nearly impossible to achieve levels of success that fakers and posers have achieved. This is why successful autistics and "autistics" alike are many times attacked.

It would be *so* nice, if people who are self-diagnosed, and people who are wannabees, just bowed out of the autism world, so that *true* autistics could know and understand what autism really is, and look to successful *diagnosed* autistic people for inspiration, guidance, and mentorship.

One Possible Solution: A Virtual Impossibility

What can be done to reverse the damage that has been done to the autism community via autism factions and factionalization?

I have one possible solution, but in practice, it wouldn't work.

If it were possible to re-diagnose everyone who claims to be autistic, be it the DSM IV-TR's Autistic Disorder 299.00, Asperger's Disorder 299.80, Rett's Disorder 299.80, Childhood Disintegrative Disorder 299.10, Pervasive Developmental Disorder Not Otherwise Specified (Including Atypical Autism) 299.80, or the DSM V's Autism Spectrum Disorder [299.00 9F84.0)], or the ICD 10's (F84) Pervasive developmental disorders [F84.0 Childhood Autism, F84.1 Atypical Autism, F84.2 Rett syndrome, F84.3 Other childhood disintegrative disorder, F84.4 Overactive disorder associated with mental retardation and stereotyped movements, F84.5 Asperger syndrome, F84.8 Other pervasive develoRettpmental disorders, F84.9 Pervasive developmental disorder, unspecified with the DSM V's Autism Spectrum Disorder [299.00 9F84.0)], and if it were possible for the diagnosed people to *prove* their diagnosis without compromising anything about themselves that they would wish to remain sacred and secret, they could then join *one* single real-world organization specifically for them, and *one* online message board run by that organization. Anyone seeking a diagnosis would not be permitted to join until such time as their diagnosis came through, and wannabees, self-diagnosed people, and undiagnosed people would not be permitted to join at all.

There would be rules that *must* be obeyed in order to maintain membership in the organization and on the online message board, and anyone disobeying those rules would be thrown out.

The advantage to such an organization and online board would be that its reach and influence would be world-wide. Anyone diagnosed with Autism Spectrum Disorder would be a member of the organization and/or board.

It would be *the* organization which would represent and voice the needs of people diagnosed with autism spectrum disorder(s) -even those who are ejected from the organization and message board. It's value politically speaking would be unprecedented.

There are many reasons why this idea *wouldn't* work, however. I will give three of them here:

1) People would have to give up their right to medical privacy and "declare" themselves autistics. In so doing, they risk persecution from people, and public, private, and government entities who are prejudiced against autistics.

2) As with the general public, seldom can such a mass of people be grouped together in one large organization without differences of opinion developing. In most countries, there are many political parties representing many different kinds of ideals, and in countries where there are dictatorships, there are usually rebels trying to overthrow it. It is almost inevitable then, that factions would develop within the single autism organization, and splinter groups would soon be created to rebel against the main group.

3) Such a group of people on the autism spectrum could not be entirely representative of the autistic population anyway, because a significant percentage of autistics are either nonverbal, incapable of making their needs known, or entirely insensible, or a combination thereof.

And so here we return to where we began. It could be said that Aspergia attempted to be the message board and "virtual" society that I am advocating for now. And of course, Aspergia failed.

Can Aspergia's ideals and idealized concepts be reformulated into something new that might actually work for autistics all over the world?

That would depend on how much autistics really want such a thing to happen.

Until then, autistics will either have to police themselves, or else they will have to be policed...by people who are *not* autistic.

Conclusory Statements: What You Need To Know

My volunteer time with Midnight In Chicago has been a boon in that I have met many different people in many different areas of the disability sector, and not just in the area of autism. By far, the majority of those whom I've met are good people, many of who work and volunteer for ethical organizations.

As happens quite often in associations such as these, we get to talking about controversies pertaining to a difference, disorder, or disease, and then on to the politics that surround those controversies.

What I have gleaned is that at the autism world seems more affected than other disabilities sectors, with infighting, squabbling, and factionalization. It also seems that some people who claim to be autistic spend a great deal of time trading on their supposed autism for personal gain even as they purport to be working for autistics.

Some people who have other disabilities are beginning to see *all* autistics with the warped and distorted incorrect stereotypes created and perpetuated by a select few selfish individuals. My hopes are that when the autism community as a whole begins to see this, they will unite together and reject the groups and individuals that are responsible for creating poor representations of autistics. The autism community depends on revamping its image if it expects to continue to get help, support, and understanding from the general public, charitable organizations, and government institutions.

At present, one of the charitable organizations disliked by many autistics, Autism Speaks, has gained considerable ground by listening less to autistics than to parents and caregivers about what should or should not be done to help autistics. As much as it would seem wiser to include autistics in consultations in developing strategic plans for helping those affected with autism, given the state of autism politics, and the activities that some political factions get up to, it seems a wise move to leave the loudest voices out of it, because the loudest voices do not appear to be representing the majority of autistics at all.

In the future, it just may be that more and more autism organizations follow Autism Speaks' lead as they try to compete. Should this happen, a small number of "autistics" and "autism activists" will be entirely responsible for alienating nearly all autistics from their own representation in charitable organizations.

Diagnosed autistics who understand the concepts I am trying to impart here should rethink their loyalty to many of the autistic advocacy organizations and representatives they subscribe to.

It may not be necessary for autistics to take any action, however. With the DSM-V redefining autism, and throwing those who do not fit the new definition into the social (pragmatic) communication disorder category, it just may be that self-diagnosed and misdiagnosed autistics, as well as wannabees, will find themselves placed there by clinicians.

Time will tell.

Afterword

I believe I have indicated that this book is not meant to impugn the autism community, but to attempt to describe its politics, delineate its political factions, and demonstrate how politics and the behaviors of political factions play out, both in real life and on the net.

There are many, many people and organizations that are worthy of acclaim for the significant and valuable contributions they have made to better the lives of autistics worldwide. I cannot name them here, not only because there are so many of them, but because if I left one or many out, it may be seen as a covert suggestion that they are *not* notably excellent contributors.

The treatment of this subject matter is an open door for further investigation and discovery by all who read this. It is not meant to be comprehensive, nor could it be. Arguably, for every autistic person and autism organization that exists, there is a separate faction, because every person and every organization has a slightly different perspective about autism.

I would encourage others to give some thought to what I have written, and to write more on the subject if it seems to be appropriate to them to do so.

Partial Annotated List of Works Cited

The following people, organizations, works or sources were cited, referenced, or discussed in passing or at length in this publication and have been included here because the author feels they may be of some interest to the reader. This list does not encompass all citations in this publication. Inclusion or omission of people, organizations, works, or sources does not constitute any endorsement or lack thereof. Supplementary information has been included where the author though it might be helpful or useful to the reader.

People:

Hans Asperger
Maxine Aston
Dr. Tony Attwood
Eugen Bleuler
Simon Baron-Cohen
Elyse Bruce
Jesus Christ
Allyson Goodwyn-Craine M.S. CCC-SLP
Eustacia Cutler
Edan Dagan
Claire Danes
Michelle Dawson
Thomas Edison
Albert Einstein
Henry Ford
M.S. Garnett
God
Temple Grandin

Adolf Hitler
Dustin Hoffman
Dr. Leo Kanner
Dr. O. Ivar Lovaas
Jenny McCarthy
Dr. Laurent Mottron, M.D., Ph.D.
President Barack Obama
Kim Peek
Dr. Stephen Scherer
Taylor Swift
Dr. Peter Szatmari
Thomas D. Taylor
Dr. Andrew Jeremy Wakefield
Donna Williams
Zoologist

Organizations:

Age of Autism
American Academy of Pediatrics
American Medical Association
Autism Genome Project
Autism Speaks
Big Pharma
Convention on the Rights of Persons with Disabilities
Fellowship of the Aspergian Miracle – Secret Society
Former Aspergia Members – Secret Society
Government
Internal Revenue Service (IRS)
Midnight In Chicago (www.midnightinchicago.com)
Nazis
Oak Ridge National Laboratory
United Nations
University of Montreal
US Centers for Disease Control and Prevention (CDC)

Blogs:

Examiner.com

Huffington Post
The <u>Midnight In Chicago</u> blog
(<u>www.midnightinchicago.wordpress.com</u>)
The <u>Thomas D. Taylor</u> blog
(<u>www.thomasdtaylor.wordpress.com</u>)

Periodicals

<u>Good Housekeeping</u>
<u>The New York Times</u>
<u>Newsweek</u>
<u>Readers Digest</u>
<u>Rolling Stone Magazine</u>
<u>Time Magazine</u>
<u>The Wall Street Journal</u>
<u>The Washington Post</u>

Publications:

By Edan Dagan:

The Aspergian Mythos

By Thomas D. Taylor:

<u>Autistic Authors, and Autistics, and Autism in Literature: A Commentary</u>

<u>Evil Creeps In: A Tale of Exorcism </u>(Copyright 2011, 2012, Thomas D. Taylor)

Other:

Bible

DSM IV-TR
(Diagnostic and Statistical Manual of Mental Disorders, Fourth edition, Text Revised)

DSM V
(Diagnostic and Statistical Manual of Mental Disorders, Fifth edition)

ICD 10
(International Statistical Classification of Diseases and Related Health Problems, 10th edition)

Movies:

Invasion of the Body Snatchers
Rainman
Temple Grandin

Websites:

www.amazon.com
Aspergia (www.aspergia.com)
www.createspace.com
EZ Board
Facebook
Midnight In Chicago www.midnightinchicago.com
http://www.ontariogenomics.ca/research/project/44
www.podomatic.com
Midnight In Chicago Podcasts www.autism.podomatic.com
Twitter
YouTube

Other:

Aspie Quiz
Australian Scale for Asperger Syndrome
The Aspergian Mythos

About the Author

Thomas D. Taylor is an author, an artist, a photographer, a songwriter, and (along with Elyse Bruce) Co-Creator of Midnight In Chicago, a 100% volunteer-run international initiative which raises funds and awareness for people with disabilities.

His short story "The Interview" won the First Place Fiction award in the 1991 edition of Towers literary magazine. Another of his stories, "A Grasshopper Cerebrates Humanity," was published in the same issue. In 2013, his political commentary, "Idle No More: A White Man Speaks," was published in The First Perspective magazine.

Taylor's artwork has sold worldwide. Taylor painted the front and back cover art for two of singer/songwriter Elyse Bruce's albums: Midnight in Chicago, and Countdown to Midnight. His photograph, "Gun" appears on the cover of this publication.

Taylor is also responsible for co-writing three songs with Elyse Bruce: "Late Night In The Borough", "Somewhere In Detroit," and "How Do I Begin To Believe (Lying In The Arms Of My Judas)."

Other Books By Thomas D. Taylor

Science Fiction

Geo-213: The Lost Stories
Geo-213: The Lost Expedition

Horror

Evil Creeps In: A Tale of Exorcism
Deadly Duo: Two Stories of Death and Murder
Gruesome Triad: Three Stories of the Macabre
Grim Quatrain: Four Tales of Terror
Ghostly Quintet: Five Tales of Ghosts, Apparitions, and the
Beyond

Mainstream Fiction
Life Is A Journey: Twenty Coming-Of-Age Stories

Nonfiction

Autistic Authors, and Autistics, and Autism in Literature: A
Commentary

www.ingramcontent.com/pod-product-compliance
Lightning Source LLC
Chambersburg PA
CBHW070850290526
45795CB00001B/55